Remembering the Past

Remembering the Past

Critical Perspectives on the Anti-Sikh Violence of 1984

Edited by

Ishmeet Kaur Chaudhry

With a Foreword by

Amritjit Singh

Orient BlackSwan

REMEMBERING THE PAST: CRITICAL PERSPECTIVES ON THE ANTI-SIKH VIOLENCE OF 1984

ORIENT BLACKSWAN PRIVATE LIMITED

Registered Office
3-6-752 Himayatnagar, Hyderabad 500 029, Telangana, India
e-mail: centraloffice@orientblackswan.com

Other Offices
Bengaluru, Chennai, Guwahati, Hyderabad, Kolkata,
Mumbai, New Delhi, Noida, Patna

First published 2025

041935

ISBN 978-93-5442-584-4

Typeset in
Calisto MT 10/13
by Le Studio Graphique, Gurgaon 122 007

Printed in India at
Kensington Printing & Packaging, Noida 201 301

Published by
Orient Blackswan Private Limited
3-6-752 Himayatnagar, Hyderabad 500 029, Telangana, India
e-mail: info@orientblackswan.com

Ravinder Randev,
*The Unsung Hero of Our Lives**

---

*Ravinder Randev was a veteran journalist. During the post-assassination violence of 1984, he diverted a mob that had attempted to attack a gurdwara in Shimla. He had given our family words of assurance and reaffirmed our faith in humanity above any communal division. This book is dedicated to the likes of Ravinder Randev.

Contents

Part III
Literary Imaginaries and Cinematic Representation

Part IV
Experience and Personal Narratives

Abbreviations

AFDR	Association for Democratic Rights
BJP	Bharatiya Janata Party
CAA	Citizenship (Amendment) Act
CBI	Central Bureau of Investigation
FIR	first information report
NCR	National Capital Region
NGO	non-governmental organisation
POTA	Prevention of Terrorism Act
PUCL	People's Union for Civil Liberties
PUDR	People's Union for Democratic Rights
RSS	Rashtriya Swayamsevak Sangh
SAD	Shiromani Akali Dal
SGPC	Shiromani Gurdwara Prabandhak Committee
SIT	special investigation team
TADA	Terrorists and Disruptive Activities (Prevention) Act

Foreword

Amritjit Singh

For many of us, 1984 continues to evoke George Orwell's well-known 1948 novel that had introduced us to *doublethink*, *newspeak* and *memory hole*—paradigms that continue to play a prominent role in many parts of the world today. However, in the South Asian context, 1984 signals the terrible events in and around the year that remain inscribed painfully in the memory of most Indian citizens. Through several years of careful and diligent work, Ishmeet Kaur Chaudhry has gathered nine substantive essays in this volume covering a wide range of issues that emerge from the then Prime Minister Indira Gandhi's decision to storm the Darbar Sahib in Amritsar (the Golden Temple) and 40 other gurdwaras in Punjab in June 1984, and the consequent violence directed at Sikhs in New Delhi and other cities in the first week of November 1984 after Mrs Gandhi was assassinated on 31 October.

More specifically, this edited volume, *Remembering the Past*, is the first of its kind to offer a critical assessment of literary texts on the 1984 anti-Sikh massacres. It addresses several crucial concerns related to the reading of communal violence through personal experiences and also offers literary analyses of selected texts—novels, short stories, films and oral narratives that explore the painful subject of 1984. The essays offer an evaluation of literary works that cover a variety of experiences connected with both June 1984 in Amritsar and November 1984 in Delhi and other locations. These experiences stem from the violence faced by innocent Sikh pilgrims who had gathered at the Harmandir Sahib in the first week of June 1984 to commemorate Guru Arjun Dev's martyrdom anniversary; the trauma resulting from the brutal killings of innocent Sikh families, especially their adult males, in Delhi and elsewhere; the humiliation and rape of women; and also how Sikh women persisted in their fight for justice without much institutional support throughout the terrible 1990s in Punjab. The essays in this volume and the editor's compelling 'Introduction' collectively signal how survivors of the 1980s and the 1990s attempted to recover from the trauma of what they had experienced and question whether full recovery is ever possible.

There have been many monographs and edited volumes dealing with the politics surrounding the 1984 anti-Sikh violence. This volume is an attempt to break the silence around the literary writings on the tragedy and to offer a critical evaluation of such output. In many ways, this is a companion volume to the book Ishmeet had published in 2019: *Black November*. The essays in the present volume discuss the personal experiences and encounters of scholars such as Nandita Haksar, Uma Chakravarti and Dilip Simeon who had been involved in the rescue of the Sikhs in Delhi in November 1984. Essays by Anshu Saluja and Yasmeen Arif focus on survivors' narratives, while the one by Anne Murphy discusses concerns related to trauma. Amutha Charu Sheela focuses on an analysis of available 1984 literature, while Diamond Oberoi Vahali and Jasmine Anand critically analyse films on the 1984 anti-Sikh massacre. Ishmeet Kaur Chaudhry's Introduction provides a detailed background to the situation, raising crucial questions regarding the responsibility of state and community towards the victims and the weaknesses of India's judicial system in delivering justice. Nothing demonstrates the truth of 'Justice delayed is justice denied' more than the slow pace at which the prominent perpetrators of the 1984 violence have received punishment for their misdeeds. For example, Sajjan Kumar was finally convicted in 2018, 34 years after the mob violence he had led. In 2005, Justice Nanavati Commission of Inquiry recommended charges against Jagdish Tytler. The Central Bureau of Investigation (CBI) filed a chargesheet against Tytler on 20 May 2023, and the court took cognisance of CBI's chargesheet against him on 26 July 2023. Meanwhile, hundreds of victims have died waiting for justice.

It is my privilege to invite you to read the essays included in *Remembering the Past*, not as a collective final word on this difficult topic but as a way of complicating and expanding our continuing conversations on many related issues. The volume invites us to further explore topics such as the importance of political dialogue; the importance of sustaining constitutional processes and institutions; the convergence of civil rights and human rights; the cultivation and propagation of negative stereotypes to target and harass minority groups in order to build majoritarian voting blocs; the role of memory and post-memory; oral narratives as testimony; and the uses and misuses of film, music and social media.

The invitation to write this Foreword also allows me an opportunity to express my own diasporic perspective on both June and November 1984. I offer in four discrete sections not only an account of how I experienced those two events from my perch in New York, but also my sense of the major blunders Mrs Gandhi made in her handling of this sensitive political situation.

Amritsar, June 1984

While Sikhs and Hindus in Punjab experienced considerable mutual mistrust and suspicion during the years immediately before and after 1984, there was no mob violence directed at Sikh or Hindu communities within the state. Paradoxically, during the same years, thousands of Sikh and Hindu individuals and families became victims of violence directed at them by either the Sikh militants or by police and paramilitary forces of the state and central governments. As Gulzar's film *Maachis* (1996) suggests, targeting of innocent Sikhs and 'fake encounters' between 'militants' and police became a common occurrence in Punjab in the 1980s and 1990s. Many observers believe that in the early 1980s, Sant Jarnail Singh Bhindranwale had also directed the killing of dissenting Sikhs and Hindus—apparently a majority of his victims were moderate and intellectual Sikhs (Singh et al. 2016: xxxi, n.22). That pattern of targeting perceived 'adversaries' on both sides continued for nearly a decade after the Blue Star invasion of the Golden Temple.

The traumatic events of 1984 shook up the fragile faith Indians had built under Jawaharlal Nehru, Vallabhbhai Patel and Lal Bahadur Shastri—their sense that India had left behind, risen above and beyond, the kind of horrific violence experienced by Hindus, Muslims and Sikhs during Partition in 1947. That partition—evoked with anger and sarcasm by W. H. Auden in his poem 'Partition' (1966) as an avoidable infliction upon the subcontinent by the departing British rulers—resulted in more than 1 million killings and approximately 14 million people rendered homeless on both sides of the India–Pakistan borders, in the east and the northwest (Cowasjee 1995: xi–xii). In her pioneering book, *The Other Side of Silence* (2000), Urvashi Butalia established a powerful link between 1947 and 1984. As a feminist who worked with refugee camps during and after November 1984, Butalia became sharply aware of how many victims of 1984 were forced to recall their painful memories of the displacement and sexual violence they had experienced in 1947. This is how Butalia makes the connection:

> It took the events of 1984 to make me understand how ever-present Partition was in our lives, too, to recognize that it could not so easily be put away inside the covers of history books. I could no longer pretend that this was a history that belonged to another time, to someone else. (2000: 6)

That 'ever-present Partition' in our hearts and minds was fully on display in the massacre of innocent Sikhs in Delhi and other cities—in response to Mrs Gandhi's assassination by two of her Sikh bodyguards on 31 October 1984. The bodyguards were not linked in any way to the militants who were the targets of Operation Blue Star, conducted between 3–10 June 1984. These bodyguards were ordinary Sikh citizens and civil servants who were deeply hurt by Mrs Gandhi's decision to violate the sanctity of the Golden Temple and 40 other gurdwaras in Punjab with paratroopers, armoured tanks and three divisions of Indian armed forces as part of the Operation (Singh et al. 2016: xxxi, n.22). Further, as noted, the attack was carried out in the middle of a holy week for Sikhs, the 378th anniversary of Guru Arjun Dev's martyrdom in June 1606.

For three days following Mrs Gandhi's assassination, a naked dance of violence found Sikhs at its centre and left the community in a state of shock and disbelief. Sikhs, a well-integrated minority, became the target not only of spontaneous rage, but also of carefully orchestrated killings of families and adult Sikh men in particular. The police in several major cities chose to look away, and in some locations, they are alleged to either have aided in the massacre or were otherwise directed to do nothing to stop the madness in the streets (Wikipedia n.d., '1984 Anti-Sikh Riots'). In 1947, Hindus and Sikhs had found themselves on the same side of the divide, resulting in the long-term demonisation of Muslims in India that continues to haunt the nation's politics and public life to this day. In 1984, Sikhs became the new targets, mostly of deputed Congress Party workers but also occasionally of right-wing Hindus and other lumpen elements. While many middle-class Hindus had risked their lives to protect and shelter Sikh neighbours, a few others felt that Sikhs deserved to be penalised for their habit of bragging about their hard work and success, and for their perceived 'arrogance' and 'masculinity' towards other citizens.

It might help to recount a bit of background to what happened in 1984. In October 1973, the Akalis, the moderate Sikh political party, had pressed the Central government in Delhi to consider a set of demands known as the Anandpur Resolution (Sikhi Wiki n.d.; Wikipedia n.d., 'Anandpur Sahib Resolution'). Among other things such as the equitable distribution of irrigation waters among neighbouring states, the Resolution asserted the need for individual states to have additional rights as part of a constitutional federal structure—an issue that was also being raised in West Bengal and Tamil Nadu. Choosing not to engage the Akalis in a dialogue, Mrs Gandhi condemned the Anandpur Resolution as a separatist move (Wikipedia n.d., 'Anandpur Sahib Resolution'). The situation in Punjab, especially in Amritsar, began to deteriorate quickly. On Vaisakhi Day in April 1978, there was a deadly confrontation in Amritsar, a short distance from Darbar Sahib, between the members of the Nirankari sect and Sant Jarnail Singh Bhindranwale's followers. By 1981–82, there were serious grounds for the state and Central government to act on the worsening situation inside the Golden Temple compound. In 1982, Bhindranwale was arrested at Mehta Chowk and then released. In July 1982, the charismatic Sant took shelter inside the Golden Temple, along with a cluster of 150–200 armed followers. To begin with, there was a level of cooperation between Bhindranwale and moderate Sikh leaders like Sant Harchand Singh Longowal, but that amity unravelled quickly. Mrs Gandhi allowed this combustible situation to smoulder for two years without taking any action to flush out Bhindranwale or reach a political settlement with Akalis on their demands. In fact, in November 1982, at the Union Cabinet's direction, Congress leader Swarn Singh had negotiated an agreement on such issues with the Akali leaders, but Mrs Gandhi backed out without an explanation (Kidwai 2023). As later events have demonstrated, and as is borne out in several commentaries by journalists and historians, Blue Star was a flawed operation in both its planning and execution.[1]

Khushwant Singh, a journalist and historian with impeccable secular credentials, protested the action by returning his Padma Bhushan, an honour that had been bestowed upon him in 1974 by the Indian government. Citing the quick, clean work of Israeli or German commandos in similar situations, Singh condemned the Army attack on the Golden Temple by pointing out that in the 'crossfire upwards of 5,000 people, a majority of them pilgrims, including women and children, lost their lives. ... Far from doing a competent job, our army commanders botched up a simple operation' (Singh 2015). In an interview on 11 June 1984 with William Claiborne, a *Washington Post* correspondent, Khushwant Singh remarked: 'I know Bhindranwale had been provoking them for months, but to flush out a rat, you don't bring down the house' (Claiborne 1984).

Prime Minister Indira Gandhi: Her Role and Responsibility

To this day, many Indians continue to believe that in June 1984, Mrs Gandhi had no choice other than to storm the Golden Temple in order to flush out the armed militants. As noted by Pritam Singh (2021), the state media (TV and radio) and non-state media outlets had 'praised the operation for saving India's "unity and integrity" from "anti-national" Sikh secessionism'.[2]

Based on my own research and reflection on the events before and during June 1984 as well as in November 1984, I find it necessary to acknowledge occasional missteps on the part of the Akalis to bring the Centre's attention to their political demands. For example, nine Akali leaders were arrested in February 1984, when they burnt copies of Article 25 of India's Constitution. Sant Bhindranwale's provocative presence and his alleged targeting of both Hindus and Sikhs who criticised him openly did not make things easier for either the Congress or the Akalis, both of whom attempted to use the Sant to their own ends. However, I must concur with Pritam Singh regarding the primary responsibility that Mrs Gandhi bears for the 1984 tragedy:

> Indira Gandhi's political decision to use the 'Hindu card' to gain electoral victories led her to choose a dangerous path of confrontation, first with the Akalis and eventually with the entire Sikh community. This miscalculation cost Mrs. Gandhi her life, and left the communities of Punjab and of India in general scarred and polarised. (Singh 2021)

As Gita Mehta, Hartosh Singh Bal and Mark Tully/Satish Jacob have all pointed out, Sanjay Gandhi and Zail Singh cultivated Bhindranwale with money and special attention, enabling him to run his own candidates for the SGPC election in 1979. Although almost all of Bhindranwale's candidates lost their bid, he enjoyed the attention he received through canvassing for his SGPC candidates and began to display his megalomania in public on a regular basis, ultimately making him a Frankenstein's monster for all sides. As noted, the Akalis allowed the Sant and his armed followers to move into the Darbar Sahib in 1982—which is when the Centre had good reasons to act. In April 1983, when DIG Police A. S. Atwal visited Darbar Sahib for prayers and became the victim of a bullet fired from inside the compound, Mrs Gandhi again failed to take action.

As the nation's leader, Mrs Gandhi failed to meet her obligation to negotiate with the Akalis in good faith regarding their well-articulated political demands. Later, for over two years, she deliberately delayed necessary action to deal with the growing presence of militants inside Darbar Sahib. By deciding in May–June 1984 to make an unprecedented move to invade the holy shrine with tanks and armed troopers, Mrs Gandhi committed a transgression that offended the global Sikh community and many other Indians at home and in the diaspora. Many Sikhs in Canada were incensed by her insensitivity and began to openly support demands for the creation of Khalistan, an independent Sikh homeland. In 1985, a couple of Sikh extremists in Canada allegedly bombed an Air India flight with 187 passengers, most of them Indo-Canadians bound for India from Toronto. My dear friend Professor Harinder Singh Marjara of Montreal lost his beloved wife and his youngest daughter in that tragedy. Harinder has never stopped grieving.

In the first national elections that took place after Mrs Gandhi's assassination, the Congress under Rajiv Gandhi's leadership won a landslide victory. Rajiv Gandhi had been a member of Parliament for three years. When he took his oath as Prime Minister on 31 December 1984, at age 40, he was still a novice in politics. He envisioned that India under his leadership would emerge as a front-rank nation in a new world order, helping to negotiate conflicts between neighbouring countries. He recognised the need to address the pending issues in Punjab and took a few concrete steps to defuse tensions. He released the Akali leaders who had been in prison since Operation Blue Star and lifted the ban on the All India Sikh Students Federation. Under his direction, the Punjab Governor Arjun Singh relaxed censorship of the Punjabi press and began reviewing the cases of thousands of Sikhs imprisoned since the 1984 assault on Darbar Sahib and other gurdwaras. He also began to respond to the economic needs of Punjab in various ways. After several weeks of negotiations, he signed an 11-point agreement with Akali leader Harchand Singh Longowal on 23 July 1985. In signing this Agreement, he ignored the opposition of orthodox Sikhs and Haryana politicians to a few contentious issues. While a few goals of this accord were met, some others (including the transfer of Chandigarh to Punjab) were never achieved. Within a month of signing the Agreement, Longowal was assassinated by a Sikh militant. In May 1988, Rajiv Gandhi carried out the Operation Black Thunder to remove arms and gunmen from the Golden Temple. Two entities called the National Security Guard and the Special Action Group were created and they surrounded the Darbar Sahib Complex in a 10-day siege to achieve their goals. For many observers, the effectiveness of the May 1988 action would highlight the excesses and failings of Operation Blue Star four years earlier.

Delhi, November 1984

1 November 1984, a Thursday, is a day I can never forget. I was a professor then at Hofstra University in Long Island, where I taught a heavy load of courses on Monday, Wednesday and Friday, each week. However, my most enjoyable teaching during 1984–85 took place every Thursday at Wesleyan University—a once-a-week course on African American drama that included well-known plays on race and identity by Langston Hughes, Lorraine Hansberry and LeRoi Jones. I would leave my home in Bayside, Queens, around 9 AM, arriving in Middletown, Connecticut, two hours later. I would teach my three-hour class from 1 PM to 4 PM, getting back home by dinner time.

On Wednesday, 31 October 1984, the news of Mrs Gandhi's assassination had flashed across the globe. As we walked together on the Hofstra campus from one building to another, my Jewish American colleague Susan had expressed serious concerns about the retribution that would most likely be visited upon innocent Sikhs in response to the dastardly act committed by Mrs Gandhi's bodyguards. In my naïve Nehruvian idealism, I had attempted to reassure my colleague that while some anger would probably be directed at Sikh citizens in the streets, the reaction would not be too extreme. Spurred possibly by the long memory of her Jewish heritage, Susan had predicted the situation much more accurately.

Driving from Queens, NY, to Middletown, CT, on Thursday morning and returning home in the afternoon, I was tuned in to the CBS News Radio. I was deeply shaken by what I heard. Driving in either direction, I was forced to face a new reality about my beloved homeland, as the number of Sikh killings reported from New Delhi kept doubling every half hour. In fact, on my return drive home to Queens, I felt compelled to turn off the radio and find solace in the Gurbani kirtan cassette tapes that were always in my small Datsun car during those years. Kabir's reassuring message came through in the melodious voice of Ragi Harbans Singh: 'Aval Allah noor upaya, kudrat ké sabh bande/ek noor té sabh jug upjaya, kon bhalé, kon mandé' (First, Allah created the Light; then, by His Creative Power, He made all mortal beings./From that One Light, the entire universe welled up. So how can some be good, and others be treated as bad?).[3] As I navigated the always crowded I-95 toward Throgs Neck Bridge to reach home, I attempted to remain focused on the road, even as Guru Nanak Dev's 1519 protest to God against Babar's brutalities upon hapless citizens roared into my memory: 'Eti maar pai kurlané, tein ki dard na aya' (In the face of such slaughter, Oh God, did you feel no pain or empathy?[4]).

At that moment, it was difficult for me to be philosophical about a pattern of human history—how individuals, families, communities and nations perpetrate actions (domestic abuse and incest, repression of Indigenous Peoples in Canada and the US, slavery and colonialism, Jim Crow and Japanese internment camps in North America, Holocaust in Germany, apartheid in South Africa) that cause multi-generational trauma—actions that would call for subsequent regret and apology, truth and reconciliation commissions, or reparations. At some point in 1999, I was shocked to learn that when Patwant Singh, Kuldip Nayar and Lt General Jagjit Singh Aurora met with President Zail Singh and Home Minister P. V. Narsimha Rao, respectively, on 1 November 1984 to seek their intervention, the two leaders took no action at all, letting the killings of innocent Sikhs go on for another 48 or more hours (Kaur 2001). Until recently, we did not have access to paradigms such as critical race theory and intersectionality. Today, we have a more layered understanding of how 'majoritarianism' plays an inverted trickster role in the creation of conflicting narratives and alternate realities. It is much easier in 2023 to recognise the need to build memorials and monuments to painful chapters in our history as a warning against their recurrence. A monument or historical park commemorating 1984 would likely serve the same goal in our national memory and imagination as the Jallianwala Bagh Memorial in Amritsar or the Partition Museum in Delhi.

Bearing Witness

The days and months immediately following November 1984 were extremely difficult for most Sikhs in India, especially those who lived in various regions of India away from Punjab. They felt vulnerable and disturbed by how they were being asked to defend or explain crimes they had not committed. Even Sikhs in Punjab and Delhi felt mistrust and suspicion directed at them by their neighbours, long-time friends and colleagues—this was evoked with great resonance by novelist Amitav Ghosh in his essay, 'The Ghosts of Mrs Gandhi'" (*New Yorker* 1995). It became easy to attach the label 'Khalistani' to suppress disagreements, even harass or expel Sikh colleagues at work. Unless you were a 'cut Surd', you were no longer viewed as a secular Indian citizen (Singh 2017). A statement made by the newly chosen Prime Minister Rajiv Gandhi illustrates the nature of the new challenges Sikhs in and around Delhi faced. Nineteen days after the assassination, at a Boat Club rally, Rajiv Gandhi said, 'Some riots took place in the country following the murder of Indiraji. We know the people were very angry and for a few days it seemed that India had been shaken. But, when a mighty tree falls, it is only natural that the earth around it does shake a little' (cited in Singh 1990: 235). The Congress party won an unprecedented margin of victory in December 1984 by using dog-whistles that inverted widely held positive stereotypes of Sikhs as honest, generous and trustworthy people (*The New York Times* 1985).

Sikhs who lived abroad on timebound or permanent resident visas faced their own challenges. Worried about the nascent unpredictability of India's political life, Sikh citizens in Canada and the US began applying for landed immigrant status for their immediate families in India. Like most other Sikhs in the US, I recall feeling compelled to deal with two issues immediately: (i) to ascertain the safety and well-being of loved ones who lived in India and (ii) to educate Americans about who Sikhs were—our origins, our beliefs, our looks and our lives. With a dear old friend, I started working on a Q&A booklet on Sikhs and Sikhism. Between stressful daily routines and our differences on what to include, that worthy project fell apart quickly. Fortunately, gurdwaras in the UK and North America reprinted publications such as *Who Are the Guilty?* (produced by Rajni Kothari and the People's Union for Civil Liberties [PUCL]), which were then widely distributed among concerned global citizens.

My young family and I lived in New York, as did my eldest sister. Four of my siblings (two brothers and two sisters) lived in north India at the time. I was relieved to connect quickly with three of my four siblings in India—they were scared but safe. Every expensive phone call was riddled with myriad stories of uncertainty and precarity: friends or neighbours who had lost their lives or barely survived the violence; Sikh homes and businesses vandalised and destroyed, including two factories owned by my uncles in the Kirti Nagar Industrial Area; neighbourhood gurdwaras attacked and the *Holy Granth* desecrated, its pages strewn in the streets; and the occasional kindness of strangers or acquaintances. My four siblings and I were deeply frustrated in our efforts to reach our youngest sister, who lived in Kanpur with her husband and two young sons. As in Delhi, scores of Sikh families in Kanpur had also suffered attacks on their lives and properties. In desperation, I contacted my dear friend Chaudhri Harish Chandra, a Punjabi Hindu who was a well-respected professor of English at the prestigious Christ Church College in Kanpur. At serious risk to his own personal safety during the curfew days of mid-November 1984, Harish managed to reach my sister's residence in Civil Lines and used his suave charm to wangle some basic information from their protective neighbour: my sister and her family were alive, having narrowly escaped getting killed; they had been forced to cut their hair and remove other symbols of Sikh identity, such as the *kara* and the turban; and all four of them were hiding in a very small space, barely enough for them to breathe in and survive. (Years later, I came to associate that space in my imagination with the 'tiny crawling space', 9x7x3 feet, that Linda Brent, aka Harriet Jacobs, describes in *Incidents in the Life of a Slave Girl*, 1861 [Chapter 21].)

Trauma is neither logical nor open to correction. Like grief in Emily Dickinson's poem ('After great pain, a formal feeling comes—'), post-traumatic stress is unpredictable and chooses its own course. Appearing and reappearing at its own will, it hits you the most when you expect it the least. The shock of what happened in 1984 has travelled across oceans to penetrate the diaspora and is likely to get passed on from one generation to the next. Forgetting may be easily, breezily recommended by well-wishers and casual observers, and it may even be attempted by those affected, but it is really hard to accomplish. A well-meaning friend, an Indian diplomat serving then in Vancouver, BC, advised me by phone to forget what happened and move on. I had to grit my teeth not to hang up on him. (On 7 April 2009, a young Sikh journalist Jarnail Singh had hurled a shoe at India's Home Minister P. Chidambaram, when the minister made a similar suggestion in response to the journalist's energetic questioning about why those Congress leaders such as H. K. L. Bhagat who had led the mobs in November 1984 had not been brought to justice 25 years after the tragedy [*The Economic Times* 2009].)

We continue to learn the value of 'bearing witness' from its skilful uses over decades in Holocaust studies: the importance of preserving human dignity on the part of victims and survivors, finding ways of processing the experience and acquiring empathy and support, and demonstrating the possibilities of resistance to prevent any group from being seen as hapless victims. In Holocaust studies, survivors' testimony and video representations are important resources towards the goal of 'bearing witness'. As an example of bearing witness to 1984, the widely travelled poetic performance *Kultar's Mime* by Sarabpreet Singh achieves a powerful representation of how November 1984 violence affected Sikh children in Delhi (Kumar 2014).

Alan Filreis, a professor of English at the University of Pennsylvania, finds the memoir (such as Elie Wiesel's *Night* [1956] and *Dawn* [1962]) more purposeful than celluloid representations in his undergraduate course on the Holocaust, easier for his young students to identify with. For him, the primary focus of his course is addressing problems of representations of the Holocaust—an issue that is very pertinent to the many book-length accounts already available. Paradoxically, Filreis can also require his students to watch Claude Lanzmann's nine-hour documentary film *Shoah* in one sitting. He would like his students to confront a basic dilemma about describing the tragedy. While the Holocaust is

> an event too enormous, too deep, too problematic, too painful, and too traumatic to describe, yet there is a need to describe it to those who did not see it, with knowledge that words will fail to convey the enormity of the depth and pain. ... I want my students to understand that dilemma so that we never take for granted the struggle that anyone who has seen trauma—whether it's the trauma of mass murder, or the trauma of the sudden loss of a parent, or the trauma of a giant catastrophe—we should never take for granted how hard it is to represent that (Johnson 2018).

In relation to the sectarian violence that South Asia has experienced in 1947, 1971, 1984 and 2002, it would help to heed Ravinder Kaur's important reminder:

> The idea is not only to honour the dead, to heal the wounds and to give voice to those silenced, but also to serve as a deterrent for future generations, as a reminder of destruction that human beings are capable of unleashing. In short, choosing to remember or forget, to publicly speak or remain silent are always deeply political gestures (Kaur 2021).

As each of us make our 'political gestures' or ethical choices, I hope that as the largest democracy in the world, as the fabled home to figures such as Buddha, Kabir, Guru Nanak Dev and M. K. Gandhi, and as the nation that was the first to honour Dr Martin Luther King, Jr, India would do well to pursue Dr King's dream of building his cherished 'beloved community', wherein no one feels left out and where every citizen feels cherished and has a seat at the table.

Notes

1. Based on several books on the subject, including Singh and Nayar (1985); Kumar et al. (2003); and Tully and Jacob (1985).

2. Pritam Singh's article (2021) in *The Wire* outlines the history of the three *ghallugharas* the Sikh community has endured, in 1746, 1799 and 1984. Singh also

reminds us of how these genocidal episodes find a place in *ardaas*—the daily prayer in Sikh gurdwaras throughout the world.

3. Author's translation.
4. Author's translation.

References

Auden, W. H. 1966. 'Partition'. Available at https://hellopoetry.com/poem/786/partition/ (accessed on 9 January 2025).

Bal, Hartosh Singh. 2019. 'How the Congress Propped Up Bhindranwale'. *The Caravan*, 8 June. Available at https://caravanmagazine.in/conflict/how-the-congress-propped-up-bhindranwale (accessed on 30 June 2025).

Butalia, Urvashi. 2000. *The Other Side of Silence*. Durham: Duke University Press.

Claiborne, William. 1984. 'India Says 450 Died in Punjab'. *The Washington Post*, 11 June. Available at https://www.washingtonpost.com/archive/politics/1984/06/11/india-says-450-died-in-punjab/c8a164f7-a4fe-445c-96c3-9899067ea79d/ (accessed on 20 November 2024).

Cowasjee, Saros. 1995. 'Introduction'. In *Orphans of the Storm: Short Stories on the Partition of India*, eds Saros Cowasjee and Kartar Singh Duggal. New Delhi: UBS Publishers.

Ghosh, Amitav. 1995. 'The Ghosts of Mrs Gandhi'. *The New Yorker*, 17 July. Available at https://amitavghosh.com/other-works-contributions/essays-and-posts/the-ghosts-of-mrs-gandhi/ (accessed on 20 November 2024)

Johnson, Greg. 2018. 'Teaching the Holocaust to Remember, to Learn, and to Bear Witness'. *Penn Today*, 12 April. Available at https://penntoday.upenn.edu/news/teaching-holocaust-remember-learn-and-bear-witness (accessed on 20 November 2024).

Kaur, Naunidhi. 2001. 'Waiting for Justice'. *Frontline*, 1 September. Available at https://frontline.thehindu.com/other/article30251717.ece (accessed on 20 November 2024).

Kaur, Ravinder. 2021. 'We Best Remember Partition When We Connect the Dots from 1947 to 1984 and 2002'. *The Wire*, 14 August. Available at https://thewire.in/communalism/how-not-to-remember-partition (accessed on 20 November 2024).

Kidwai, Rasheed. 2023. 'Opinion: How Indira Gandhi Lost a Chance to Solve Punjab Tangle 40 Years Ago'. *India Today*, 9 July. Available at https://www.indiatoday.in/opinion-columns/story/negotiations-subterfuge-how-indira-gandhi-lost-opportunity-solve-punjab-tangle-forty-years-ago-2404023-2023-07-09 (accessed on 20 November 2024).

Kumar, Ram Narayan, Amrik Singh, Ashok Agrwaal and Jaskaran Kaur. 2003. *Reduced to Ashes: The Insurgency and Human Rights in Punjab*. South Asia Forum for Human Rights.

Kumar, Umang. 2014. 'Kultar's Mime—A Play that Recreates the Anti-Sikh Violence of 1984'. SikhNet, 14 October. Available at https://www.sikhnet.com/news/kultars-mime-play-recreates-anti-sikh-violence-1984 (accessed on 20 November 2024).

Singh, Amritjit, Nalini Iyer, and Rahul K. Gairola (eds). 2016. *Revisiting India's Partition*. New Delhi: Orient BlackSwan.

Sikhi Wiki. n.d. 'Anandpur Sahib Resolution'. Available at https://www.sikhiwiki.org/index.php/Anandpur_Sahib_Resolution#:~:text (accessed on 20 November 2024).

Singh, Harmeet Shah. 2017. 'How "Cut Surd" has Stealthily Gained Currency among Indian Sikhs', *DailyO*, 12 August. Available at https://www.dailyo.in/variety/sikhism-turban-guru-nanak-intolerance-indian-diaspora-punjab-cut-surd-18926 (accessed on 20 November 2024).

Singh, Indu Prakash. 1990. *The Aborted Revolution*. University of Michigan Press.

Singh, Khushwant. 2015. 'Operation Blue Star "Was a Well-calculated and Deliberate Slap in the Face of an Entire Community": Khushwant Singh'. *Scroll.in*, 6 June. Available at https://scroll.in/article/732469/operation-blue-star-was-a-well-calculated-and-deliberate-slap-in-the-face-of-an-entire-community-khushwant-singh (accessed on 9 January 2025).

Singh, Khushwant, and Kuldip Nayar. 1985. *Tragedy of Punjab: Operation Bluestar & After*. New Delhi: Vision Books.

Singh, Pritam. 2021. 'Wounds that Never Heal: Remembering Operation Bluestar'. *The Wire*, 6 June. Available at https://thewire.in/history/wounds-that-never-heal-remembering-operation-bluestar (accessed June 2025).

The Economic Times. 2009. 'Journalist Throws Shoe at P Chidambaram, Let off', 7 April. Available at https://economictimes.indiatimes.com/news/politics-and-nation/journalist-throws-shoe-at-p-chidambaram-let-off/articleshow/4369411.cms?from=mdr (accessed on 9 January 2025).

The New York Times. 1985. 'Opinion: Why India Voted for Rajiv Gandhi', 16 January. Available at https://www.nytimes.com/1985/01/16/opinion/l-why-india-voted-for-rajiv-gandhi-218074.html (accessed on 20 November 2024).

Tully, Mark, and Satish Jacob. 1985. *Amritsar: Mrs Gandhi's Last Battle*. New York: Rupa.

Wikipedia. n.d. '1984 Anti-Sikh Riots'. Available at https://en.wikipedia.org/wiki/1984_anti-Sikh_riots (accessed on 9 January 2025).

———. n.d. 'Anandpur Sahib Resolution'. Available at https://en.wikipedia.org/wiki/Anandpur_Sahib_Resolution (accessed on 9 January 2025).

———. n.d. 'Rajiv-Longowal Accord' . Available at https://en.wikipedia.org/wiki/Rajiv%E2%80%93Longowal_Accord (accessed on 24 March 2025).

Acknowledgments

This book would not have seen the light of the day without the contributions of many people. It is not possible to mention each one of them but I am indeed extremely grateful to all of them and they shall stay on in my heart forever.

Nevertheless, I need to mention a few names, beginning with Ravinder Randev, who saved my family's life during *Chaurasi*, and to whom I dedicate this book as a sign of my gratitude. I am extremely grateful to my mentor Prof. Girija Sharma (Himachal Pradesh University), Prof. Amritjit Singh (Ohio State University), Prof. Rachel Bari (Kuvempu University) and Prof. Atanu Bhattacharya (Central University of Gujarat, Kundhela, Vadodara).

Thanks are due to the library staff members of Indian Institute of Advanced Study (IIAS), Shimla, and Panjab Digital Library. I thank EduSikh, Bombay, for having given me extremely encouraging responses and a platform to speak on the subject while I was working on it.

I thank Davinderpal Singh of Panjab Digital Library, and Paramjeet Singh of EduSikh.

Words fall short to thank Dr Charanjeet Kaur, a soul-mate. My friends are my stress-busters, I remember each one of them as I thank them.

Thanks are due to all the contributors who waited patiently with me in the making of this book: Nandita Haksar, Uma Chakravarti, Dilip Simeon, Yasmeen Arif, Diamond Oberoi Vahali, Anne Murphy, Jasmine Anand, Anshu Saluja and Amutha Charu Sheela.

Most importantly, my family has been by my side to bear with my academic commitments, and particularly my various moods as I worked on issues related to trauma and violence (it does get infectious). Many thanks to my husband Avtar Singh, my strength and support system, for being by my side, and my daughter Harsheel Kaur, who may find some meaning in my work when she grows up. My parents, Gursagar Singh and Gurnam Kaur—these are actually their experiences that I am trying to comprehend, and I would not miss mentioning that I drive my strength from these two, very strong people.

Above all, special thanks to Roopa Sharma, editor, Orient BlackSwan; our chance meeting at a book exhibition seems to be pre-ordained as this book was to be born through her hands. I am extremely thankful to Roopa for being an amazing person, extremely honest and amicable. Her personal touch and commitment with this book went beyond a purely professional endeavour, and the work on this book is very close to my heart.

Introduction

In a Discordant State

1984 and its After-Life

Ishmeet Kaur Chaudhry

In the Present

Forty years later, the survivors of the 1984 anti-Sikh violence (referred to as *Chaurasi*, hereafter) are still awaiting justice. Incidents of brutal violence were reported across the country following the assassination of the then Prime Minister Indira Gandhi on 31 October 1984. On 13 August 2021, the newspapers reported reopening of a case after a special investigation team (SIT) was formed by the Uttar Pradesh government regarding the killings of Sikhs in Kanpur. Even though several representations, cases, first information reports (FIRs) and affidavits have been filed by the victims in Delhi, not much attention was paid to cases in Kanpur, Bokaro and other parts of the country. This does not suggest that the survivors in Delhi received due justice. Successive governments in the last four decades have failed altogether in bringing justice to the victims of Chaurasi. The cases kept lingering on, judgments were delayed with a perpetual postponement of hearings and procedural complications. Victims continued to live with a sense of betrayal, distrust and disappointment.

It took 34 years for the courts to pass a judgment on the 89 convicts (in December 2018). While the official number of the killings was 2,733 in Delhi alone and 3,325 across the country, only 89 perpetrators were convicted (Ahooja Committee Report 1987). Sajjan Kumar, one among the numerous senior leaders of the Congress party involved in the violence, was given a life sentence (*The Economic Times* 2018). For years, other senior leaders against whom complaints were filed in the courts have been roaming scot-free. Many of them, including Sajjan Kumar prior to his conviction, were given accolades and ministerial positions in the

Congress-led government at the Centre in the years after the violence. It is ironic that the verdict on Sajjan Kumar was declared around the time when another senior leader of the Congress party, Kamal Nath, suspected to be one of the instigators of the violence, was sworn in as the chief minister of Madhya Pradesh, though he later lost his position mid-term.

The slow pace of the judicial system allowed perpetrators to enjoy prestigious positions without being held accountable for their acts in the past. Such a situation threatens the security of common citizens, leading to distrust of state institutions and judicial structures amongst people. This is evident from the fact that at times some of the survivors, now wearied, refuse to talk about their experience anymore. One of the survivors,[1] speaking off the record, stated that she felt awfully hurt that H. K. L. Bhagat, a senior Congress leader (who was spotted leading mobs by many survivors, as stated in their affidavits), had passed away without being brought to book. She was inconsolable, and reported that her life had been compromised as she had lost seven members of her family and was given the job of a peon in a school. Her younger son had passed away at the age of 31 years due to complications from drug addiction. She refused to forget and forgive H. K. L. Bhagat as she had seen him herself. She remembered how, before Chaurasi, he had always visited their homes, campaigning for votes, and how her family had always supported the Congress party. When I contacted her in the wake of Sajjan Kumar's conviction, she refused to comment. Another survivor, when called on the mobile phone,[2] said there was some solace, but it was not enough. She said that it was the election time and as always Chaurasi was being used as a political tool to win votes. On the conviction of Sajjan Kumar, a young poet Harnidh Kaur (2018) persuasively analysed the conviction thus:

> Justice, especially where genocide is concerned, is an intangible concept. Yes, it is easy to claim that a conviction is a step towards justice, but what are the principles of this justice? Is it just retributive? Does putting a man already at the end of his life into prison help? Every party that comes to power throws us some kind of piecemeal 'deal' and pats itself on the back for buying our silence for a little while longer. Do they not realise this silence is ours by creation? It is a silence we chose because we know it is the only way to keep our future relatively safe. …
>
> This is desolation. And any half-baked attempt at telling us that we have been 'gifted' justice is one in the long, insulting string of consolations that offer us Sikhs no succour or rest.

The questions raised by Harnidh Kaur are extremely significant, especially when countless human lives are involved. Justice, despite being an 'intangible concept', is concrete. The protectors of justice are accountable to ensure security for their citizens by setting strong examples. Punishing the perpetrators is one aspect of justice, while taking responsibility of the crimes is another. Until someone accepts responsibility for what has happened, reassurance is impossible. Legal procedures with respect to the assassins of the prime minister were quick, but delayed justice towards the survivors of Chaurasi has caused irreparable loss. For example, the latest report submitted by the SIT that comprised of former Delhi High Court judge S. N. Dhingra and IPS officer Abhishek Dular clearly pointed out that the police's lack of interest resulted in 'crimes remaining unpunished and culprits going scot-free'. The report also criticised judges for dealing with the court cases in a perfunctory sense, as a routine matter. The report lamented that 'nobody approached the SIT with any specific evidence related to the culprits or witnesses' (Krishnan 2020). Therefore, it became clear that the culprits would go unpunished.

All through these years, the Congress has refused to take responsibility for the killings, dismissing the events as an emotional outburst and as revenge for the assassination of the 'people's prime minister'. Ironically, it was ultimately Dr Manmohan Singh, a Sikh himself, who after becoming the prime minister tendered an apology to the Sikh masses (Samyuktha 2010). The Gandhi family, in contrast, has always failed to show remorse or sympathy for the victims of the mass killings. Rahul Gandhi has callously denied Congress's involvement in the pogrom (Tandon 2018). Senior advocate H. S. Phoolka, in a recent interview, responded to the question of whether 'expected an apology from Congress and what form should that apology take' thus:

> Protecting the life and liberty of citizens is a government's responsibility. Any government which fails to do so owes an apology to the nation and victims. The Congress was in power when the riots took place, so it owes an apology, but it has to be sincere. It doesn't mean that you apologise and then reward those who conduct the riots. (*Indian Express* 2019)

PM Manmohan Singh's apology is understood better on humanitarian grounds than as an apology by the Congress. It is even more considering that in 1984, Singh's 'Hindu' son-in-law had to stand outside his house to protect it from the mob. Furthermore, even as the governor of the Reserve

Bank of India at the time, he had to return to Bombay without being able to present a wreath at the body of the assassinated prime minister (Daman Singh 2014: 169). In hindsight, he is worthy of receiving, rather than tendering, an apology. The indifference of the Gandhi family and other Congress leaders adds another painful layer of impunity to Indian history. While the perpetrators involved in Chaurasi enjoyed powerful positions, the survivors walked to the courts, sat on *dharna* with their little children, managed a living on petty wages and continued to remember every minute detail of their experience of Chaurasi. They struggled with the judicial procedures, ignorant of the paperwork and other legal formalities, speaking with tearful eyes, hoping for justice to come their way someday. Though the government failed to ensure protection, many common citizens, the good samaritans, displayed extraordinary strength amid chaotic times, stood for what was right and supported the afflicted. This act of theirs reinstated faith in humanity.

Thus, the silences need to be broken and common concern for human rights needs to be voiced. The Sikhs and many other people who witnessed the mass killings during Chaurasi have never been able to forget the disastrous outcome of the violence. This became evident in February 2020, when Delhi was once again witness to communal violence. The violence broke out in the wake of a clash between pro–Citizenship (Amendment) Act (CAA) and anti-CAA protesters in Jaffrabad, spreading to parts of north-cast Dclhi and continuing for four days. This reminded people of a similar situation during Chaurasi. Around 53 innocent people, including an officer of the Intelligence Bureau (IB) and a policeman, lost their lives, while hundreds of people were left injured and vandalised (Chaturvedi 2020). The brutal violence against the Sikh community in Chaurasi too had prevailed for four days; it continues to affect the life of survivors to this day and people have neither been able to forget nor forgive. Many Sikhs in Delhi stood in solidarity with the victims of the 2020 violence because of their own experience.

Defining Chaurasi

'Chaurasi',[3] or '84' in Punjabi, has became a significant word that now connotes a descriptive definition for the Sikh community. The political atmosphere of Punjab which remained very disturbed in the 1980s, leading to an army-led attack on the Golden Temple in Amritsar (known as Operation Blue Star) in June 1984, the assassination of the prime minister of India, followed by years of terrorism and militancy in Punjab are together termed as Chaurasi. The years following Chaurasi have been years of struggle for justice for Sikhs. This struggle brought never-ending anxieties and uncertainties with it. Therefore, Chaurasi was no longer to be read as a date, but much in line with an Orwellian dystopian tale of brutality and betrayal. Thousands of innocent pilgrims were killed during Operation Blue Star in the gurdwara complex; this was followed by the killings of thousands of others across the country after the assassination of Indira Gandhi. The repeated tales and narrations of what had happened on those fateful days became a major concern for every household. During gatherings of Sikh communities, conversations were not about health, lifestyle or travel but about killings, loss and politics around Chaurasi. Concerns were being raised and critiqued regarding the secular nature of the nation, autonomy of the state and the security of ordinary people. Issues involving institutional responsibilities of the police system, minority status, identity markers and debates related to nation vis-à-vis its citizens were common. The children of these families grew up struggling, managing challenges of life thrust upon them at a very young age. They began to be identified as '*chaurasi wale danga peedrik*'[4] or being looked upon as suspected terrorists (popularly called as *ugarvadi*, *khardku* or *Khalistani*).

With this evolved a new vocabulary related to Chaurasi. Discussions in various forums began about revisiting the word 'riot' and suggesting that 'riots' are majorly accidental in nature; owing to the nature of the killings in Chaurasi, calling it 'state-led violence' seemed apt; also, the use of the term 'pogrom' or 'carnage' featured in discussions. Moreover, emphasis is being laid on calling this event a 'genocide', equating it with the Holocaust. One of the survivors[5] remarked that during 'riots' people of all communities are affected, injured or killed; 'riots' are not targeted at selected communities; therefore, the word 'riot' would be inappropriate to address the 1984 anti-Sikh violence. This survivor's observation emerged from her experience and not from an academic discourse. She laid emphasis on the fact that it was a state-orchestrated attack that targeted a particular community.[6]

A thin line of difference prevails in the usage of words such as riot, pogrom, carnage, genocide or massacre, terms that have been repeatedly used for the anti-Sikh violence of 1984. The etymology and contexts in which they are used are important for this study. Beginning with 'riot'—the word finds its origin in the thirteenth century, from the old French word meaning 'dispute, quarrel, (tedious) talk, chattering, argument, domestic strife', compared to medieval Latin 'riota' meaning 'quarrel, dispute, uproar, riot' and Latin *rugire* 'to roar', meaning 'public disturbance' (late fourteenth century) (Harper, 'Riot (n)' 2001–08).

The second word 'pogrom' was used to describe the violence against Jewish people in the Russian empire in the late nineteenth and early twentieth centuries. The term can be better understood through the historical understanding of hatred against Jews, or antisemitism, both in Russian as well as English contexts, dating back to the first two crusades, 1096–1102 and 1147–49.[7] The Online Etymology Dictionary entry dates it as '1882, from Yiddish *pogrom*, from Russian *pogromu* "devastation, destruction," from *po-* "by, through, behind, after" (cognate with Latin *post-*; …+ *groumu* "thunder, roar," from PIE imitative root **ghrem-*' (Harper, 'Pogrom (n)' 2001–08). Interestingly, encyclopedia.com (2018) lists the 1984 anti-Sikh violence following Indira Gandhi's assassination under the entry 'pogrom'. Antisemitic pogroms from the late eleventh century to the early twentieth century have been attributed to religious reasons, though another factor appears to be the economic prosperity of Jewish people, which was met with trade jealousy among the mainstream populations. In many cases related to anti-Sikh violence, religio-political concerns along with a similar jealousy towards economic prosperity were important reasons for the mass execution of the Sikhs. Many people identified the participants of the mobs as those who plundered shops and houses for their selfish motives; for example, many of them were tenants of Sikh property owners who thought they could usurp the shops by killing the owners; a few who led the mobs had borrowed money from affluent Sikh businessmen or were involved in disputes related to land issues.[8]

The next word is 'carnage' whose origin is 'c. 1600, from Middle French *carnage* (16c.), from Old Italian *carnaggio* "slaughter, murder," from Medieval Latin *carnaticum* "flesh," from Latin *carnaticum* "slaughter of animals" from *carnem* (nominative caro) "flesh," originally "a piece of flesh," (from PIE root *sker-(1) "to cut")'. The word has been used for the slaughtering of people rather than beasts (Harper, 'Carnage (n)' 2001–08). The term may justifiably be used for the anti-Sikh violence, as it points to the manner in which the Sikh men were slaughtered, burnt alive, put to fire by 'garlanding' them with burning tyres around their necks; individual and mass burnings using flammable powder and kerosene oil exemplify deeply dehumanising and vicious forms of violence.

Finally, the word 'genocide' is the most controversial, though there has been a continual demand by some within the Sikh community to call

Chaurasi a genocide. The Online Etymology Dictionary refers to *genos* in Greek, meaning 'race or kind' and *cide* meaning 'killing', but for a definition, it refers to a Polish-born US jurist Raphael Lemkin (1900–59). Lemkin states:

> Generally speaking, genocide does not necessarily mean the immediate destruction of a nation, except when accomplished by mass killings of all members of a nation. It is intended rather to signify a coordinated plan of different actions aimed at the destruction of essential foundations of the life of national groups, with the aim of annihilating the groups themselves. (Harper, 'Genocide (n)' 2001–08)

The same survivor[9] who critiqued the word riot also corroborated the popular knowledge that this was a community-based attack, where people of the Sikh community were singled out, identified, their houses spotted, marked and attacked based on their identity markers.

The demand to declare the anti-Sikh violence as 'genocide' has been repeatedly voiced on various forums for many years, and most recently in December 2018 by Shiromani Akali Dal leader Prem Singh Chandumajra, who raised this demand in the zero hour soon after the Delhi High Court released its judgment announcing life sentence to senior Congress party leader Sajjan Kumar (Aschom 2018). It would not be wrong to mention that Indian politicians, particularly Sikh leaders from Punjab, have remained oblivious to the cause for all these years and have shown whatever little interest in Chaurasi only recently. They maintained an unjustified silence on the issue for a very long time, even though the victims in India and among the diaspora commemorate such events from time to time. Those who had to migrate, irrespective of their caste, class or gender, continue to remain fixed in the memory of the time of their migration—for them that moment of movement defines their existence. This may be true for all communities, but for some innocent Sikhs who were forced into political asylum or exile during Chaurasi, their experiences and memories of the past remain stuck in that very moment of their movement. The reason for this may be that while Sikhs from Punjab were struggling to re-establish themselves, those who were forced to leave the country on various pretexts, including threats from militants as well as multiple interrogations by the police, remain rootless.

In this context, effective motions were moved in the international spaces; for example, in 2012, Warren Enstch, an Australian MP and lawmaker, tabled the petition recommending that the 1984 anti-Sikh pogrom be declared as a 'genocide'. This petition was filed on 1 November 2012, 28 years after the event. He stated that:

> It is important to note that today, Nov 1, is 28 years to the day that these attacks took place. And as long as they continue to be referred to as 'anti-Sikh riots' there can be no closure for the Sikh community. Discussions around mass violence and genocide will always be controversial but the continued denial of such historical injustices can only encourage modern day crimes against humanity. (*India Today* 2010)

Later, the US government refused to declare the anti-Sikh violence in India as 'genocide' in April 2013 (*Times of India* 2013). This was disappointing for members of the Sikh community in the US. On the other hand, in April 2017, the Ontario Assembly carried the motion that described the anti-Sikh violence as 'genocide', making it the first legislature to do so. This was heavily criticised by the Indian government, which termed it as a 'misguided' understanding of the concept (Bhattacharya 2017). The motion was moved by Harinder Malhi, a member of Provincial Parliament (MPP) belonging to the ruling Liberal Party. Following this, the then defence minister of India, Arun Jaitley, met Harjit Sajjan, minister of national defence, Canada, on the latter's visit to India in April 2017 and told him that the resolution was 'unreal' and 'exaggerated'. The Canadian minister is 'understood to have distanced the Canadian federal government from the resolution' (Sen 2017). He clarified that 'the resolution of the Ontario Assembly did not reflect the official stand of Canada' (ibid.). The refusal of successive Indian governments to accept the anti-Sikh violence as 'genocide' and Harjit Sajjan's differential stand on the issue indicate the milder treatment being meted out to the entire issue. The official narrative characterises the violence as a politically motivated attack by the Congress government in power and portrays the other political parties as non-participants in the entire affair. Had this been true, there would have been stronger voices in favour of the Sikhs and against their killings from the Opposition, but they too chose to remain silent. The official version seeks to provide a justification that it was not a national agenda to eradicate the Sikh community from the nation (even though the Sikhs were being killed nation-wide), denying the killings be termed as 'genocide'. Ironically, the attack by Indian army on the Golden Temple was led under the supervision of the ruling government, excluding all possibilities of Chaurasi to be read as a singular party-led attack. Therefore, governments have failed in supporting the Sikhs on this matter.

The People's Union for Civil Liberties (PUCL) and People's Union for Democratic Rights (PUDR) in the report *Who Are the Guilty?* on investigations from 1 November to 10 November 1984 clearly stated that the violence was a 'well-organised plan':

> A fact-finding team ... has come to the conclusion that the attacks on members of the Sikh Community in Delhi and its suburbs during the period, far from being a spontaneous expression of 'madness' and of popular 'grief and anger' at Indira Gandhi's assassination as made out to be by the authorities, were the out-come [*sic*] of a well-organised plan marked by acts of both deliberate commission and omission by important politicians of the Congress(I) at the top and by authorities in the administration. (Mukhoty and Kothari 1984: 1)

The report stated that the 'arson is the work of an expert' (ibid.). Many eyewitnesses confirmed the use of white flammable powder during the violence, which corroborates this finding. One survivors and his friends agreed that while Indira Gandhi's assassination was a trigger point, the perpetrators were already prepared for an attack. They felt that even if Gandhi had not been killed, the anti-Sikh attacks would have taken place.[10] Thus, the Sikh community began to feel threatened and 'othered' in their own nation. One bore the brunt of a transformed image in the national imagination: from a chivalric, brave soldier in the service of humanity and nation, to a so-called terrorist, an anti-national element.

More recently, the term 'genocide' was used by Justice Guaba, in his judgment in December 2018, when he sentenced 89 people accused of killings. He referred to Chaurasi as a 'genocide' (Datta 2018). Jyoti Grewal suggests that even though 'naming the problem is essential to analysing its intent and meaning', conceptualising Chaurasi is exceedingly problematic because, most importantly, 'the unique situation of Sikh–Hindu violence does not fit into any established paradigm of communalism' (2007: 11).

Therefore, defining or naming the event continues to be critical and complicated, and the significance of revisiting it thus remains central. Where the Sikhs struggle with an anti-national image, their religio-cultural practices have helped them heal and evolve from the setbacks they have faced. It would not be wrong to say that the impression of Chaurasi seems to have resulted in sublimation of an experience for the survivors who may have sought healing and recovery in empathising with others. With a deep understanding of being othered as a minority community, many Sikhs have chosen to return to their history and culture. They have made renewed attempts to understand the principles of their faith by implementing them practically in life, especially principles like that of 'seva' (community service) and 'sarbat ka bhala' (welfare of all). Even more, the participation of people from other communities who stood in solidarity with the victims of the recent riots in Delhi in 2020 is also worth noting. This time the people of Delhi immediately compared this violence to the chaos of Chaurasi and rejected its recurrence. Chaurasi continues to shock the Sikhs as those years were underlined by humiliation, injustice and disgrace, resulting in a future full of fear, distrust, betrayal and uncertainty. Therefore, at many sites of conflict, violence or natural disasters, whenever the common people needed help, Sikh organisers and volunteers have reached sites of distress and provided support in several ways, particularly by serving 'langar' (meals from the community kitchen), following the principles of Guru Nanak Dev, primarily, with a spirit of rendering service to the humankind irrespective of religion, caste or creed.

Principle of 'Seva' and the Sikh Image

In Sikhism, the concept of 'seva', meaning 'selfless service unto others', is pivotal. Rooted in the ideological principles of the Guru Granth Sahib and Guru Nanak Dev's idea 'Nam Japo, Kirat Karo and Vaand Chako',[11] sharing one's earnings with those in need is the founding principle of Sikh ideological thought that has been integrated with practical living. Sohi et al. (2018) explain Guru Nanak Dev's efforts towards the betterment of society and how he institutionalised the concept of 'seva' as a socio-religious concern:

> Contributing to the welfare of humanity be it by giving one's labor, resources, or any other form of assistance was espoused as a way of life for the Sikhs right from the time of the first guru, Guru Nanak Dev who himself worked immensely for the betterment of the people. Efforts were made by Guru Nanak Dev to institutionalize this practice in order to encourage people to make it a part of their way of life. We find emphasis on seva in the lives of the other Sikh gurus as well. Thus, seva has been central to the Sikh way of life. (2018: 2068)

The social aspect of 'seva' is to treat all individuals equally, irrespective of their caste, class and status. This concept needs to be understood in the historical, political and spiritual sense as well. In Sikh history, the spirit of martyrdom depicts selfless service ('seva') through body, with heart and wealth (*tan, man, dhan*). Incidents from the life of Gurus and their families are seen to have a universal impact as they do not limit themselves to the Sikh community or one nation alone, but are applicable to humanity in general. The Gurus laid down their lives to protect faith of other communities[12] and to save the common citizens from the atrocities of oppressive forces. Anne Murphy suggests that these historical narratives are 'utilized to emphasize the importance of "Seva" in Sikh tradition, binding the community together in a shared past and theology' (Murphy 2004: 343).

Such practices of the Sikh faith have enabled the community to reinstate its identity, image and honour through 'seva' every time it faced threats in contemporary times, be it during the Partition in 1947, when the anti-national narrative and propaganda circulated against the Sikhs in 1984, during the years of militancy and insurgency in Punjab in the 1980s and 1990s, or during the times of famine. The principle of 'seva' offered an alternative to the tarnished image of the Sikhs. Sohi et al. (2018) suggest that 'Sikhs have established their unique identity in the multicultural Indian society and the distinct principles and practices of this community have made this possible. The ritual of seva is one such distinctive feature of the community' (2018: 2068). This is also evident from the Viakom Movement, launched in 1924 by people belonging to the so-called low castes. They were protesting the ban imposed on the entry of the lower caste people onto the roads approaching Sri Mahadeva temple. This was the first anti-caste movement in Kerala. The news of this movement attracted nation-wide attention. Following a discussion of Sardar K. M. Panikkar (an Indian statesman and diplomat from Kerala and a minister of the Maharaja of Patiala) with Mangal Singh (the ad-hoc president of the Shiromani Gurdwara Prabandhak Committee [SGPC]) and the committee members of SGPC, a group of 12 Sikhs was sent to Kerala to help the agitators where a langar (a community kitchen that provided free meals) was set up (Dharam Singh 2020: 83).

More recently, members of the Sikh community remained committed to 'seva' throughout the lockdown period during the Covid-19 pandemic. Packaged food was provided to hospitals, both in India and among the diaspora, and also to migrant labourers in India who were forced to walk long distances to return to their native places. The migrant labourers were forced to undertake the journey due to the sudden declaration of a national lockdown, as a result of which all economic activities came to a sudden halt in cities, leaving the working classes in the lurch. They provided free oxygen and bedding facilities at gurdwaras in the National Capital Region (NCR) to patients suffering from Covid-19 during the second wave of the pandemic in 2021, when the country was facing a shortage of oxygen cylinders.

The Political Conflict

The twentieth century saw some crucial developments for the Sikh community, particularly between the 1920s–40s, and the 1970s–90s. The early years redefined the Sikh identity as separate from other religious communities, particularly from the Hindus, who are commonly considered their nearest counterpart, as was evident during Partition violence. This period is also known for the establishment of Sikh politics within a democratic framework. The Sikhs remained politically engaged right from the beginning, with Guru Nanak Dev's dialogue with Babur, Guru Arjan Dev's martyrdom, Guru Hargobind Singh's military activities, Guru Teghbahadar's martyrdom and Guru Gobind Singh's opposition of the ruling oppressors in power, and the rising of the Sikh Raj under the able leadership of Maharaja Ranjit Singh. Continuing ever since, with the independence of India in 1947, a new government independent of the colonial rule also redefined the Sikh identity as a separate identity. The separation of identity and the evolution of Sikh politics, with its leaders like Master Tara Singh, his daughter Rajinder Kaur, Giani Kartar Singh and Sardar Hukam Singh, gave the community a new form in accordance with the new set of government in place post Independence.

The Sikhs had merely resettled by the 1970s and the 1980s that another upsurge took place to redefine them. This time it was shielded with a narrative of negative militarianism and a demand for Khalistan which was heavily misconstrued with the state politics of the Congress government. Further, the separation of Haryana, Himachal Pradesh and Punjab had already reduced the large and a very fertile area of Punjab (3.57 lakh sq km before separation) into a small area, only about 50,000 sq km. Punjab thus not only struggled for its land, but also witnessed a huge cultural loss, with a threat to the religion as well as language of its people. It is rightly said that to attack a community, attack its language. Owing to this, the language dispute was clearly visible in Punjab in 1957 when the Hindi language movement opposed the designation of Gurmukhi as a state language in Punjab. A lot of Punjabi-speaking Hindus in Punjab declared Hindi as their mother tongue, with a prominent Punjabi accent, during the 1961 census. Finally, because of different linguistic belts, Punjab was divided into three parts—Haryana, Himachal Pradesh and Punjab. This new Punjab had to bear the animosity of the neighbouring states, and Haryana and Punjab's unresolved water dispute and sharing of the capital city, Chandigarh, remain contested till date.

In the 1970s, Punjab witnessed massive political conflict in which the state, political parties and several local extremist groups were involved. Amritjit Singh et al. (2016) explain the situation as a complicated one, where Sant Jarnail Singh Bhindranwale was being used both by the Congress and Akali leaders for their political benefit. The Akalis presented a memorandum of demands, which were included in the 1973 Anandpur Sahib Resolution, to the then Prime Minister Indira Gandhi. She paid little attention to these demands, and even though there was no demand for a separate Sikh nation in the resolution, Mrs Gandhi 'touted its focus on the enhanced state rights as a step toward secession' (Amritjit Singh et al. 2016: xxxi). Singh et al. report the happenings during the 1970s and the cold attitude of the central government concerning the memorandum as follows:

> She did not respond to the issues and demands raised by Akali leadership in good faith or in a timely fashion, instead letting the situation fester into the early 1980s. In 1982, Congress leader Swaran Singh negotiated an agreement on behalf of the central government with the Akalis on the distribution of water and key issues from the Anandpur Sahib Resolution, but Mrs Gandhi quickly backed out without any explanation. Around 1977, when the Akali–Janata coalition came to power in the Punjab after the defeat of Congress Party in assembly elections, Sant Jarnail Singh Bhindranwale, a charismatic religious leader, had emerged on the Punjab scene. (Ibid.: xxxi)

A Sikh majority in Punjab resulted in the Akalis coming to power, even though for a short period. However, they soon lost owing to a split within the party, and this inter-party conflict consequently paved the way for the Congress to come to power in the state. The Akali Dal, which had reformulated itself as a party 'with a base among the Sikhs' (Judge 2005: 54), joined hands with Sikh religious leader Bhindranwale in 1982. By this time, Bhindranwale had grown suspicious of the Congress, and felt that they had ulterior motives in offering him support. Paramjit Singh Judge explains how many of these matters remained independent of each other till the coalition between the Akalis and Bhindranwale. The demand for

Khalistan was evidently not of interest to Bhindranwale. That demand had appeared in 1971 when Jagjit Singh Chauhan got a half-page advertisement published in the *New York Times* that raised the issue of Khalistan (Judge 2005: 64). Bhindranwale did not express an interest in these demands. The media had been creating anti-nation narratives, painting Sikhs as terrorists or Khalistanis.[13] The ruling party used the media to project the entire issue for their electoral benefits and against Bhindranwale. But one should also remember that the militant groups also used the media to reach out to people. Judge clearly states that

> Chauhan had no connection with the Bhindranwale phenomenon, which started seven years after the advertisement. Similarly, the passing of Anandpur Sahib Resolution in 1973 by the Akali Dal was a strategic document on the autonomy of states for electoral gains. Bhindranwale picked up the Anandpur Sahib Resolution as the demand charter of the Sikhs. The significant rise of the Sikh diaspora till mid-1970s contributed to the development of the idea of the independent Sikh state. Some of the prominent Sikhs abroad raised the issue of Khalistan. The Congress party too had its share in this process when Giani Zail Singh virtually sponsored the formation of Dal Khalsa, which articulated the glory and autonomy of the Sikhs. The Congress and the Akali Dal—the two major political parties competed with each other on capturing the votes of the Sikhs. In the process both revived Sikhism in their own ways showing holier-than-thou behaviour. (Judge 2005: 64)

Therefore, the discourse and narrative of Khalistan emerged parallel to Bhindranwale's politics. It did not have an immediate connection to him, though the narrative grew and was attributed to him as well as to the other militant groups that openly demanded Khalistan. Similarly, Joginder Singh, in his book *Myth and Reality of the Sikh Militancy in Punjab* (2006), describes the involvement of political parties and the role played by the media in projecting various narratives and creating divisions between the Hindus and the Sikhs in Punjab:

> The political parties indulged in mutual mudslinging and accused their political opponents for [*sic*] generating communal violence. The Akalis and the Sikh press accused Hindu organizations and Congress politicians. Whereas, the mahashay press and the Congress accused the Sikh communal organisations. The government accused both Hindu and Sikh communalists. The Congress alleged that some foreign powers were behind the communal violence. (Singh 2006: 63)

With this, violent clashes were on the rise in Punjab with every passing day. Raids became common; arrests of suspects by the police and retaliation by local groups and supporters of Akali Dal and Bhindranwale in the name of revenge became the order of the day. Planned killings of both Hindus and Sikhs at different times and at different places made matters worse. Sikh history began to surface both as motivation for the youth to participate in and join the local groups, and as justification for the killings, whether in retaliation, self-defence or even vengeance. At the same time, Bhindranwale was now more clearly being projected as a national threat by the government. The Government of India attacked the Golden Temple in June 1984 to arrest Bhindranwale as he was residing there. At the same time, more than 37 historical gurdwaras in and around Punjab were damaged under the Army's control (Talta 2015: 318). Darshan Singh Talta presents an estimate of the causalities in Harmandir Sahib as follows:

> Total casualties inside the Golden Temple remain contested, between the official counts of 300 army officer and men, with 500 civilians, while impartial observers put 700 army officers and men and about 5000 civilians. The army also took control of 37 other historic gurdwaras around Punjab with some resistance at some places and casualties too. (Ibid.)

Even though Bhindranwale could have been arrested outside the Golden Temple, heavy military ammunition and tanks were forced into the premises of the temple, reducing the Akal Takhat, a symbol of political sovereignty for the Sikh community, to debris. This incident had a deep emotional impact on the Sikhs, who felt deeply humiliated. Even those Sikhs who did not support militant violence were shaken in the aftermath of Operation Blue Star. Punjab was in mayhem, and in a quick succession of events, on 31 October 1984, two Sikh bodyguards of Indira Gandhi, Satwant Singh and Beant Singh, assassinated the prime minister. This was followed by a massacre of Sikhs openly in the streets of the capital and across different parts of the country.

Over the 1980s and 1990s, many Punjabis within the state of Punjab faced charges of having carried out 'anti-national' activities. Certain anti-terrorism laws like Terrorist and Disruptive Activities (Prevention) Act (TADA), and later the Prevention of Terrorism Act (POTA), were also enforced in Punjab during this period by the Government of India. TADA came into effect in May 1985 and lapsed in 1995, after being given five extensions by Parliament. It was enacted in 1985 when the Congress was in power at the Centre. TADA was a special law under which a person who advocated cession or secession directly or indirectly was liable to be punished. Such a person could be detained without formal charges or trial against him for a year. Under this act, one could be detained in police custody up to 60 days which, in all probability, increased the risk of torture. At the same time, the detainee may not be produced before a judicial magistrate, but may be produced before an executive magistrate who may be a police officer or in administrative service. The executive magistrate was not answerable to the high court. The trials could be held anywhere, and the witness's identity could be concealed or kept secret. This was in violation of the standards of a fair and just trial. A person may be accused of committing a terrorist act based on suspicion or information by anyone. This person shall be presumed to be guilty unless proven otherwise. Finally, a person could appeal only to the Supreme Court.

In 2002, TADA was replaced by POTA. This Act was defeated in the Rajya Sabha but was passed in a joint session of Parliament. POTA was initiated as a response to increasing terrorist attacks, particularly the 2001 attack on Parliament. Jaijee and Suri write that POTA 'expanded the definition of terrorist act with an "intent to threaten the unity, integrity, security or sovereignty of India"' (2020: 48). They explain that while 'TADA vaguely referred to "intent to overawe the government", POTA also swept up anyone who was the member of an unlawful association' (ibid.). POTA was repealed in 2004 and replaced by the Unlawful Activities Prevention Act (UAPA). Unlikc TADA and POTA, UAPA is a permanent law. Jaijee and Suri explain that it is 'all of TADA, all of POTA, plus it broadened the definition of the terrorist act still further':

> Now it's any act that makes use of 'bombs, dynamite … or any other substances … of a hazardous nature', or 'any other means of whatever nature.' Speak, write, publish, organise, mobilize … aren't these activities 'likely to threaten' the government or 'likely to strike terror in (certain segments of) the people'. (Ibid.)

Under this law, one can be arrested by the police without charge for six months. Such laws are instrumental for the state to have an absolute control on the individual, whether or not they are proven criminals. Suspicion is enough to hold them in custody. It was such laws that were applied to countless citizens in Punjab in the name of restoring normality. Many young boys went missing. They were arrested by the police, never to be found again. Similarly, the police personnel who did not support such illegal killings were also murdered and went missing. Jaswant Singh

Khalra, a human rights activist, engaged himself with investigating the countless illegal killings and cremations that involved the Punjab police. Khalra's research, and later his murder, was evidence of the role played by the police in misusing laws like TADA (Kumar et al. 2003).

Kirpal Dhillon explains that Chaurasi resonates

> with similar episodes in Sikh history, such as the *ghallugharas* or the organised massacres of Sikhs during Mughal rule. Together with Operation Bluestar, the 1984 Sikh bloodshed contributed significantly to the sharpening of separate identities and agendas between Hindus and Sikhs worldwide, despite the two having much in common in social and familial terms. They would henceforth look at every major event, starting with Operation Bluestar itself, in a sharply antagonistic manner. While the Sikhs began to see themselves in terms of a marked minority .... (2016: 22)

Moreover, terrorism and the tensions in Punjab added to the tainted imaging of Punjab and Punjabis, particularly the Sikh community. One wonders how the separation between the Hindu and the Sikh creeps in, and how it widens by the time Chaurasi is organised.

Collective Memory and a Methodology of Remembering

The past can be relocated in the present through a reconstruction of cities, sites and narratives, both literally and metaphorically, in the form of stories, songs, poems, slogans and sometimes festivals,[14] and with collective community gatherings on several occasions in gurdwaras. The annual commemoration events held at memorial sites on the dates related to Chaurasi are significant.[15] Radhika Chopra rightly remarks that

> We do not leave our past behind; it's a palpable presence in our present and we actively commemorate and remember the past in monuments and memorials, in texts, images, songs, stories, rituals, art, space and time and, I would add, in evocations of the spirit of persons. (2010: 120)

She reiterates the contention of Halbwach and Eves, 'It is in society that people acquire memory, localizing the present in the past … the memory is collective not because its content is shared but because the process of remembering is shared' (ibid.). Chopra engages with the split between the memorial and memories—while 'memorials are placed in the dialogical relations of reference … remembrance is layered, weaving historical pasts and contemporary politics' (ibid.: 125). She recalls how the public places and the bazaars surrounding the site of events are also sites of remembrance. The bazaars surrounding Darbar Sahib are 'replete with artefactual remembrance available as religious souvenirs'. They

> amplify the messages of memory portrayed within the shrine and its museum. Despite the overwhelming presence of shrine-centric rituals, shop keepers have their own take on politics of memory promoted by orthodoxy. In and through the language of this the commemorations within the shrine in the aftermath of Operation Bluestar are both supported and critiqued. The folk of the bazaar see themselves as custodians of belief and their shops as sites of sanctity which are as significant as those within the complex of the shrine. (2018: xvii)

Apart from the commemorative events organised annually by Akal Takhat or gurdwaras in Delhi, there is a continual streak of remembrance for the survivors on the days when they have hearings in the courts and when *dharna*s are organised by the survivors, and these protest sites become sites of commemoration. For the survivors, demonstrations and protests have become a part of life as politicians make fake promises as political gimmicks. The survivors reported returning to dharnas for fulfilment of these promises (Chaudhry 2019: 27). Recalling, therefore, is a collective form of memory, as one of the survivors described how they empathised with onc another in moments when their spirits began falling.[16] They looked around at each other to find the same experiences and similar pain, very much in line with Chopra's claim that people acquire memory in society as a group.

These concerns raise a series of considerable research questions: Is it possible to remember the traumatic experience that remains unforgettable? How to remember? Or is it possible to forget and move on? Why is remembering important and what could be the possible ways in which remembering is documented and presented? Giorgio Agamben, in the context of holocaust survivors, suggests, 'The survivor's vocation is to remember; he cannot *not* remember' (1999: 26). Every attempt to remember also brings to life the traumatic events. How does that affect the subject whose experience is being revisited? What purpose would 'remembering' solve? Does remembering lead to recovery? Is recovery ever possible? Primo Levi, a holocaust survivor, brings out how the memory of the traumatic events, in case of a prisoner in the Nazi camp, remained fixed in his memory. He may have forgotten what happened before or after the camp but the prisoner vividly remembered every detail of his life in the camp: 'I still have a visual and acoustic memory of the experiences there that I cannot explain ... sentences in languages I do not know have remained etched in my memory, like on a magnetic tape' (Agamben 1999: 26–27). At the same time, there may not be one single method to recall or remember. Remembering can surface in several ways, in different forms of expression and even through silences that may be considered as an inability to recall. While, for some, articulating may be therapeutic or healing, for others silence may represent a sense of resignation. This was evident in the visit to a gurdwara within the Tilak Vihar widows' colony, where photographs of men and children killed during the Chaurasi violence have been displayed in a very small room. Due to the paucity of space, hundreds of frames have been piled up on each other. On entering the room, several women walk in to talk about their children and men, pointing at the photographs hanging on the wall. The expressions on the face of a boy about 4–5 years old, in a photograph, sends shivers down the viewer's spine, and the manner of his killing freezes one's nerves. One wonders how this little kid could harm anyone. What danger did he pose to those in power? Did he deserve such a death?

Inadequacies and Injustice

Studies on violence, trauma and experience involve personal and subjective perceptions that provide a sense of alternate history from a survivor's point of view, testimonies about all that went unrecorded. While it is understood that the judiciary follows a systemic procedure, rules, regulations, evidence and official records, those responsible for inadequacies at various levels, in maintaining records, or falling prey to the political pressures, or those who have to blindly follow orders of corrupt officers, are neither questioned nor made accountable. Pav Singh states:

> Security forces, including both the police and the army, are rarely held accountable for abuses they commit, which at times are all too prevalent. In such circumstances, the normal rules of security and policing are often circumvented, and human rights abuses become rife, as they were in Punjab during 1980s and 1990s. (2017: 183–84)

Such action, or rather inaction, sets precedents for the perpetrators and ensures the possibility of similar events in future. The impact of such incidents is manifold. Meenakshi Ganguly, South Asia Deputy Director at the Human Rights Watch, spells out the bearings of repeated examples of impunity on society in general: 'India's failure to prosecute those most responsible for the anti-Sikh violence in 1984 has not only denied justice to Sikhs but has made all Indians more vulnerable to communal violence' (Human Rights Watch 2014). The repeated obstruction in investigations by the authorities in order to 'protect the perpetrators of atrocities against Sikhs, [has led to] deepening public distrust in India's justice system' (ibid.). During Chaurasi, the involvement of many senior Congress leaders was ignored due to the lack of evidence regarding their direct involvement with the killings, though the affidavits submitted by the victims have named different Congress leaders who were supporting the mobs. Sanjay Suri in his book *1984: The Anti-Sikh Violence and After* (2015) devotes a chapter to Kamal Nath as Suri himself, as a beat reporter at the Rakabganj, was an eyewitness to his presence. He saw how Kamal Nath controlled the mobs by signalling them. The mob was more obedient to him than to the police present there on the site. Suri reports:

> What did the police know about the crowd that they could stand back and decide to leave it in the hands of Kamal Nath? Indisputably, before their eyes, this was a Congress crowd. Just as indisputably, men from this crowd had killed two people, and were ready to advance to kill again. For a police force to stand by watching all this was itself illegal. The stillness of the police was actionable … . It is outside of law for a police force to stand and watch a political leader make moves to exercise control that was for them to enforce. (2015: 50)

Suri also expresses his disappointment when the affidavit that he submitted to both Mishra and Nanavati commissions were not considered and were noted as 'not [having] been "very clear"' (ibid.: 48). The complexity of the system fails to facilitate the survivors. Many affidavits reported instances where police remained insolent towards the victims.[17] Manoj Mitta and H. S. Phoolka state, 'The police, incidentally, did not register cases related to any of the incidents witnessed … In fact, not a single case of anti-Sikh violence was registered that day throughout Lutyens' Delhi' (2007: 20). The role of police is quite questionable. Virginia Van Dyke (1996) discusses three different methods employed by the police while dealing with violence during Chaurasi. She explains that 'they were either "conspicuous by their absence," passive observers, or acting in complicity by encouraging or actually participating in the violence' (Van Dyke 1996: 210). Therefore, in such cases where the institutional machinery seems to have crumbled, one of the ways to expose the truth is through first-hand narratives of the survivors, mostly women. Unfortunately, their accounts are never considered as sufficient evidence.

Women of Chaurasi: A Subject of Neglect

These 'tales of mourning' will continue to reverberate from generation to generation. Thousands of women lived on with a feeling of humiliation, having experienced multiple forms of mutilation themselves and having helplessly watched their girls being molested in front of them by the mob.[18] Unfortunately, the complaints remain absent in the legal records. This is primarily because women remained a subject of neglect. Their concerns regarding sexual assault remained unaddressed. Moreover, other socio-cultural factors also prevented the women from recording their experiences and registering legal cases against the perpetrators. Often, a woman's body and her honour are associated with the honour of the family itself. Pratiksha Baxi reports that many families, where there was even a single man, chose to remain silent about the violation of women's body as it was seen as a marker of the 'weakness' of the man who could not protect the women of his family (Baxi 2007: 83). The ones who chose to speak informally were those who had lost all the men of their family. Baxi informs, 'We find that in the aftermath of the 1984 violence, not a single case of molestation or rape was ever registered. A number of fact-finding reports published in the aftermath of Delhi 1984 reported narratives of rape of women, yet these did not enter legal records' (ibid.). Since women continued to live with such humiliation, they struggled for a living and had to live through great difficulties and challenges. Many women reported their experiences to doctors (ibid.: 84); these informal narratives and some others as reported by Madhu Kishwar (1984) testify to the rapes during Chaurasi. Another thing that is frequently omitted is the impression on the minds of children; many girls were physically assaulted and many boys either watched their sisters or mothers being humiliated in front of them or were at least not unaware of such happenings. The repression of this experience resulted in continuous depression and frustration amongst the youth. Forty years hence, some of these children have been lost to drugs and petty crime as they were unable to tackle their mental trauma.

Personal Experiences

On 31 October 1984, as my family and I peeped out from our window, watching the mob attacking the gurdwara right opposite our house, there was a knock on our door. It was our neighbour, veteran journalist Ravinder Randev, who called us and assured us of our safety. He went out and began hurling stones at the mob; consequently, people began to disperse, primarily as they were scared of being identified, particularly by a journalist. Soon after, other neighbours came to our house and reassured us. My grandfather, who had moved from Kahuta, Rawalpindi, to Shimla in Himachal Pradesh during Partition, was very uncomfortable and feared that the mob might return. He related the communal experiences of Partition violence to Chaurasi. His memory had taken him 37 years back in time. Suddenly, a feeling of 'rootlessness' creeped into his mind.

Similarly, Karnail Singh[19] narrated how his father's experience of Partition violence in 1947 saved them during Chaurasi in Delhi. The family had taken shelter in the house of a Hindu Lala[20] in Punjabi Bagh, but the Lala behaved a bit erratically. Karnail's father understood that he was plotting something against them, and he immediately moved his sons from there. Based on his experience from Partition when neighbours and even some close friends had betrayed them, he led his sons to change places and hidings, moving from one house to another for the first two days. On 3 November, they were driven to Fateh Nagar, a relatively safer place, by a family friend, a mona-Sikh[21] man, who carried a licensed gun with him and pretended to shoot at the sight of a mob.

Similarly, people who had experienced Partition violence referred to Chaurasi as a second partition, as they felt a similar sense of communal discrimination; the difference being that during Partition violence, all communities were involved in attacking each other, but during Chaurasi, only the Sikhs were singled out and targeted.

Moreover, a navy officer from Uttar Pradesh, Ramesh Singh, now retired, remembers how as a child he was influenced by his Sikh neighbours. He wore a *kara* (a steel bangle)[22] right from his childhood and adorned a beard. He was in Delhi when the massacres were taking place. He was to go on leave to Dehradun, and had to shave his beard and remove the kara as he was given to understand that the unruly mob was targeting all persons who remotely looked like or resembled a Sikh.[23] Being in the defence services mattered little to a mob, who in their frenzy could not distinguish between right and wrong. There is no doubt that the Sikh population was a target of the mobs during Chaurasi, but to understand it as Hindu–Sikh hate violence would be incorrect, as the violence was orchestrated by the leaders of the ruling Congress party. At the same time, it is true that several neighbours, civil rights organisations and people of other religions affiliations, including Hindus, also risked their lives to save the Sikhs. Many such people became victims of the fury of the mobs for having protected their Sikh neighbours, friends or even strangers. These people have moved on as unnoticed victims. But the solidarity they showed has restored deep faith in humanity during times of acute distress.

Karnail Singh remembers how a rickshaw-puller, a migrant labourer, reported the burning of their showroom at Moti Bagh in a step-wise sequence through repeated phone calls: how some people had marked a cross on their glass, broken open the furniture showroom, began looting the material and finally set the empty showroom on fire. Since he was calling from the showroom's phone, in his last call (probably before the phone wires would have completely burnt out) he stated that some people had set fire to the shop, with a policeman overseeing the violence, and on the rickshaw-puller's attempt to douse the flames by throwing water, the policeman had threatened him. This rickshaw-puller stands tall in the memory of Karnail Singh who spoke of deep admiration for him.[24]

Jarnail Singh in his book *I Accuse: The Anti-Sikh Violence of 1984* describes how those institutions that are supposed to protect and care for citizens were supporting the killings: 'The police was instructed to either turn a blind eye or help the mobs' (2009: 29).

Similarly, Sanjay Suri refers to a close encounter with a Sikh man who asked him for help lest he be killed that night at Sultanpuri. He describes the eyes of that man: 'The eyes looked like he was some prey being hunted' (Suri 2015: 56). Suri himself had a narrow escape and wonders till date as to what happened to that man (ibid.: 56–57).

The inhuman brutality of these incidents puts the nation to shame. Some survivors reported that they were supporters of the Congress party as they had benefitted from the macro-loans introduced during the Congress government.[25] They felt betrayed when they were targeted. For these people, life has been the toughest and they continue to struggle, waiting for closure, some day.

Perspectives

The essays in this volume provide a critical examination of Chaurasi. They address various aspects related to the reading of violence, ranging from personal experiences to commemoration of trauma, and its after-effects, dealing with the concerns related to women, violence and rape; recovery and survival; and matters of representation, be it oral narratives, cinematic depiction or literary representations.

Nandita Haksar explains the complexities of the judicial procedures and the gaps within the system in her essay, 'Multiple Narratives of 1984: The Importance of Remembering'. Haksar assesses the efficacy and importance of the interventions made by human rights activists; at the same time, the interventions did not address the root causes of the conflict. Her chapter addresses the criticalities of the judicial system, as she was a part of the fact-finding team whose report 'Who Are the Guilty?' was published by the PUDR and PUCL (Mukhoty and Kothari 1984). The report was dismissed on the ground that PUDR and PUCL had no locus standi.

Uma Chakravarti in her chapter 'A Personal Account of 1984' recalls her own experience of helping their Sikh house-owner, followed by her participation in the rescue camps, recording interviews of the survivors, and working for years with the subjects of violence. In the essay, she states that eventually, Chaurasi simply became a way to justify impunity, and communal and sexual violence in other parts of the country, particularly Gujarat. Only some feminists and civil rights activists, like Chakravarti herself, were left to point out that one does not justify the other; there were many like her who had stood against all forms of communal and state-sponsored violence and continue to do so, no matter what.

Dilip Simeon in 'The Broken Middle' discusses how the violent events of Chaurasi signify the breakdown of consensual politics and the ideal of composite and inclusive Indian nationhood. When communal animosity spreads across society, it corrodes the social conscience and (directly or subliminally) produces a genocidal consensus. It is time to see beyond parties and pay attention to the functions of communal ideology. The essay draws a clean history of events, focusing on the role played by political leaders and the party supporters. Moreover, how the simultaneous formation of relief camps provides a sense of productive involvement of ordinary citizens of the country.

Anshu Saluja's chapter 'Engaging with Oral Narratives: Contextualising the Dialogue on 1984' opens up the innumerable ways in which the nuances of violence, its nature and after-effects are enumerated, remembered and recalled. Employing the oral history techniques, she suggests that for studying incidences of ethnic violence across the world, survivor testimonies and memories have been extremely important. Her respondents included social workers, legal and human right activists, journalists, writers and film-makers who became involved in the immediate aftermath, and in particular cases are still associated with either the issues of relief and rehabilitation or the quest for justice along with the survivors.

Yasmeen Arif's essay 'Enduring Exile and Lasting Loss: The Widows of the 1984 Delhi Sikh Carnage' is an ethnographic depiction of experiences of survivors read together with the discourse offered by the state documentary practices, inquiry commission reports and other public representations. Exploring the nuanced afterlives of loss and grief, the queries that contour the essay are: what kind of subjectivities does the state engender in these people? What conditions of enablement or vulnerability does 'legitimate' victimhood provoke, especially when justice continues to elude these people? The answers lead to the idea of an exile, both in a material and metaphorical sense. Though these biographies are allowed to be grasped as recovered lives that continue within ostensible normalcy, but as identities of those that are forsaken, they track a course embedding the burden of memory into the terrain of the future, tainting the realm of hope rather than remaining in the past.

Anne Murphy brings out the complexities involved in building memorial sites and how these constructed sites of memory tend to remove the social public from within it. She draws parallels between the memorial in Gurudwara Rakab Ganj on 'Chaurasi' vis-à-vis a smaller memorial site in the heart of Tilak Vihar widows' colony, where the site becomes more functional and worthy for the survivors. One of the models presented in her chapter, 'The Politics of Possibility in the Commemoration of Trauma', is the commemoration of trauma offered by the museological and other forms of memorialisation of the Holocaust and that of the Canadian first nations. These parallels extend the discourse of commemoration from a singular identity of the Sikhs to a wider context of human beings, as well as 'othered' communities in particular.

Jasmine Anand's essay, 'It was a Dog's Life: Evocation in Gurvinder Singh's movie *Chauthi Koot*', provides a background to the Delhi carnage by depicting the situation in Punjab in 1984, a year of curfews, state-initiated control, insurgency, Sikh militancy and religio-political extremism. The essay sets parallels between the difficult life of humans and a dog (a significant character in the movie *Chauthi Koot*) that metaphorically became synonymous in the grind of the 1980s. The various paths of turbulence and gorging repression and terror have found expression in the movie, registering the accounts of gruesome brutality.

Amutha Charu Sheela in 'Demonising the Dear: Identity and Violence in Vaasanthi's *The Silent Storm*' discusses the power struggle between two ideologies—secular nationalism and religious nationalism. Though brutal violence is condemned by everybody, opinions were always divided. Some of them blamed the militants for their anti-social activities while others held the Indian state responsible for inciting violence in the state. The analysis of the novel *The Silent Storm*, translation of Tamil novel *Mauna Puyal* by Vaasanthi, probes the reasons behind the violence, its effect on the local communities and how both the groups try to justify it.

Diamond Oberoi Vahali in 'Trauma and Restitution, the Healing Power of Compassion: A Psychoanalytical and Cinematic Analysis of *Kaya Taran*, a Film on the 1984 Massacres against the Sikhs in India' analyses the film *Kaya Taran* set in the backdrop of the 1984 anti-Sikh violence in Meerut. It depicts the face of humanity in a situation of mob violence wherein a group of Christian nuns in a convent give protection to a Sikh woman and her young son Jagpreet even at the risk to their own lives. This chapter while focussing on the 1984 anti-Sikh violence analyses the power of compassion and delves into the glimpses of humanity. The movie captures the pitiable state of the innocent people who become victims of their times and personal revenge.

Conclusion: 'Injustice Anywhere is a Threat to Justice Everywhere'

'Injustice anywhere is a threat to justice everywhere': this powerful quote by Martin Luther King, Jr., is extremely appropriate in the context of Chaurasi and other similar situations time and again. The impact of injustice is not visible singularly but affects plurally all communities and masses irrespective of class, caste or race. The Universal Declaration of Human Rights of the United Nations moves beyond nations, caste, race, sex and other boundaries. The strength of the declaration lies in ensuring justice to human beings irrespective of any divisive factors. In the same light, H. S. Phoolka appropriately remarks that injustice in cases related to Chaurasi signified a failure to deter those who would prey on the powerless:

> People who are in majority in a particular area, they attack a community and then they get political patronage. This kind of violence started from 1984. I have said this many times, if the people guilty in the 1984 riots had been punished, we wouldn't have seen Mumbai riots of 1993, Gujarat riots of 2002 or Kandhamal, or whatever is happening these days, these lynching[s] etc. (*Indian Express* 2019)

Ironically, with changing times, the dynamics of the aforesaid structure have undergone immense transformation. One case of injustice enables several kinds of injustices faced by the minorities, Dalits, tribal and women. Even though the legal systemic procedures fail the citizens, the citizens' commitment and resilience to fight for their rights instils hope. It is the ability to display hope even in the most sombre conditions or forbidding time that keeps humanity alive.

Acknowledgments

This book could not have seen the light of the day without the support of the Central University of Gujarat, where this work was undertaken as a pilot project.

Notes

1. This conversation is based on fieldwork at Tilak Vihar widows' colony in April 2014.

2. Conversations on the mobile phone, 28 December 2018; name not revealed due to confidentiality.

3. See Kaur (2017).

4. 'The survivors of 1984 riots'. The word 'riot' is contested as riots are accidental but the nature of the 1984 anti-Sikh violence was identified clearly as a state-led well-organised pogrom, as declared in the PUDR report (Mukhoty and Kothari 1984).

5. Attar Kaur was interviewed during the field visit to the Tilak Vihar widows' colony in April 2014.

6. Interview with Attar Kaur in April 2014.

7. For more details, refer to Encyclopedia.com (2018).

8. Information retrieved from affidavits filed with the Nanavati commission. These affidavits are available in a CD (provided to the author by a confidential source), 'Carnage 84: Massacre of 4000 Sikhs in Delhi', A Delhi Sikh Gurudwara

Managing Committee (DSGMC) presentation. Material put together by Sr Advocate H. S. Phoolka, Prof. N. S. Bawa, Wing Commander R. S. Chhatwal, Commodore J. M. S. Sood; consultant editor Manoj Mitta; designed and programmed by Simran Kaur and Hitesh Wadhwa; legal and technical research Satinder Singh (2001).

9. Attar Kaur, interviewed in April 2014.

10. Karnail Singh, Delhi, a furniture merchant, and his friends in conversation with the researcher. 14 April 2014.

11. Guru Nanak Dev introduced the idea of remembering God ('Nam Japo'), while also self-earning for livelihood, individually on daily basis ('Kirat Karo'), and sharing a part of the earnings with the needy ('Vaand Chako').

12. Guru Teghbahadar, the ninth Guru of the Sikhs, was martyred in Delhi by Aurangzeb because the Guru tried to prevent the forcible conversion of Kashmiri Pandits.

13. Paramjit S. Judge in his book *Religion, Identity and Nationhood: The Sikh Militant Movement* (2005) and Joginder Singh in *Myth and Reality of the Sikh Militancy in Punjab* (2006) have presented a detailed analysis of the role played by the media around the years of militancy and its crucial impact on the psyche of people.

14. Indira Gandhi's assassination followed Diwali, which is a major festival in India, and a lot of survivors interviewed during my fieldwork in April 2015 reported never celebrating Diwali since 1984 anti-Sikh violence.

15. Some of these memorial sites are personal, such as the events held by the families of survivors; some are more formal, like those organised by gurdwaras, but the state does not commemorate at all.

16. Attar Kaur, interviewed in April 2014.

17. These affidavits arc available in the CD (provided to the author by a confidential source), 'Carnage 84: Massacre of 4000 Sikhs in Delhi' (2001).

18. '"Chaurasi Cannot be Forgotten": Attar Kaur and Relatives', in Chaudhry (2019: 11–19).

19. Karnail Singh, Delhi, a furniture merchant, in conversation with the researcher on 14 April 2014.

20. Lala is a shopkeeper.

21. A man born in a Sikh family who has cut his hair and does not adorn a turban.

22. *Kara* is one of the five Ks. It is an iron/steel bangle, borne by the Sikhs in their right hand.

23. Based on interview with Ishmeet Kaur Chaudhry, 16 June 2018.

24. Karnail Singh, Delhi, a furniture merchant, in conversation with the researcher on 14 April 2014.

25. Attar Kaur and Relatives, 'Chaurasi Cannot be Forgotten', in Chaudhry (2019: 11–19).

References

Agamben, Giorgio. 1999. *Remnants of Auschwitz: The Witness and the Archive*. Trans. Daniel Heller-Raozen. New York: Zone Books.

Ahooja Committee Report. 1987. Available at https://1984sikh-archive.org/wp-content/uploads/2023/02/ahoojacommitteereport.pdf (accessed on 23 June 2020).

Aschom, Dibanish. 2018. 'Declare 1984 Anti-Sikh Riots as Genocide, Says Lok Sabha Member'. *NDTV*, 17 December. Available at https://www.ndtv.com/india-news/declare-1984-anti-sikh-riots-as-genocide-says-lok-sabha-member-prem-singh-chandumajra-1963777 (accessed on 7 January 2019).

Baxi, Pratiksha. 2007. 'Adjudicating the Riot: Communal Violence, Crowds and Public Tranquility'. *Domains* (Special Issue) 3: 70–105.

Bhattacharya, Anirudh. 2017. 'Ontario Passes Motion Calling 1984 Riots Genocide, India Says Move Misguided'. *Hindustan Times*, 8 April. Available at https://www.hindustantimes.com/world-news/ontario-passes-motion-describing-1984-anti-sikh-riots-as-genocide/story-1YPs2tiMkvtW2Tp7UDyydK.html (accessed on 7 January 2019).

Chaturvedi, Amit. 2020. 'IB Staffer Ankit Sharma, Killed in Delhi Riots, Was Stabbed 51 Times: Police Chargesheet'. *Hindustan Times*, 3 June. Available at https://www.hindustantimes.com/india-news/ib-staffer-ankit-sharma-killed-in-delhi-riots-was-stabbed-51-times-police-chargesheet/story-eLcOABeHFIjNJNCV14gOlO.html (accessed on 12 July 2023).

Chaudhry, Ishmeet Kaur. 2019. *Black November: Writings on the Sikh Massacres of 1984 and the Aftermath*. Delhi: Speaking Tiger.

Chopra, Radhika. 2010. 'Commemorating Hurt: Memorializing Operation Bluestar'. *Sikh Formations* 6(2): 119–52.

_____. 2018. *Amritsar 1984: A City Remembers*. Lanham, MD: Lexington Books.

Datta, Saurav. 2018. '1984 Pogrom was a Genocide, Says Delhi High Court'. *News Click*, 3 December. Available at https://www.newsclick.in/1984-pogrom-was-genocide-says-delhi-high-court (accessed on 15 December 2018).

Dhillon, Kirpal. 2016. '1984: An Overview'. In *1984: In Memory and Imagination*, ed. Vikram Kapur, 3–23. New Delhi: Amaryllis.

Dyke, Virginia Van. 1996. 'The Anti-Sikh Riots of 1984 in Delhi: Politicians, Criminals, and the Discourse of Communalism'. In *Riots and Pogroms*, ed. Paul S. Brass, 201–20. Hampshire and London: Macmillan Press.

Encyclopedia.com. 2018. 'Pogroms'. 14 May. Available at https://www.encyclopedia.com/history/modern-europe/russian-soviet-and-cis-history/pogroms (accessed on 27 December 2024).

Grewal, Jyoti. 2007. *Betrayed by the State: The Anti-Sikh Pogrom of 1984*. New Delhi: Penguin Books.

Harper, Douglas. 2001–08. 2001–08. 'Carnage (n)'. Maoning Tech. Available at https://www.etymonline.com/search?q=carnage (accessed on 24 November 2017).

——. 2001–08. 'Genocide (n)'. Maoning Tech. Available at https://www.etymonline.com/word/genocide (accessed on 24 November 2017).

——. 'Pogrom (n)'. Maoning Tech. Available at https://www.etymonline.com/word/pogrom (accessed on 24 November 2017).

——. 2001–08. 'Riot (n)'. Maoning Tech. Available at https://www.etymonline.com/word/riot#etymonline_v_15091 (accessed on 24 November 2017).

Human Rights Watch. 2014. 'India: No Justice for 1984 Anti-Sikh Bloodshed'. 29 October. Available at https://www.hrw.org/news/2014/10/29/india-no-justice-1984-anti-sikh-bloodshed (accessed on 13 October 2020).

India Today. 2010. '1984 Sikh Riots Petition Tabled in Australian Parliament'. 2 November. Available at https://www.indiatoday.in/india/north/story/1984-sikh-riots-petition-tabled-in-australian-parliament-120394-2012-11-02 (accessed on 7 January 2019).

Indian Express. 2019. 'If 1984 Guilty had been Punished, There wouldn't be Mumbai 1993, Gujarat 2002, These Lynchings: HS Phoolka'. 6 January. Available at https://indianexpress.com/article/india/anti-sikh-riots-1984-guilty-sajjan-kumar-mumbai-1993-gujarat-2002-lynchings-hs-phoolka-5524891/ (accessed on 7 January 2019).

Jaijee, Inderjit Singh, and Dona Suri. 2020. *The Legacy of Militancy in Punjab: Long Road to 'Normalcy'*. New Delhi: Sage Publications.

Judge, Paramjit S. 2005. *Religion, Identity and Nationhood: The Sikh Militant Movement*. Jaipur: Rawat Publications.

Kaur, Harnidh. 2018. 'After Sajjan Kumar Conviction, Everyone has Become an Expert on Sikh Trauma'. *The Print*, 19 December. Available at https://theprint.in/opinion/after-sajjan-kumar-conviction-everyone-has-become-an-expert-on-sikh-trauma/165860/ (accessed 10 January 2019).

Kishwar, Madhu. 1984. 'Gangster Rule: Massacre of the Sikhs'. *Manushi*, December.

Kaur, Ishmeet. 2017. 'Religious Intolerance and Cinematic Representations: A Study of Selected Short-films on the 1984 Anti-Sikh Pogrom in India'. *Indi@logs: Spanish Journal of India Studies* 4: 63–78.

Kumar, Ram, Amrik Singh, Ashok Agrwaal and Jaskaran Kaur. 2003. *Reduced to Ashes: The Insurgency and Human Rights in Punjab*. Kathamandu: South Asia Forum for Human Rights.

Krishnan, Murali. 2020. 'Police Tried to Hush up 1984 Riots Cases: SIT'. *Hindustan Times*, 16 January. Available at https://www.pressreader.com/india/hindustan-times-chandigarh/20200116/281483573331411 (accessed 7 February 2020).

Kushbeen Kaur Sohi, Purnima Singh and Krutika Bopanna. 2018. 'Ritual Participation, Sense of Community, and Social Well-being: A Study of Seva in the Sikh Community'. *Journal of Religion & Health* 57 (6): 2066–78.

Mitta, Manoj, and H. S. Phoolka. 2007. *When a Tree Shook Delhi: The 1984 Carnage and Its Aftermath*. New Delhi: Lotus.

Mukhoty, Gobinda, and Rajni Kothari. 1984. 'Who Are the Guilty? Joint Inquiry into the Causes and Impact of the Riots in Delhi from 31 Oct to 10 Nov'. Joint Inquiry, Delhi: People's Union for Democratic Rights (PUDR) and People's Union for Civil Liberties (PUCL).

Murphy, Anne. 2004. 'Mobilizing Seva (Service): Modes of Sikh Diasporic Action'. In *South Asians in the Diaspora: Histories and Religious Traditions*, eds Knut Axel Jacobsen and Pratap Kumar, 337–72. Leiden: Brill.

Samyuktha. 2010. 'Manmohan Singh Apologizes "on Behalf of Government" for 1984 Anti-Sikh Disturbances'. Oneindia.com, 28 June. Available at https://www.oneindia.com/2010/06/28/manmohansingh-apologizes-on-behalf-of-government-for.html (accessed on 27 December 2024).

Sen, Sudhi Ranjan. 2017. '1984 Anti-Sikh Riots Were Not "Genocide", Arun Jaitley Tells Canadian Defence Minister'. *HuffPost*, 18 April. Available at https://www.huffingtonpost.in/2017/04/18/1984-anti-sikh-riots-werent-genocide-india-to-canada_a_22044717/ (accessed on 7 January 2019).

Singh, Amritjit, Naini Iyer and Rahul K. Gairola. 2016. 'Introduction: The Long Partition and Beyond'. In *Revisiting India's Partition: New Essays on Memory, Culture, and Politics*, eds Naini Iyer, Rahul K. Gairola and Amritjit Singh, xiii–xxxv. New Delhi: Orient BlackSwan.

Singh, Daman. 2014. *Strictly Personal: Manmohan and Gursharan*. HarperCollins Publishers.

Singh, Dharam. 2020. 'Sikhism and Religious Pluralism'. In *Interfaith Dialogues: A Sikh Perspective*, ed. Hardev Singh Virk, 74–90. New Delhi: Guru Nanak Dev Foundation.

Singh, Jarnail. 2009. *I Accuse: The Anti-Sikh Violence of 1984*. New Delhi: Viking.

Singh, Joginder. 2006. *Myth and Reality of the Sikh Militancy in Punjab*. Delhi: Shree Publishers & Distributors.

Singh, Pav. 2017. *1984: India's Guilty Secret*. New Delhi: Rupa Publications.

Suri, Sanjay. 2015. *1984: The Anti-Sikh Violence and After*. Noida: HarperCollins Publishers.

Talta, Darshan Singh. 2015. 'The Third *Ghallughara*: On the Sikh Dilemma Since 1984'. *Sikh Formations: Religion, Culture, Theory* 11 (3): 316–42.

Tandon, Aditi. 2018. 'Rahul Denies Cong Hand in '84 Riots'. *The Tribune*, 26 August. Available at https://www.tribuneindia.com/news/nation/rahul-denies-cong-hand-in-84-riots/643015.html (accessed on 2 January 2019).

The Economic Times. 2018. '1984 Anti-Sikh Riots: Sajjan Kumar Sentenced to Life Imprisonment'. 17 December. Available at https://economictimes.indiatimes.com/news/politics-and-nation/1984-anti-sikh-riots-sajjan-kumar-sentenced-to-life-imprisonment/2013-verdict-reversed/slideshow/67123913.cms (accessed on 27 December 2024).

Times of India. 2013. 'U.S. Refuses to Declare 1984 Anti-Sikh Riots in India as Genocide'. 2 April. Available at https://timesofindia.indiatimes.com/world/us/US-refuses-to-declare-1984-anti-Sikh-riots-in-India-as-genocide/articleshow/19342076.cms (accessed on 7 January 2019).

I

Revisiting 1984

Human Rights and Justice

one

Multiple Narratives of 1984

The Importance of Remembering

Nandita Haksar

I began my human rights practice in the Supreme Court in the 1980s, which meant that a large number of the cases I was involved with related to the violation of human rights of Sikh youth. As an active member of the People's Union for Democratic Rights (PUDR), I travelled often to Punjab for fact-finding missions, frequently co-ordinating with the Punjab-based Association for Democratic Rights (AFDR); the general secretary of AFDR at the time was Jagmohan Singh, the nephew of Bhagat Singh.

The chief concern of the AFDR was the growing divide between the Sikhs and the Hindus. Jagmohan's mother, Bibi Amar Kaur, sat in protest[1] when a statue of Bhagat Singh was erected in Ludhiana without Rajguru and Sukhdev, the two comrades who were hanged with him. She said that she had three brothers and protested against the honour being given only to one of them.

When Bibi Amar Kaur died, she left behind a will that was very moving. A friend, Chaman Lal, translated it from Punjabi into Hindi; it was published in *Jansatta* but the *Indian Express* refused to publish it when I gave them the English translation. In her will, Bibi Amar Kaur said she had nothing to leave except the principles and values she had learnt from her brothers—and her brother Bhagat Singh had warned against communal politics.

I was in Amritsar a few days after Operation Blue Star. Although I am not at all religious, I was shocked by the large hole made by a tank driven through the wall into the Akal Takhat. It is an image which has stayed with me.

And in October–November of 1984, I saw how Sikhs were targets of vicious violence in which 10,000 Sikh men lost their lives, women were raped, and properties, including gurdwaras, burnt down. More than 3,000 Sikhs were murdered, many burnt alive, in the capital of democratic India (PUDR and PUCL 1984). I was one of the members of the fact-finding report which was published under the title, 'Who Are the Guilty?'. The report documented the attack on Sikhs in Delhi after the assassination of Prime Minister Indira Gandhi and stated that it was not a spontaneous reaction to her assassination but a planned and organised massacre.

I was also deeply involved in litigation before the Delhi High Court and the Supreme Court, and appeared before the Mishra Commission on behalf of the Nagrik Ekta Manch. In addition, I interviewed the victims as well as members of the communities who were involved in the violence against the Sikhs. Those interviews were a part of the work which was jointly edited by Uma Chakravarti and me and published under the title: *The Delhi Riots: Three Days in the Life of a Nation* (1987).

I remember the terror of those days, the stories of torture, arson and murder. The images of Sikhs being garlanded with burning tyres and being burnt alive are cauterised in my mind. But I also remember the amazing spirit of the Sikhs who, a few hours after they had been under murderous attacks, could form disciplined lines at the camp to get their first hot meal; their courage and their enormous dignity in the face of the violence and hatred directed against them.

It is more than four decades since those momentous events took place. It is important that we honour the memory of those who perished and show solidarity with those who survived. It is also equally important to remember the remarkable show of solidarity to the Sikh community by the citizens of Delhi, and I was witness to the way complete strangers came together, risking their lives to save the lives and property of the Sikhs; just as it is to remember the Sikhs in Punjab who laid down their lives protecting their Hindu neighbours.

However, commemoration must go hand in hand with analysis of the context of the violence and we must have a deeper understanding of the root causes. In this chapter, I assess the efficacy of the interventions made by the human rights activists, and try and understand why these were very important; but at the same time, the interventions did not address the root causes of the conflict.

Guru Harkrishna School

It is well documented that the police refused to respond to calls by Sikhs whose homes were being burnt and who were facing murderous mobs surrounding their homes. I, myself, saw how a police jeep stood by as a mob attacked the Guru Harkrishna School which was opposite my flat in Munirka Enclave.

I was standing at the gate of our colony watching the fire spread in the school when I heard someone say: 'Aunty, let's go and rescue the Sikhs.' I do not know who said this but it galvanised five or six young men to rush with me across the field and rescue the Sikhs trapped inside the school. Among the six young men was Ravindra Bhatt, who was a junior lawyer and later became a judge of the high court.

We managed to persuade all the Sikhs to come with us to my flat but in one room I saw a young married Sikh couple who refused to leave their grandfather who was in a wheelchair. The picture of their courage and dignity is etched in my mind. I was so relieved to find that another young man rescued the venerable gentleman on a two-wheeler while the couple rushed to my flat.

There was an army officer in uniform who stopped me and almost shouted at me for putting the entire colony in danger by bringing the Sikhs into our colony. I shouted back at him that he could burn all of us alive but first he should remove the uniform of the Indian army he was wearing.

Looking back, what is absolutely remarkable is that those of us who went to rescue the school teachers did not know each other, and I still do not know their names. Apart from the five or six of us from Munirka Enclave and the unknown man on the two-wheeler, there was another young man who rescued the principal by breaking the glass door with his bare hands and bringing him out. Then there was a Jat man from the Vasant *gaon* (village) who helped me take the Sikhs across and to whom I handed over the keys of my flat; and the woman with a baby who told me to take her baby so she could guard the school building.

It is truly remarkable that there was so much trust and perfect understanding among us, strangers to each other and to the Sikhs.

Someone living across my house made *khichiri* for everyone and later I discovered that she was the mother of Poonam Mutreja, who was one of the persons behind the formation of the Nagrik Ekta Manch.

But not all the people in colony were happy; many of the men were scared and kept quoting rumours about how the Sikhs were poisoning the water, etc.; so we had to move the rescued families to the only place I knew they would be safe—my alma mater, the Jawaharlal Nehru University (JNU). I do not know who sent the large vehicle in which we put the male school teachers and hid them under blankets and drove them to safety inside JNU. But I do know that for the four days of curfew they were safe and looked after by the students and teachers of the university.

Farash Bazar Police Station

I do not remember how the Nagrik Ekta Manch came to organise a camp for the Sikh refugees at the Farash Bazar police station near Jhilmil Colony in Shahdara. But I do remember that there were two blocks of four-storeys-high buildings which were occupied by 3,000 Sikhs who had taken refuge there.

Most of the people organising that camp belonged to various non-governmental organisations (NGOs). I remember that someone said we should make hot tea for the Sikhs because they were suffering from shock. I accompanied someone in her car, I do not now remember the person. She very efficiently went to South Extension and got the *tentwala* to open his shop from the back (since there was curfew) and give us a large utensil for the tea; next we looked for sugar but none of the shops were open so she bought *batasha*s (solidified form of sugar of the size of a biscuit), and then we bought tea.

I was trying to make the tea and can never forget the Sikh youth making fun of me, 'Why, you have never made tea?' And I said, 'No, not for 200 people.' They stopped me from emptying the box of tea and asked how I would strain it; then one of them told me to use a dupatta to tie the tea and put it into the boiling water. I asked how much milk we should put in and someone said, 'Just put in one or two buckets…' and there was much laughter. These were people who had barely escaped death; they had seen their relatives being burnt to death and they could laugh and tease.

All this was being done under the protection of the station house officer (SHO) of the Farash Bazar Police Station, Daryao Singh. This policeman refused to follow the other policemen and officers who declined to help the Sikhs and were complicit in the violence, the murders and the arson.

I do not know where the SHO is, but it would be worth recording his story and he should be given a citizen's award for providing a safe haven to the Sikhs and saving their lives.

It was here that someone suggested that we, human rights activists, do fact-finding rather than trying to manage a refugee camp. It was decided that it would be a joint fact-finding team of the People's Union for Civil Liberties (PUCL) and the PUDR.

Who Are the Guilty?

The four members of the fact-finding team were: Summanto Bannerji and myself from the PUDR; Dinesh Mohon and Smitu Kothari from the PUCL. Smitu Kothari had to leave for Rome, so that left the three of us.

Everywhere we went, people had made lists of the names of the people who attacked the Sikhs. These lists included senior Congress leaders as well as the local goondas. Soon, we had so much material that a team of PUDR members sat in Summanto's flat at Press Enclave under the competent guidance of Sudesh Vaid and collated and compiled the list of people.

Summanto then sat at his red typewriter to write the report, while Dinesh and I went around interviewing people. By the time we landed at the residence of I. K. Gujral, who later became the prime minister, we realised that the attacks on the Sikhs were not spontaneous expression of anger directed at them for the assassination of Indira Gandhi. The opening paragraph of the report stated clearly and categorically:

> ... the conclusion that the attacks on members of the Sikh Community in Delhi and its suburbs during the period, far from being a spontaneous expression of 'madness' and of popular 'grief and anger' at Mrs Gandhi's assassination as made out to be by the authorities, were the outcome of a well-organized plan marked by acts of both deliberate commissions and omissions by important politicians of the Congress (I) at the top and by authorities in the administration. (PUDR and PUCL 1984: 5)

How did the arsonists get access to so much kerosene to burn huge houses in New Friends Colony, especially when there was a curfew and all the depots were closed? How did the mob know where the Sikhs lived? The people had told us that the local leaders carried voters' lists with them. How did they get these lists when the whole country was mourning?

And how did the entire police force become paralysed and could not rescue the Sikhs? After all, the Farash Bazar police station had done a commendable job.

We recorded in our report:

> All through the period from October 31 to November 4, the heights of the riots, the police all over the city uniformly betrayed a common behavioural pattern marked by (i) total absence from the scene; or (ii) a role of passive spectators or (iii) direct participation or abetment in the orgy of violence against the Sikhs. On November 1, when we toured the Lajpat Nagar area we found the police conspicuous by their absence while Sikhs' shops were being set on fire and looted. Young people armed with swords, daggers, spears, steel trishuls and iron rods were ruling the roads. The only sign of police presence was a police jeep, which obstructed a peace procession brought out by a few concerned citizens (who later organised themselves into the Nagrik Ekta Manch) on the evening of November 1. When the procession was on its way to the Lajpat Nagar main market, a police inspector from the van stopped the procession, warned it not to proceed reminding its members that the city was under curfew and Section 144. (PUDR and PUCL 1984: 10)

All the evidence we gathered pointed to the involvement of the political leaders at the highest level; it showed that the violence, the massacre was planned, directed and well thought out.

This was really shocking for me, especially since my father had been secretary to Prime Minister Indira Gandhi, and I knew so many of the senior Congress men and women. I asked I. K. Gujral: 'Can they [the Congress] be party at the highest levels to such violence?'[2] He did not deny the possibility.

Back at Summanto's place, the PUDR members sat arguing whether we should publish the names of the Congress party leaders. Suppose the Sikhs used our list as their hit list? We argued late into the night. Someone said we would be putting the members of the fact-finding team into danger so our names were not mentioned but then that night someone set fire to Mr Govind Mukhoty's car parked outside his Jor Bagh home. He was a senior counsel and the president of PUDR.

Despite these threats that we were facing, we decided to go ahead and publish the names. There were two other fact-finding reports which came out around the same time; they did not publish the names of the perpetrators of the violence.

'Who Are the Guilty?' was sold out within a fortnight. The printer was threatened and was too scared to print another edition. The report was translated into Punjabi and sold like hot cakes but was banned by the Central government. An organisation close to the Khalistanis wanted our permission to print thousands of copies of the report. Now we were in a dilemma. PUDR was a human rights organisation and could take strong stand on human rights issues, mainly state violence. But we did not want our reports to become tools in the hands of Sikh or any other communal or extremist organisations. We refused them permission.

But the report served one very important purpose. Many Sikhs, in Delhi and in Punjab, told us that after reading our report they felt that they were not alone and that many people from the majority community were with them. This act of solidarity stopped them from being completely alienated from India.

The Law, the Courts and the Justice System

It was in the first few years of my law practice that I realised that the justice system was not equipped to deliver justice when a large number of people from one community were targets of state violence. Till this day, the men involved in the murder of the Sikhs in 1984 have not been punished; men who raped Sikh women roam around free; and those who were part of the mobs which committed arson have no fear of being punished for their criminal acts.

The police would not register complaints by the Sikhs and PUDR decided to file a petition before the Delhi High Court asking it to direct the police stations to register the FIRs and to set up an independent commission to enquire into the causes of the killings. The case came up before Justice Rajinder Sachar. He was a man known for his integrity and courage. He directed that the FIRs be registered. However, the case did not come in his court again. It went to a bench of two judges, Yogeshwar Dayal and B. N. Kirpal. When Govind Mukhoty filed the report 'Who Are the Guilty?', they dismissed it. They questioned the veracity of an affidavit we submitted of a woman who had watched her daughter being raped. And they dismissed the petition on the ground that PUDR and PUCL had no locus standi.

I drafted a special leave petition in the Supreme Court in January 1985 but was shocked to find that it was listed before the Constitution Bench. It came up without following the usual procedure and I found myself facing the judges. I was asked to withdraw the petition in the 'interest of the country' and when I refused, it was thrown out.

Case after case of torture, illegal arrest and one case of mistaken identity of a woman wrongfully arrested during Operation Blue Star were all dismissed. No reasons given, no appeals possible.

It is not possible to give an account of all these cases but let me give one example. Amarjeet was a young wife of a garage mechanic who lived near the Golden Temple. She had just had a baby girl and wanted to go to the gurdwara to pray on the day of the Operation Blue Star. The irony is that she gave tea to the CRPF men who had taken position on her roof and she never returned.

Her husband heard the shooting and the thunder of the tanks and waited for his wife to return. His two older daughters held the baby while he looked madly for his wife and found her in the hospital, her right eye had been damaged. He was not allowed to speak to her. She was taken along with the militants, including three women militants, and lodged in Jodhpur jail.

The garage mechanic heard a human rights lawyer had come from Delhi and was staying at Gursharan Singh's home. Gursharan Singh was a legendary theatre personality and I was staying with him. I took the particulars and filed a petition before the Supreme Court. The case came up before Justice Bhagwati and I was sure he would issue notice but he said he could not take up this case. The reason was left unsaid.

Amarjeet spent four years in Jodhpur jail. Her oldest daughter gave up her studies in order to look after her baby sister; the middle sister was traumatised and needed psychological help which she did not get. When the mother came out, the baby screamed and refused to go to the strange woman. That was what broke Amarjeet.

But Amarjeet and her husband phoned to say she was back from jail. She came with Amritsari *papad* and thanked me for trying to save her.

Press Council of India

The media continued to call the massacre of Sikhs in the aftermath of Indira Gandhi's assassination 'anti-Sikh riots'. Girilal Jain, editor of *The Times of India*, rationalised the violence: The Hindu cup of patience was full to the brim. N. C. Menon, who succeeded Khushwant Singh as editor of *Hindustan Times*, wrote of how Sikhs had 'clawed their way to prosperity'. Some students of the Indian Institute of Mass Communication (IIMC) filed a petition against Girilal Jain before the Press Council of India. It was written in rather abusive language and Professor Baxi advised them to come to me to re-write the petition.

The question that came up was this: How could the Council find an objective criterion to judge whether an editorial was communal or not? I filed a petition asking for permission to produce an expert witness who could help the Press Council; the Council gave its consent. This was the first time such an expert was produced before the Council.

I asked Peggy Mohan, the linguist, to analyse the editorials and come to her own conclusions. Many years later she recollected this incident in these words:

> In an earlier case in 1984, I was asked by some students of Mass Communications if I could analyse an editorial written by Girilal Jain, editor of *The Times of India*, during the anti-Sikh violence. They had complained about the article to the Press Council, and there was to be a hearing to decide whether Girilal Jain should be censured. Could I find a way of demonstrating that his editorial was excessively communal? I decided, for comparison purposes, to look at all the editorials in Delhi newspapers on that day. I chose three indices of communal content: phrases where 'we' referred to Hindus, phrases where 'they' referred to Sikhs, and phrases that showed an approval of violence. I counted the total number of words in each category for each of the editorials, and calculated it as a percentage of the total text. By adding up all three categories, I got a score for how communal that editorial was. Plotting all the scores of all newspapers for the same day on a graph showed where the spikes were: which paper had the most communal editorial. *The Times of India* won hands down. (Mohan 2012)

I had taken the case seriously because I thought the Press Council could play an important role in checking the excesses of the media. The Press Council did give me a patient hearing. Girilal Jain was represented by senior counsel L. M. Singhvi, and he would himself come for the hearings. It was of course naive of me; but then I had just started my law practice. Of course, the Press Council was not going to rule in favour of some students of journalism represented by a young lawyer. We lost.

The Ranganath Mishra Commission

It was the common demand of all the human rights organisations as well as Sikh organisations, including the Shiromani Akali Dal, that an independent commission be set up to look into the causes of the violence against the Sikhs. Finally, in April 1985 the government set up a Commission of Enquiry headed by Ranganath Mishra. I was asked to represent the Nagrik Ekta Manch before the Commission.

From the beginning, it was clear that Ranganath Mishra Commission was not committed to bringing out the truth. It barred the PUDR and the PUCL from appearing even though they had brought out the only report ('Who Are the Guilty') which listed the names of the perpetrators of the crimes, including 3,000 murders in three days in the capital of India.

The Commission decided to hold the hearings in camera and did not allow the media to report the proceedings. Then it rejected 2,905 of the affidavits filed before it and accepted only 128 (PUDR and PUCL 1987: 4).

By March 1986, the Citizens Commission, the Akali Dal and Nagrik Ekta Manch decided to walk out of the Commission. It was thoroughly discredited.

Justice Ranganath Mishra became a Supreme Court judge and also the chairman of the first Human Rights Commission of India.

Root Causes of the Violence against the Sikhs

Even in the middle of the violence, we in the PUDR struggled to understand its causes. In the course of interviews for the book *The Delhi Riots*, I came to realise the complexities at the ground level. For instance, the mob which attacked the school was largely from the Vasant Gaon which harboured a deep resentment against the school which stood on the land which had once belonged to the villagers. In fact, when the land was first taken away, the villagers used to defecate on the land as a protest. That deep resentment had burst into the vicious attack on Guru Harkrishna School.

The interviews for the book revealed how the Hindu–Sikh divide was rooted in the days of Punjab's formation in independent India. As the Punjabi language was increasingly subordinated to Sikh religious demands, Punjabi Hindus attempted to disavow their mother tongue; but Sikhs, in turn, saw this as a betrayal of a shared identity. There were often sharp differences in perception between the Hindus and Sikhs of their relationship in the past. For instance, in my interview of Gurbachan Singh, a senior retired diplomat, he said the Hindus and Sikhs did not see themselves as antagonistic communities in the past:

> There was constant intermarriage. My grandmother came from a Hindu family. My mother comes from a Hindu family. My wife comes from a Hindu family, my daughter-in-law comes from a Hindu family ... so in our family—at least in those days in Rawalpindi there was no conception, no idea, that so and so is a Hindu or so and so is a Sikh (Chakravarti and Haksar 1987: 276).

But after Partition, when Kanta Arora (not her real name), an Arya Samaji, came to Delhi from Multan, she definitely perceived the Hindus and Sikhs as separate communities. When I asked her why the Punjabi Hindus had declared that Hindi was their language, she said, 'Actually it was because the Hindus used to learn Hindi. They never learnt Punjabi' (ibid.: 491).

She went on to say that the Sikh girls studied Urdu and Gurmukhi whereas the Hindu Punjabi girls studied Hindi and Gurmukhi.

The Arya Samajis continue to revere Dayanand Saraswati and his preachings written in *Satyarth Prakash* or the 'Light of Truth'. Chapters 11 to 14 contain vitriolic attacks on Buddhism, Islam, Christianity and Sikhism. But it is hailed as the best exponent of Vedic religion.

There have been many times that various organisations have called for a ban on the book. Girija Kumar, former librarian of JNU, has documented many of the early debates on the issue of banning *Satyarth Prakash* in his book titled *The Book on Trial* (2008).

The *Satyarth Prakash* or the Arya Samaj cannot be held to be direct cause of the massacre of the Sikhs in 1984; many Arya Samajis were active in the rescue, relief and rehabilitation of the Sikhs. Most prominent among them was Swami Agnivesh who faced an angry mob in the flaming orange robes of a swami.

However, what our report 'Who Are the Guilty?' failed to document was the role of the cadres of the Rashtriya Swayamsevak Sangh (RSS) in the massacres of the Sikhs in 1984. Former Chief Minister of Punjab Capt. Amarinder Singh of the Congress has pointed out that 14 FIRs were registered against 49 BJP–RSS leaders for their role in the anti-Sikh violence of 1984 (*The Pioneer* 2014).

It has also come to light since 1984 that the attack on the Golden Temple was carried out on the advice of the British. The documents released after 35 years by the National Archives of UK include a letter from the foreign secretary's principal private secretary Brian Fall to his opposite number in the Home Office, dated 6 February 1984, referring to an 'Indian request for advice on plans for the removal of dissident Sikhs from the Golden Temple' (Calamur 2014). It states that the then British prime minister, Baroness Thatcher, is 'content that the foreign secretary should proceed as he proposes' (Nayar 2018).

The other letter, dated 23 February 1984, said a SAS officer visited India and drew up a plan which was then approved by Mrs Gandhi (Graham and Nelson 2014).

The matter has been subject of an enquiry in the UK, but Sikh organisations have expressed their dissatisfaction with the enquiry.

Conclusion

The interventions by the human rights community were crucial at the time but they were rather like emergency first aid rather than addressing the root cause. Even though we did indicate the causes of the Hindu–Sikh divide, we could do little to stop it from sharpening over the years.

As a human rights lawyer, what I remember most about 1984 was the failure of the state to respond; the police, the judiciary, the commissions of enquiries—all failed to intervene and stop the massacre. How could the entire state machinery be so quickly mobilised to attack a community and turn them into a persecuted minority? Now the question has acquired urgency when another community, the Muslims, is being attacked and the institutions for the protection of democracy are even more weak and corrupted by money and communal politics.

In 1984, human rights activists worked without any funding; the lawyers did all the work pro bono and there was a great deal of cooperation among different groups, organisations and parties. Now there is money and funding for human rights work done by NGOs which do not seriously challenge the state as they are dependent on its goodwill to allow the funds.

Even in 1984 some of the more political groups and organisations were critical of the role of NGOs, including the Nagrik Ekta Manch, for making the victims dependent on them instead of promoting self-help and political understanding of the events.

The human rights movement itself is now divided along caste and communal lines. This is a reflection of the divisions in the wider society.

The leadership of the human rights groups has overwhelmingly been in the hands of the majority community.

A growing alienation from Indian democracy and the idea of India has taken root and the roots are growing deeper, sustained by Hindu majoritarianism. The violence against minorities and those who show solidarity with them is deeply entrenched; it has been institutionalised and normalised. It is a tribute to George Orwell's vision of 1984.

Notes

1. Bibi Amar Kaur died in 1985, so the protest must have taken place sometime between 1982 and 1985.

2. In conversation with I. K. Gujral during the course of fact-finding.

References

Calamur, Krishnadev. 2014. 'U.K. Aided India in Raid on Sikh Shrine, Documents Suggest'. *National Public Radio*, 14 January. Available at https://www.npr.org/sections/thetwo-way/2014/01/14/262400978/u-k-aided-india-in-raid-on-sikh-shrine-documents-suggest (accessed on 21 November 2024).

Chakravarti, Uma, and Nandita Haksar. 1987. *The Delhi Riots: Three Days in the Life of a Nation*. New Delhi: Lancer International.

Graham, Georgia, and Dean Nelson. 2014. 'Britain "Backstabbed" Sikhs by Advising India on 1984 Golden Temple Raid'. *The Telegraph*, 14 January. Available at https://www.telegraph.co.uk/news/worldnews/asia/india/10571223/Britain-backstabbed-Sikhs-by-advising-India-on-1984-Golden-Temple-raid.html (accessed on 21 November 2024).

Kumar, Girija. 2008. *The Book on Trial: Fundamentalism and Censorship in India*. New Delhi: Har Anand Publications.

Mohan, Peggy. 2012. 'Linguist in a POTA Court'. *Open*, 16 December. Available at http://www.openthemagazine.com/article/india/linguist-in-a-pota-court (accessed on 21 November 2024).

Nayar, Kuldeep. 2018. 'Key to Operation Blue Star in British Hands'. *The Citizen*, 25 March. Available at https://www.thecitizen.in/index.php/en/newsdetail/index/4/13375/key-to-operation-bluestar-in-british-hands (accessed on 21 November 2024).

People's Union for Democratic Rights (PUDR) and People's Union for Civil Liberties (PUCL). 1984. 'Who Are the Guilty? Report of a Joint Inquiry into the Causes and Impact of the Riots in Delhi from 31 October to 10 November 1984'. Available at https://ia601600.us.archive.org/26/items/WhoAreTheGuilty_201502/Who%20Are%20The%20Guilty.pdf (accessed on 21 November 2024).

——. 1987. 'Justice Denied: A Critique of the Mishra Commission Report on the Riots in November 1984'. Available at https://www.pudr.org/publicatiosn-files/1987-Justice%20Denined.pdf (accessed on 21 November 2024).

The Pioneer. 2014. 'Amarinder Names BJP, RSS Leaders Involved in 1984 Riots'. 8 February. Available at https://www.dailypioneer.com/2014/state-editions/amarinder-names-bjp-rss-leaders-involved-in-1984-riots.html (accessed on 22 December 2024).

two

Enduring Exile and Lasting Loss

The Widows of the 1984 Delhi Carnage[1]

Yasmeen Arif

> In Poussin's painting, *Gathering the Ashes of Phocion*, Phocion's wife bends down outside the boundary wall of Athens to scoop up his ashes, in an integral *gestus* which gathers her own soul and body into this act of perfect devotion. The tension of political defiance and the fear of being discovered appear only in the taut *contrapposto* of the woman servant, which is juxtaposed to the utter vulnerability of the stooping wife. Arising above the two foregrounded figures is a combined land and townscape of classical magnificence and gleaming temples and municipal buildings, perfect displays of the architectural orders, which convey no hint of malign intent. Yet Phocion's condemnation and manner of dying were the result of tyranny temporarily usurping good rule in the city.
>
> ... In Poussin's painting, this transcendent but mournable justice is configured, its absence given presence, in the architectural perspective which frames and focuses the enacted justice of Phocion's wife, her response to the implied act of injustice by the city. To see the built forms themselves as ciphers of the unjust city would be to perpetuate endless dying and endless tyranny—unending disaster. (Rose 1996: 150)

This chapter begins with a few days in 1984, when the seeming 'usurpation of good rule in a city' caused one of the worst carnages in independent India. The assassination of the then Prime Minister Indira Gandhi by her Sikh bodyguards, in the morning of 31 October 1984, had incited an onslaught of violence against the Sikh community in Delhi, the capital city.[2] With genocidal intensity, several Sikh localities in Delhi were targeted and men, both young and old, were annihilated through some of the most grotesque methods of mass murder. Countless women were raped, houses burnt and looted, business establishments and even entire colonies were razed to the ground. This essay describes and attempts to make meaning of the continuing lives of some of those who survived this carnage. These lives are those of the widows and their children who live in the Tilak Vihar Widows Relocation Colony (hereafter the Colony) situated in a dense neighbourhood of west Delhi.[3] Tucked away beyond the edge of a bustling, fairly prosperous neighbourhood, this is a place which, by virtue of its nomenclature and its residents' profile, becomes, as I intend to argue, an address of exile. The particular nuance that I would like to draw from the words of Gillian Rose quoted earlier is this sense of 'cast away-ness' that the residents of the Colony articulate, denounced by the powerful 'structures' of the city. Perhaps the lofty city buildings that provide the backdrop for Poussin's painting represent an iconic view of the high ideals of a city-state—an imagined and aspired space that can sustain the honourable governance of a contract between the individual and society, partly mediated by the techniques of statecraft as well as a rational, critical public sphere. Foregrounded against this could also be the Colony residents—forsaken by justice as they perceive it, removed from a 'normal' society they were familiar with and defined by deaths that remain meaningless, they appear to remain outside the scheme of the 'legitimate' order of the city. Several decades have passed since the event and while monetary or material compensation has been the measurable mode of 'justice' offered to the survivors, convictions made against the murders committed continue to be absurdly disproportionate.[4]

The metaphorical 'banishment' to a place is heightened by a loss made private and insular in the lives of these survivors because they perceive their mourning to have failed in achieving formal retribution. By this fact, their loss seems invisible in the formal remembrance of the city. The image of Phocion's wife against the mighty structures of the city in Poussin's painting brings to relief unaccountable death that has to be disregarded, cast outside the limits of the ordered city, which, in turn, renders the survivor threatened and threatening. This essay mirrors this portrayal by describing, on the one hand, the authority of the state and its institutions in either acknowledging or disregarding disorderly deaths, of withholding or dispensing benevolence/justice. On the other, it is about an afterlife of loss and injustice that constitutes an ongoing vulnerability amongst those who were left behind. If the metaphor of the city were to stand for a conglomeration of the state (as in the Athenian city-state of Phocion's painting), the arenas of the public and those other agencies that come into effect in these circumstances, the subjectivities engendered by the 'city' with reference to un-retributed death suggest a powerful aspect of state practice and its ramifications in taking away individual agency from personal biography and in its place inscribing a seemingly futile future. In the manner that Gillian Rose indicates earlier, this is an opposing relationship constructed and sustained as an aggravated opposition between the agonies of suffering inside against the seeming relentless injustices of the outside. The discussion is thus about the interstices of the violent event and those who survived, of state practices, justice and quotidian existence. It attempts to trace the metonymic domains[5] of affect that such interactions perpetuate into the socialities of these lives and their futures. In another way, it is about how the ordered city/state can perpetrate, through its forms and structures, an unending of the 1984 disaster as it unfolds in the future realm of these lives.

Survivors, Perpetrators and Benefactors: Domains of Affect

The relationship of opposition or the engendering of subjectivities in this exploration engages primarily with the figure of the widow and her children. These are figures whose constitutive bodies appear to be split down the middle with the singular stroke of an event of mass violence. One side is made up of an alleged 'enabling' public bureaucratic classification[6] of a victim that counts as an index of entitlement. The other is the stigma and burden of private grief and loss, made acute and apolitical to the extent that it has not found its closure in legal justice.[7] However, it is not the alleged lack of justice alone, but public knowledge that constantly reminds/reiterates this and makes this an 'open', public wound. There is an ironic twist which causes this wound to be nursed as if it is intensely private, as an internal subjectivity alone, but its intensity appears to have been also fuelled by the fact that it is 'known' to be an open wound, as it were, by an outside, by an arena of the 'public'.[8] It is the same reason why the impotency of the outside makes this burden a private one, yet sustained by a public.

For instance, as per official figures, there were a total of 707 cases filed in relation to the massacre (Grover 2002). The following detail about these cases, as reported by Vrinda Grover as part of an investigation into the role of justice in the events of 1984, indicates the overall situation:

> Of these, 322 cases were sent as un-traced and cancelled. As many as 320 cases had ended in acquittal. While 25 cases were pending in trial courts, only 30 cases, which did not even constitute 10 percent of the total, resulted in conviction. (2002: 75)

It has to be mentioned that most of these convictions are not about the murders but are rather about looting, arson, rioting, and so forth. In Vrinda Grover's analysis of a representative sample of 126 trial court cases, the following description indicates the general pattern that these cases have taken:

> … only 8 cases resulted in convictions while the rest resulted in acquittals. Of these 8 convictions, 2 were overturned by the High Court while the death sentences awarded in 3 of the cases were reduced to life sentences by the Supreme Court. In this sample, 99 of the Trial Court Cases relate to the offence of murder under section 302 IPC. An analysis of the judgment reveals a pattern—that a combination of grave lapses in investigation, inordinate delays, insufficient evidence, procedural lacunae led to a majority of cases concluding in acquittals. (2002: 75)

Clearly, there has been a 'failure' of law or due process by which the most heinous of acknowledged offences—murder—has remained unaccounted for.[9] However, these murders themselves, by rendering a group of women as widows, give them and their children a classificatory label—'victims'[10]—with rights of claim to compensation.

Two sorts of material compensation were made available. First, single-room apartments in the four-storeyed blocks of Tilak Vihar. All of these houses in the Colony were originally meant to be grade IV housing for government employees, which were then reassigned as accommodation for these survivors and their children. Approximately 950 families were given allotments here from around March 1985; around 700 of these were widow families.[11] Monetary compensation for loss of lives had initially been stipulated by the state at a rate of Rs 10,000 (approximately US$ 250) per life in 1984. In 1997, this amount was increased to Rs 2 lakh (approximately US$ 2,300), which together with retrospective interest amounted to Rs 3.5 lakh.

It is interesting to note that this increased compensation amount was based on a Delhi High Court judgment[12] that directed the Delhi government to pay the required amount to all the survivors within four months. The judgment states:

> It is the duty and responsibility of the State to secure and safeguard the life and liberty of an individual from mob violence. It is not open to the state to say that the violations are being committed by private persons for which it cannot be held accountable...
>
> Thus those lives which are endangered or lost during the riots, clearly come under the purview of the violation of Article 21[13] of the Constitution... If it is not able to do all that then it cannot escape the liability to pay adequate compensation to the family of the person killed during the riots as his or her life has been extinguished in clear violation of Article 21 of the constitution.[14]

By taking recourse to the Constitution, the courts make the state responsible and liable to the survivors and assign a calculable value to the lost life. Between this and the complicity of the state[15] in dis-allowing convictions for murder lies the future of the widow's life world. For the widow, it is the loss that has made possible a quasi-enabling moment, producing the subjectivity of a claimant (in relation to the giving authority—the state or other organisations that demonstrate a capacity to provide some form of support) potentially into the temporal extent of an entire lifetime.

Apart from state compensation, another source was the Delhi Sikh Gurudwara Management Committee that had provided a monthly pension to these widows, which has now been discontinued. One of the main non-governmental organisations (NGOs) providing support in the Colony is the community establishment called Nishkam Sikh Welfare Council (hereafter, Nishkam), which has been working in the area since it was established as a relocation colony. Apart from providing healthcare and schooling, vocational training and counselling to young people of the Colony, it also maintains a sewing centre which was started with the main aim of providing some form of livelihood for the widows. One of the dominant themes in many of our conversations with the Colony residents has been the kind of everyday support received or denied from various sources. A consistent complaint has been the changing nature of Nishkam and how their intentions have changed from charity to profit-making even in essential areas like healthcare.[16] The tone of these complaints always posits an underlying sense of 'right' to the facilities that Nishkam has to offer. Nishkam officials, however, maintain that it is quite impossible to continue the initial kind of support for 20 years, suggesting that nothing is quite enough when the 'habit' of entitlement sets in.

In addition, there is a substantial amount of talk about everyday facilities like water and electricity, supply of which, like in other similar localities of the city, remains illegal and sporadic at best. The Colony residents report how some bills show up from time to time, none of which are ever paid because, as they say,[17]

> (Elderly widow A):[18] They had said they would give us a house in place of a house. My man was killed, my brother was killed, my whole family has been killed—for what reason should I pay a bill. We said bring our men back, we will pay our bills. We do not have jobs, work, we have small children ... how are we to educate them, feed them? Even our little ones have to go and earn.

There continues to be insecurity about the houses as well; for instance:

> (Elderly widow B): They have fixed Rs 42,000 for these houses. The government has allotted but they have not paid their dues to the DDA.[19] Only when the government pays up will our houses be free. ... They ask us for money—sometimes a notice shows up. They should make a concrete decision on this. Today, I am alive. Tomorrow when I die, they will throw my children out because our allotments are still uncertain.

This kind of material insecurity stems from a deeper affect, from an experience of failed justice that extends, in my opinion, from this seemingly mundane everyday terrain to a more negative interiority, one that ties in the outside, the public to the private and the local.

> (Elderly widow B): Whatever has happened to us was very bad. What can we do now? What has happened to us has happened. But then, even our Guru Granth Sahib has been de-sacralised. What has been done to our men has been done. Our Sardars have always been martyred. We are a community of martyrdom, but Durbar Sahib has been burnt—it has been vandalized. What fault did it have? Many gurdwaras have been burnt. The people who had done this, their killings, nothing has been done. Nobody has been caught. There are these hearings and then our people say, 'well, this government is supporting us'. No government is supporting us. We are just sitting peacefully, waiting for when God will Himself act.
>
> ... We do not want anything from them, the justice we should have been given has been denied to us.
>
> ... Whatever has happened in whatever way, the Sikh Community has forgotten everything. They have forgotten everything—they garland those people, today our murderers have won and come back and our brothers are garlanding them. There is no one to listen, no justice. They gave us jobs but with the jobs our children were left behind, no one to look after them. The children kept going wrong without us ... when women leave their children behind, what can happen, they will go wrong—under whose

> care could we have left them. No one child here has been reformed—some are drug addicts, some gamble. Our community should have settled us—the gurdwara has stopped our pension—they say, your children are now earning—they have done nothing for us. They have done whatever they wished. They might go on making Prime Ministers, but till we do not get justice we will remain tormented like this. Now we do not want to talk about all this. When we don't get any justice in our own home—those homes where 10 men were burnt, what will be our condition. ...
>
> Go to Nishkam, they tell you—forget '84. How can we forget, even if a dog in the house dies, we are sad. We have lost our young children, our world has burnt with them. 12 men, we are just waiting for them to come home, we are waiting and on the way, petrol is poured on them and they are burnt.
>
> ... Our living is not living.

At the time when these narratives where recorded, in 2004, the Congress party had returned to power with a startling and sweeping victory, and, ironically, with a Sikh prime minister. As the woman's narration suggests, destiny and time have worked to seal their misfortune because the perpetrators of their misery have returned to power. This betrayal is not just about politics; it is also about a community that has appeared to have 'forgotten' the gravity of 1984. Thus, it would seem, intertwined in these stories is a mingling amongst and between the party and the politician, the state and its executives, the community and its institutions, all pitted against a loss. A loss that remains without retribution because justice in the sense of attaining legitimacy has remained unattainable, relegating it not just to the inner domain of personal pain but also as a social frustration, a community betrayal. Left alone, so to speak, to carry the burden of injustice, it seems that the energy required to fuel this sense of injustice comes not only from the private trauma but also from the incessant reminders to it.

Simultaneously, in the lives of these women, healing cannot come easily also because of a double bind that renders the state both as enabler and as perpetrator through the dynamics of the same event. These women bear the knowledge, in their daily remembrances and their narratives, that the state represented by the police or the politicians has been responsible for their loss. At the same time, it is the state itself that becomes the only meaningful benefactor because their attempts at reclaiming a life are made possible by the largesse of the state in giving them a sense of entitlement. It is a strange facing-off of subjectivities, of conditions of affect that the state seems to initiate, which in turn haunts these biographical trajectories as they unfold into everyday corporeal life.

I do not suggest that a conviction is the only form of justice that these women would have found acceptable or would have liberated them from their sense of victimhood. Rather, it is a 'public' and 'private' subjective personhood that the lack of legitimate death engenders in these women, it is the morass of meaninglessness of their loss that makes them believe in their state of diminished existence. It may not be hazardous to describe these phenomena in these survivors as a situation that sometimes provides some recourse when faced with one's own inadequacies. Although the limitations of this essay do allow a deeper exploration of the experience of coming to terms, of rebuilding lives, I do not find enough analytical comfort in rendering these biographies as entirely without succour. In another sense, there is some sense of recovery that such lives clearly manifest; however, it is the peculiar entanglement of the public and the private and its intersection with state practices that makes a sense of victimhood more acute, or more permanent. Because there is another side to this story—some in the Colony, arguably very few, have indeed remarked on the fact that the 'habit' of receiving under the label of victimhood has rendered the Colony into an irresponsible society attuned to entitled deserving rather than to earning. Nonetheless, it would not be correct to represent my ethnographic findings in just one way, and although not explored in this essay, the possibility of life going on by whatever means is and has to be a part of this discourse. My representation of these phenomena should not arrest these biographies as I suspect some of the issucs I dcscribe here have.

However, what remains striking is that the condition of affect moves far beyond the lifetime of a single generation. In fact, it seeps invariably into a future, seemingly encompassing temporality within its grip of futility. It could be said that the 'unending disaster' is most poignant at the level of the young. While it remains implicated in the narratives of the elders, the sense of doom becomes literal amongst the young—a few instances of these are apparent in our conversations with some young men of the Colony, illustrating how far into the future this double bind continues. These young men are between the ages of 19 years and 24 years. Most of them were infants or very young during 1984 or were born soon after.

> A: We have not received any support from the government. They had said that they will give you these things, they will give your children jobs, they will make your children stand. They have done nothing …
>
> Some time ago there was a fire in a cinema hall in the city. The government has given them a lot, they are still giving them a lot. That was an accident. But with us, it was done to us, still they give us no help.

> With us it was no accident, it was done to us. The government should have once thought, there were riots, let us look at them—do they have all facilities or not. There is nothing here. They send 2–3 people—they talk to the leader here and that's all.
>
> … It's twenty years since 1984. But the government has not thought of keeping 15 seats for the children of the '84 people. They have not done anything till now.

Flowing underneath, in the same breath, was also an undercurrent of revenge:

> B: … But, the day we get our turn, this is just a matter of opportunity, those people took advantage of the situation, the mistakes of the police …
>
> A: … you know what kind of mistakes these police made. All of our people had come together, do you know what the police said? No fights are taking place, go home and leave your weapons with us.
>
> B: Never mind a day, if we could get just an hour. They had three days. They should give us an hour and see. The day we get a chance we will show them. The community can say what they like, but anger inside never dies. Those who can kill their own and win cannot be considered manly (*namard*). I cannot live like that. What are the sardars (men of the Sikh community) doing these days? There is no sardar now who has any humanity—in spite of them showing their piety. Tytler has come again to contest—the man who killed our fathers, burnt them alive, he is again being put up. Why do the sardars have no courage, couldn't they have shot this Tytler, this Sajjan. Why are they standing again? They only keep fighting behind the gurdwara.[20]

Clearly, these narratives are domains of affect, reproductions of those expressed by their mothers, ones that are peculiarly produced and reproduced in time and space through these biographies. These are the instances that illustrate the relationships of subjectivity that the metaphorical city/state bring about, particularly when there is usurpation of good rule and whose reminders are not made to go away.

Beyond the Limits of the City: Addresses of Exile

These generations in the Colony, both past and future, are now a 'community' of victims bound together by their common loss and grief to follow a common destiny, remembered on occasion as anecdotes in discourses of other 'similar' events in the country.[21] But their lives have continued for 20 years of ordinary living—at least till the time of my meetings with some of them—in one way or another. What is the nature of this life? Have these lives been assigned any proper political subjectivity? Did their loss make for a 'grievable life', that is, a public political existence that moved into the realms of justice, closure or any form of retribution (Butler 2004: 19–49)? Have they been blended back into some form of cohered social fabric? If from Judith Butler's idea of a grievable life, I am to understand the legitimacy of their widowhood, their entitlement to legal or to any other kind of right, then the widows of the Colony do not have grievable lives. Their grief and mourning are the continued private trauma and memory (constituted 'publicly' as well) that constitutes the other part of the widows' entity. It is this other part that reproduces itself into a terrain of exile, as I suggest in the following.

It may be said that the Sikh widow of 1984 is not just a post-facto figure after 1984, in the discourse that surrounds her. The history of Sikh militancy[22] that preceded 1984 could also suggest a vulnerability to this community of women who could have had no other outcome but to eventually become a 'community' of widows. There appears to be a terrible legacy that condemns these women to a life of loss even before the loss could occur. They bear the cross to a political and violent struggle that bore the sign of the entire historic group of Sikhs which has left its scars on some, not all, from amongst the community and on behalf of them. As victims living in a city who could not or did not exercise the option of 'returning' to or finding shelter in some other refuge, like a family home, in order to remake their lives, they became a constructed community within a beleaguered community.[23]

This is a community not only in physical exile from the familiarity of their known 'secure' past homes, but they are also in exile from a certain sense of personhood, or, in another way—in their sense of womanhood. The 'masculine' militancy of the Sikhs could be thought of as a pre-emptive condition for this community of widows, a preceding vulnerability. I will also maintain that this is a vulnerability that extends to the younger generation by the very virtue of being a part of the widow's[24] world. This is a world (and a word) that is made up of an acute relationality to others, the men, whose loss and absence reduces them to a life of incompleteness, a life of eternal lack. The women are incomplete insofar that they are widows rendered so unnaturally and violently, a fact that does not gain them a 'whole' right. Even during the brief temporal span when they had become the rightful claimants to compensation, their legitimate claims to the monetary relief that they were offered had its own vagaries. Community prescription decreed that the widows were in fact only partial claimants because the money had to be divided equally with the dead men's fathers (see Das 2004: 229–30).

In addition, their children are to be always fatherless (again, rendered so unnaturally) and therefore somewhat lesser than other 'complete' youth. The young men speak with the grief of their mothers and the passion of their youth, while the young women live surrounded not by men who can offer protection but those who themselves threaten or are threatened. These are not circumstances that are born out of a 'common' misfortune of death or poverty, but they are afflictions that are caused—conditions that have an externality in blame. These are not changeable conditions that could be or that are meant to be dealt with by personal or social means. In fact, they are impediments to the movement of biography because they remove even a consciousness of agency from private life.

At another level, there seems to be a temporal bracketing to the colony as well, one that removes these lives from 'ordinary time' to a 'limited' temporal frame with a very distinct moment of origin. During our first visit to the Colony, we met a group of widows in the stitching centre maintained by Nishkam. While trying to introduce ourselves and the purpose of our interest in their lives, we took pains to elaborate how we did not want to reopen old traumas, we did not really want a retelling of the event; rather we were interested in their lives after, in the ways they coped and continued with their lives. As we discovered in that first visit and in the subsequent first meetings with most, the narratives were inevitably anchored around a beginning and that point was the days of the event. In seemingly accurate recall, most told us about the way in which the mobs appeared, how they ran through alleys, through houses, trying to find places to hide. They described how they tried to hide their sons, fathers or husbands; they remembered how a father was beaten to death, how little boys were burnt in heaps, how young men were cut up and left to die. In whatever multiple trajectories the narratives took after that initial moment, it seemed significant that life as constructed by these narratives bound, even stopped, time within the limits of the event. It would seem that temporality in these biographies does not spill out beyond the limits inscribed by the event. The future appears trapped as an afterlife of the event itself rather than as an accumulated unfolding of time.

Giving meaning to these initial moments of the narrative, it seems to me that the desire in these women to start the conversation with a vivid recollection of the event itself and moments of tragic horror suggests the following. Did the past for them only start from that one event, and no remembrance was possible unless it started from that one point which became an anchor on which hinged the possibility of remembrance? This point comes into sharper focus when it is juxtaposed against similar recollections that I could elicit in Bhogal.[25] In Bhogal, the recollection of the past extended into a different kind of anchor, a different kind of excavation of the past. While some detailed the events of 1984 in the way they unfolded in their immediate neighbourhood, most founded this event through a historical loop that brought together their community with the Partition and 1984. We were told that the Partition was an attack by those 'others', but this time it was the neighbours themselves, making the latter event doubly tragic. Survival and triumph over the second episode was just a matter of time. For most in Bhogal, 1984 and beyond was the triumph of a proud, hardworking, noble community whose ability to survive is just an echo of another time, of another experience. This is a very different kind of community experience of memory in the present than the experience in the Colony. Two parts of a community who had undergone the same tragic event (notwithstanding the difference in terms of the losses), yet their excavation into their past, from the vantage point of today, differs. What sets them apart?

I am persuaded to understand this separation in the community through a separation of the notions of loss, grief and mourning. If in Bhogal, there is a notion of triumph over a history of persecution—the future of their memory of past events is a narrative of recovery, of reclaimed normalcy. Their utterances of reclaiming a life emanate from notions of a hardworking, noble community whose ability to triumph over their tragedies is readily apparent in the way they have been able to replenish their losses. Most have been able replace the trucks that were burnt, rebuild the houses that were destroyed and recover the businesses that were interrupted. In Bhogal, material loss has been compensated by material recovery, there appears to be an apparent sense of equitability between the before and after. Normalcy is restored through a kind of substitution.[26]

In the Colony, in contrast, there is no retribution, no lost life has been replaced by a life 'taken' in conviction. The widows in the Colony have been suspended in 'futile' mourning, as Butler (2004: 19–49) could suggest, because compensation has not replaced their fundamental loss of life.[27] That in itself extends the grief into a future, or the past extends to a future which does not yet provide any tangible sign of recovery in the public personhood of the widow. Insofar that there has been no retributive formal justice for the violence committed against them, their grief remains illegitimate or, in Butler's terms (ibid.), they do not attain the political subjecthood of 'grievable lives'. Apart from attaining a bureaucratic label and some material compensation, justice still remains impotent when it comes to the balance between lives lost, life worlds transformed on one side and perpetrators named through a system of justice on the other. Perhaps this is the reason why the narration of the widows' lives always starts with the point at which their relationship with 'normal life' breaks. Every moment of the past, the present and future evolves out of the infinite event of transformation. Had there been any formal closure achieved, there might have been the possibility of a different temporal bracketing to the narration.

Not only is there an exile of these lives from the 'normal' unfolding of personal biography, there is also a corporeal crystallisation to this, precisely because these are lives led in relation to other city spaces. In other words, there is an actual address of exile in which the widows inhabit. By founding a colony for widows of the 1984 anti-Sikh violence, it was as if bureaucratic injunction, by demarcating a spatial limit to a place, had not only 'produced' a space of victimhood but also with the same stroke ascribed a possible destiny of exclusion to its residents. A newspaper report (Ghatwai 2005) suggested a similar zoning adopted, by 'choice' and not by formal rule, by victims of the post-Godhra violence in certain Gujarat villages, echoing patterns already prevalent in Surat and Ahmedabad. Instead of returning to their original homes, most of these people are choosing to relocate themselves in areas they deem safer; thus, Muslims are choosing 'safety in numbers' by moving to predominantly Muslim villages, as the report suggests. One of the reasons cited for this is the victims' continued involvement in court cases and so long as some of the neighbours continue to figure in the names of the accused, the returnees are unlikely to find much peace or personal security.

Although these instances need not necessarily be read as comparable, a pattern takes form, one that is most likely to crystallise into long durations in the spatial future of the city. It is the mapping of an urban topography by which identifiable, recognisable groups of people who are most unlikely to be successful in shedding their label are 'allotted' their designated space in the density of the city; in other words, the *emplacement* of victims. The colony thus becomes a place with a label, a label that pre-empts biographical trajectories of its inhabitants with a sign that works both as a private mark as well as a public burden. Although, at first glance, the topography of the area would suggest nothing different from other similar colonies around the city, there is an important difference. It is as if the event of 1984 has constructed, brick by brick, in these people's lives, perhaps even sustained by the outside world, a veritable wall that insulates the community within. On the one hand, it is a circumscribed geography of mourning. One of our informants, who was a very young widow in 1984, had spent the last 20 years in thc colony and was also successful in putting together a reasonable life for her family (the children were educated, one had a job), said to me when I asked whether she ever thought of leaving the Colony for a better place, 'Here I can talk everyday about '84. I can share my burden every day. But anywhere else, people will just be tired of me, the mad woman who only talks about one thing.'[28]

On the other hand, it is a bounded locale of social crisis. Most of the widows who had initially formed the small community of residents here came in with their remaining family members, either very young children or elderly relatives.[29] As mentioned earlier, soon after their relocation to the Colony, almost all the widows had to leave their homes to eke out a living. Some availed the sewing work provided by Nishkam that required them to work at a designated sewing centre nearby. Others had to travel further away for jobs that were provided in government offices. The children had to fend for themselves or, more appropriately, as we were told by some of our informants, they grew up free from the supervision of any male guardian. Naturally, we were told, these children, particularly the boys, grew up to fall prey to the predictable evils of poverty and deprivation—drug abuse, petty crimes, etc. Drug related deaths in the Colony were considered very high—about 200, possibly an exaggerated number, in the first half of 2004 alone.

This deprivation of proper, meaning 'male', parenting had allegedly created a whole generation of misguided young men, which led to the whole Colony acquiring a bad name. Some of the younger informants we talked to told us how their efforts at looking for jobs were routinely thwarted. One of them told us the story of a friend:

> A: A friend of ours had learnt the work of air conditioners. He went to an interview and everything was fine. At the end they asked him, where do you stay? And he said Tilak Vihar. They said you have to go, we cannot take you. Because you are from Tilak Vihar. Just because of this word. They say, everybody is aberrant here, we are disreputable. Someone is a

> pickpocket, someone is a thief—you catch them and they say they are from Tilak Vihar.
>
> … They say you are from 1984. There is such dirt there (in the Colony), you must also be doing the same. We can only say that five fingers are not the same. If along with four bad ones here there is another, he will also be considered bad.
>
> C: Shahpura is even worse than Tilak Vihar. All bad things happen there—chain snatching, kidnapping but only Tilak Vihar is considered disreputable.

Moreover, a whole colony composed mostly of young widows and their potential sexual availability could not have remained long from speculation. Remarks came our way from the younger informants about how the local police, in small everyday incidents, refer to the women using very abusive language. The women also told us about their early years when neighbours close to the Colony considered them to be potentially 'bad' women. Like some other poorer localities of the city, this Colony could also have been explained away by the various factors of urban deprivation. But this is a special colony, rendered so not only by its inmates but also by a society outside, both of which negotiate the place as one saturated with meaning more than what poverty can bestow. It is a society of victimhood that has moved, in time, into a grievance of entitlement. This stems from an episode of violence, of a loss, that bizarrely creates a milieu that combines a relentless but impotent public consciousness with the sharpness of continued private agony.

In a sense, a converse reflection of Poussin's painting could perhaps be possible if and when the city/state brings the survivor back into its fold. When their past has been given due presence in the history of the ordered city/state, can these lives liberate themselves from their temporal bond, from their suspension in an exile from the flow of ordinary time, so that their biographies achieve a sense of ordinariness?

Concluding Comments: The Future of Memory

In the period that has passed between then and now, in the era when lives were meant to be reclaimed, it seems that another future to these memories has been manifested. It is not as if these stories have not found a future; in fact, they have taken the form of repetitive representation in public consciousness—cinema,[30] media, non-governmental or community archives, public debate, etc. They have become a discursive motif with which to identify civil violence in independent India (very different from the Partition), to make visible the political and legal negligence in attributing accountability or justice. However, in the realm of private telling and listening, these stories appear as motifs of failed mourning, of unsuccessful grief, as persistent interruptions in biographies that were to be recuperated. The stigma of injustice and bad fate continues to falter any process of healing. These are not memories of experience that give their subjects a status of noble suffering. Rather they seem to overwhelm the project of continued life with the spreading decay of deprivation and victimhood.

Several years have passed since entitlements and compensations have been allotted and dealt with, life in the Colony has continued in hues composed by both an irremovable stain of a past event and the newer tones of an ongoing everyday life of new generations and transformed lives. In such futures of memories of violence, what is the modality of recovery? The notion of recovery in the social anthropological grasp of lives after violent devastation has been hinged on the reclamation of the everyday, on regaining normalcy.[31] It is the idea of normalcy and everydayness that intrigues and complicates the idea of recovery in the Colony.

In the ethnographic depiction of life in the Colony, normalcy should be defined within its contextual limits. There is perhaps nothing extra-normal in the bare daily running of these households. The routine and rhythm of life goes on, even beyond the everyday to emerging life stories. Just as an everydayness goes on with people going to work, with children going to school or staying behind, with household chores being attended to, other ordinary events of daughters and sons getting married, someone dying or being born, someone finding or losing a job go on. However fleeting the sense of the everyday, there is a stable sense of ordinary life that goes on amongst the widows, their families and their neighbours. Insofar that return to normalcy is the reclamation of the everyday, it is there.

At the same time, we were also told repeatedly that not a day goes by when 1984 is not mentioned. I would argue that this is a normalcy, in its essence, engendered and then sustained by a moment of transformation, following Butler's (2004: 19–49) idea of mourning and transformation. This moment in the biographies of these women is the event of the pogrom. While a particular material side to life for most of these women—for instance, a house, a bit of income, some accumulated 'goods' and expenses—suggest a standard of corporeal normalcy, they lead a life anchored to a moment in their past which has made them live with the consciousness of a profound transformation. In Butler's words:

> … one mourns when one accepts that by the loss one undergoes one will be changed, possibly for ever. Perhaps mourning has to do with agreeing to undergo a transformation (perhaps one should say *submitting* to a transformation) the full result of which one cannot know in advance. There is losing, as we know, but there is also the transformative effect of loss, and this latter cannot be charted or planned (2004: 21).

The widows of 1984 lead transformed lives made acute by the fact that the perpetrators of the violence inflicted on them continue, in the eyes of their victims, their ostensibly unchanged lives. It is this acute contrast between two sides of normalcy—the ostensibly normal lives of the perpetrators who remain unaccountable and that of the widows whose apparently normal lives are led in futile mourning—that makes their possible recovery to normalcy an irredeemable burden.

In the course of this chapter, I have tried to show the various axes along which a survivor has to fragment in order to make ordinary life possible. Once marked by violence that continues to remain unresolved, a certain trajectory of multiple selves seems to take course, on one hand in relationship to the city/state and to public socialities, on the other. As regards the former—as victims, as claimant, as a threat (to the transparency of statecraft, to the recovered community); as regards the latter—as a stigma and as an unfulfilled grieving subject. It becomes schizophrenic terrain for the work of anthropology itself—how does one bridge the gap between lies and fact, its knowing and validation, when it appears to be the same gap that sets up schisms between the institutions of state, the legal, the political and the executive just as it fragments public spheres, civil societies and communities.

Afterword

At the time of this volume going to press, over 40 years have passed since the carnage and more than 13 years since the first publication of this essay. Much more has been written during this time on the carnage—my own interpretations and concerns on this event have developed in different ways (for instance, Arif 2015, 2016). Recent occurrences connected to the carnage like Sajjan Kumar having been brought to justice, as one of the leading politicians involved in the killings, are undoubtedly continuing concerns in this event's afterlife. However, this essay reflects concerns that, I expect, are conceptually enduring and arising out of ethnographic vignettes that are about a particular position in time—and thus best retained as it is rather than subjected to any kind of updating. Episodes of communal violence in India since 1984 have multiplied and are tragically recurring with unrepentant themes similar to the ones mentioned in the essay—our human science involvements are perhaps one way of retaining testimonies of our times.

Notes

1. This essay was published in 2007 as part of a larger collection of essays on riots called 'Riot Discourses' under a series called *Domains* published by the International Center for Ethnic Studies, Sri Lanka. It was previously called 'The Delhi Carnage of 1984, The After Life of Violence and Loss'. It remains the same except for a few editorial changes and a brief afterword.

2. The assassination of the prime minister by her Sikh bodyguards was connected to the prevailing Sikh militancy. The period from 1 November to 4 November 1984 is considered to be the worst 72 hours of the carnage, an event unparalleled in the city since the partition of 1947. Some other parts of the country were affected as well. Official figures estimate the dead to be 2,733, most of whom were men in the age group of 20–50 years, although other sources place the figure at 4,000 or above. There are yet no official figures of the injured, of raped women or of the houses and businesses looted and destroyed.

3. The ethnographic information in this essay is based on our interviews with approximately 30 households in the neighbourhood. Simi Bajaj and Harpreet Kaur from the Institute for Socio-Economic Development and Democracy (ISERDD) research team helped me with these interviews. Most of the original allottees came from two of the worst hit colonies in the city—Sultanpuri and Mongolpuri. There were others from various parts of the city. The variations amongst the families in economic status or social classification in terms of caste groups were significant. This is not a point that I can elaborate here, suffice to note that apart from visible differences in material goods (although the overall colony could be loosely lower middle class), there were internal social differences made apparent by our informants with reference to caste groups.

4. A longer discussion on this follows. It is virtually impossible to trace the trial proceedings or exact number of convictions for any given charge filed during the 1984 carnage (or most other case proceedings in India) given the incredible long

time spans and wide geographical dispersal of cases. I have taken recourse to a specific report compiled by Grover, *Quest for Justice* (2002), which investigated a sample of the 1984 cases in order to provide an adequate overview of the state of affairs.

5. Understood literally, the 'metonymic' domains of affect here point to an assemblage of contiguous emotions and subjectivities that arise amongst the group I have observed, both conceptually and existentially. These are framed by the event but the frame also encompasses the idea of an afterlife—a temporal extension beyond the event itself.

6. The term 'enabling' as it is used here cannot be understood in its positive connotation alone. By 'enabling' in this context, I am alluding to the brief moment of entitlement that a survivor/victim may find themselves in, as compared to a large number of others who simply disappear from bureaucratic accounting. To have one's loss acknowledged and then compensated does suggest a quasi-enabling moment, when complete hopelessness appears to be the alternate condition.

7. The lack of legal closure is part of the *after* life of the event. However, this splitting starts from the first moment of interaction with state practice. Veena Das (2004: 229) writes about how the writing of the first information report (FIR) by the police during the carnage becomes a compelling illustration of the 'lie' of the state. The FIR, in the first place, was required to claim compensation, but it itself was a gross misrepresentation of facts because the police failed/refused to record the repeated incrimination of their own officers or politicians in the massacre.

> Thus, ironically, those who were locked in a combative relationship with the state and who had direct evidence of the criminality of the state nevertheless ended up being pulled into the gravitational force of the state through the circulation of documents produced by its functionaries. (Das 2004: 229)

8. By the public here, I do not refer to any particular discursive concept but rather the entire discursive and empirical range that would include the media, the law, citizens' groups and their activities, state directives, etc., that have been formed over time. All of this cannot be mentioned or discussed here in any adequate detail, so I have concentrated on the 'public knowledge' of legal justice as an illustrative category.

9. *The Hindu*, Tuesday, 17 May 2005, reported that five persons were sentenced to life imprisonment by a Delhi court for the murder of Baba Singh. The five men had pulled him out of his home, poured kerosene on him and burnt him alive. In 2018, Sajjan Kumar, a senior Congress MP, was sentenced to life in connection with his involvement in seven murders during the 1984 event. This was considered a high-profile conviction after almost 34 years (NDTV 2018). The first death penalty was also announced in November 2018 by the Delhi High Court to convict Yashpal Singh for the murder of two persons (India Today 2018).

10. I have used the word victim here because of its usage in the various judgments/court orders and other public documents relating to the 1984 carnage. However, the category of those who survive mass violence has been discussed through tropes of the witness, the survivor, the testifier and the victim, following Giorgio Agamben (1999), Ana Douglas and Thomas A. Vogler (2003), Cathy Caruth (1995), among others. My usage of the term 'victim' here merely replicates the category that is employed both in bureaucratic and other public terms, because the discussion is more about reiterating how the public–private world of this group is constructed. The emphasis, therefore, is not predominantly about the location of this group in the literature that addresses the constitution of these categories.

11. Figures quoted from information available at www.nishkam.org (accessed during March 2005).

12. Bhajan Kaur v. Delhi Administration 1996 III (Delhi) 333 (as quoted in Grover 2002).

13. Article 21: Protection of life and personal liberty—No person shall be deprived of his life or personal liberty except according to procedure established by law.

14. *Bhajan Kaur v. Delhi Administration 1996 III (Delhi) 333.*

15. Apart from popular knowledge, various citizens' reports (Report of the Justice Ranganath Misra Commission of Enquiry 1986; Report of the Ahooja Commission of Inquiry 1987; Report of the Kusum Lata Mittal Commission of Inquiry 1990; Report of the Jain Aggarwal Commission of Inquiry 1993; People's Union for Democratic Rights [PUDR] and People's Union for Civil Liberties [PUCL] 1984; PUDR 1992) have categorically documented the manner in which the police in conjunction with powerful politicians organised the riot. The failings of the police or their cooperation with the perpetrators and the subsequent mishandling of case procedures is a significant part of this.

16. For example, we were told that renowned film star and parliamentarian Sunil Dutt had gifted an x-ray machine to Nishkam. X-rays are, however, only available at a price to the residents.

17. For lack of space, I will not include biographical details on each informant here.

18. The names of informants are not mentioned in order to protect their privacy.

19. DDA: Delhi Development Authority. All government housing in the city comes under its purview.

20. B is referring here to Jagdish Tytler and Sajjan Kumar, both prominent Congress politicians who had a number of cases filed against them. However, lack of evidence and other procedural irregularities prevented any concrete outcomes. Fighting behind the gurdwara implies the internal politics within the religious authorities.

21. I am referring to the many events of communal violence that India has witnessed since 1984.

22. See Axel (2001), amongst others, for an overview of the Sikh militancy and its historical background.

23. I would emphasise the fact that while it is indeed the Sikh 'community' at large that suffered this attack, the burden of its afterlife is different within different sections of the community depending on a variety of factors. This has very significant implications in understanding the afterlife of an event of this proportion. Later, in this section, I will mention an aspect of this with regard to another neighbourhood in Delhi explored with similar queries.

24. Widowhood in India does establish itself as a special social category, a 'community' on whom very stringent social control is often practised. For an exploration of widowhood in rural India, see Chen (1998, 2000). The generally disadvantaged life of the widow, in the larger context of Asia and Africa, is explored by Owen (1996). The notion of political widowhood is somewhat closer to the Sikh widows insofar that the deaths of these men become like symbolic capital of a community which is used politically. It also throws up issues that interface a personal loss against a public death. An example of political widowhood is in Ramphele (1996).

25. Bhogal is the second neighbourhood in Delhi that we had explored for the same research agenda. Bhogal, however, is not a relocation colony. It is a predominantly Sikh neighbourhood that was attacked during the carnage, but there was no loss of life. One of the main reasons ascribed to this is that the community in the neighbourhood itself could come together quickly to put up a far stronger physical resistance. However, very substantial damage to property, businesses was incurred. Many homes, shops were burnt—goods-carrying trucks, which were a main trade amongst the residents, were destroyed.

26. Elsewhere, I have discussed this particular aspect by placing the differences within the community in a larger discourse on recovery, by suggesting that recovery has to be conceived as an assemblage of values and constituents—work/livelihood, justice, restitution/compensation, and so on (Arif 2015).

27. This brings out an important difference between life and property and their implication in reclaiming worlds after devastation.

28. One reading of this kind of repetition could be what Laub (1992: 69) writes with reference to her recording of Holocaust testimonies:

> Trauma survivors live not with memories of the past, but with an event that could not and did not proceed through to its completion, has no ending, attained no closure, and therefore, as far as its survivors are concerned, continues into the present and is current in every respect. … To undo this entrapment is a fate that cannot be known, cannot be told, but can only be repeated, a therapeutic process—a process of reconstructing a narrative, of reconstructing a history and essentially, of *re-externalizing the event*—has to be set in motion. This re-externalization of the event can occur … only when one can articulate and

transmit the story, literally transfer it to another outside oneself and take it back again, inside.

Perhaps, the geographical proximity of a community of victims provides for this kind of therapeutic externalisation and then internalisation here, in a compelling act of mutuality. This aspect ties in also with the kind of temporal bracketing mentioned earlier.

29. In our current fieldwork, we came across some male members in certain households who did not belong to the category of fathers or sons. Their relationship to the 'widow' was hard to establish, at any rate this was not information that was easily forthcoming. We sensed that it would be very detrimental to broach the topic of remarriage—nonetheless, if pursued, it could have led to a further analysis on how the constructed nature of this community of widows influences the engagement with the usual social sanctions and taboos of widowhood.

30. *Kaya Taran*, *Amu* are the feature films which portray stories whose protagonists' lives are woven through by the anti-Sikh violence of Delhi.

31. See Das et al. (2001). The authors list a few notions by which to approach the ethnographies and analysis of social suffering and recovery, amongst which is the idea of a return to the everyday.

References

Agamben, Giorgio. 1999. *Remnants of Auschwitz: The Witness and the Archive*. New York: Zone Books.

Arif, Yasmeen. 2015. 'Communitas and Recovered Life'. In *Wording the World: Veena Das and the Scenes of Inheritance*, ed. Roma Chatterji, 54–171. New York: Fordham University Press.

———. 2016. *Life, Emergent. The Social in the Afterlives of Violence*. Minneapolis: University of Minnesota Press.

Axel, Brian. 2001. *The Nation's Tortured Body: Violence, Representation and the Formation of the Sikh Diaspora*. Durham: Duke University Press.

Butler, Judith. 2004. *Precarious Life: The Powers of Mourning and Violence*. London: Verso.

Caruth, Cathy. 1995. *Trauma: Explorations in Memory*. Baltimore: The Johns Hopkins University Press.

Chen, Martha Alter. 1998. *Widows in India*. New Delhi: Sage Publications.

———. 2000. *Perpetual Mourning: Widowhood in Rural India*. New Delhi: Sage Publications.

Das, Veena. 2004. 'The Signature of the State: The Paradox of Illegibility'. In *Anthropology in the Margins of the State*, eds Veena Das and Deborah Poole, 225–52. New Delhi: Oxford University Press.

Das, Veena, Arthur Kleinman, Margaret Locke and Mamphela Ramphele, eds. 2001. *Remaking a World: Violence, Social Suffering and Recovery*. Berkeley: University of California Press.

Douglas, Ana, and Thomas A. Vogler, eds. 2003. *Witness and Memory: The Discourse of Trauma*. New York: Routledge.

Ghatwai, Milind. 2005. 'No Homecoming for Gujarat Riot Hit'. *Indian Express*, 6 March. Available at https://indianexpress.com/article/news-archive/no-homecoming-for-gujarat-riot-hit/ (accessed on 26 December 2024).

Grover, Vrinda. 2002. 'Quest for Justice: 1984 Massacre of Sikh Citizens in Delhi'. Mimeo.

India Today. 2018. 'Delhi Court Awards Death Penalty in 1984 Anti-Sikh Riots Case: Chronology of Events'. 22 November. Available at https://www.indiatoday.in/education-today/gk-current-affairs/story/delhi-court-awards-death-penalty-in-1984-anti-sikh-riots-case-chronology-of-events-1394041-2018-11-22 (accessed on 15 January 2025).

Laub, Dori. 1992. 'An Event without a Witness: Truth, Testimony and Survival'. In *Testimony: Crises of Witnessing in Literature, Psychoanalysis, and History*, eds Shoshana Felman and Dori Laub, 75–92. New York: Routledge.

NDTV. 2018. 'Sajjan Kumar Gets Life Term in '84 Riots; Courts Says "Truth Will Prevail"'. 17 December. Available at https://www.ndtv.com/india-news/congress-sajjan-kumar-convicted-in-1984-anti-sikh-riots-case-delhi-high-court-cancels-acquittal-1963593 (accessed on 15 January 2025).

Owen, Margaret. 1996. *A World of Widows*. London: Zed Books.

People's Union for Democratic Rights. 1992. '1984 Carnage in Delhi: A Report on the Aftermath'. Available at https://www.pudr.org/publicatiosn-files/1992-Nov-1984%20Carnage%20in%20Delhi.pdf (accessed on 21 December 2024).

People's Union for Democratic Rights (PUDR) and People's Union for Civil Liberties (PUCL). 1984. 'Who Are the Guilty? Report of a Joint Inquiry into the Causes and Impact of the Riots in Delhi from 31 October to 10 November 1984'. Available at https://ia601600.us.archive.org/26/items/WhoAreTheGuilty_201502/Who%20Are%20The%20Guilty.pdf (accessed on 21 December 2024).

Ramphele, Mamphela. 1996. 'Political Widowhood in South Africa: The Embodiment of Ambiguity'. *Daedalus* 125 (1): 99–117.

Report of the Ahooja Commission of Inquiry. 1987. Available at https://carnage84.com/official/ahooja/menu.htm (accessed on 15 January 2025).

Report of the Jain Aggarwal Commission of Inquiry. 1993. Available at https://www.carnage84.com/official/jain/menu.htm (accessed on 15 January 2025).

Report of the Justice Ranganath Misra Commission of Enquiry. 1986. Available at https://www.mha.gov.in/sites/default/files/RanganathMishra Vol_I_22102019_0.PDF (accessed on 15 January 2025).

Report of the Kusum Lata Mittal Commission of Inquiry. 1990. Available at https://www.carnage84.com/official/kusum/post.htm (accessed on 15 January 2025).

Rose, Gillian. 1996. *Mourning Becomes the Law: Philosophy and Representation*. Cambridge: Cambridge University Press.

II

Oral Narratives and Commemoration

three

Engaging with Oral Narratives

Contextualising the Dialogue on 1984

Anshu Saluja

> *It was a bright morning. When I stepped into the sunshine, I came upon a sight that I could never have imagined. In every direction, columns of smoke rose slowly into a limpid sky. Sikh houses and businesses were burning. The fires were so carefully targeted that they created an effect quite different from that of a general conflagration … Protected by certain politicians, organizers were zooming around the city, assembling the mobs and transporting them to Sikh-owned houses and shops.*[1]

The violence that began on 31 October 1984, the day of India's then Prime Minister Indira Gandhi's assassination, and which continued unabated till 4 November, was not a communal riot. It did not involve any semblance of matched confrontation between two sides. Rather, the Sikhs were being hunted down through the length and breadth of the national capital and in several other parts of the country in a series of fully orchestrated and planned attacks. These attacks were typically one-sided and there were hardly any incidents of retaliation by members of the Sikh community. The offensive involved the pursuit of Sikhs by mostly Hindu mobs, actively supervised by Congress(I) politicians, with clear connivance, and in some cases active participation, by the police.[2]

More than four decades on, in spite of the appointment of 10 commissions and committees to investigate and inquire into the events of first week of November 1984, 'those four days in which about 2733 people were killed in the capital of our Republic' still remain largely unaccounted for, with most organisers and perpetrators of violence going unpunished (People's Union for Democratic Rights [PUDR] 1992: 11). In this respect, it set a dangerous precedent for future riots and pogroms in India.

Here, it is worthwhile to keep in mind the distinction between a riot and a pogrom. The former 'carries the appearance of spontaneous, intergroup mass action', while the latter refers to 'deliberately organised—and especially—state-supported killings and the destruction of property of a targeted group' (Brass 2006: 3). Das (1990) underscores how contending explanations of such destructive events jostle and chafe, calling each other into question and upsetting the evolution of a single generalised narrative. The strenuous attempts to understand, absorb and work through what happened, their why and how, characterise the aftermath of these events for survivors and witnesses.[3] '... [T]he official story of a riot is always challenged by alternative interpretations ... these alternative interpretations constitute the meaning of the violence for people located in different social positions' (Das 1990: 15). The multiple embedded layers of meanings demand engagement and exploration, for they reveal different ways of experiencing and remembering.

Detailing the Approach and Method

For tapping into the experiences of the 1984 survivors and for capturing their largely muted voices, I have worked with oral history. Survivor testimonies and memories have been vital in studying incidents of ethnic and sectarian violence across the world. It is the survivors who have to shoulder the onerous burden of resuscitating fractured life-worlds and reformulating splintered trajectories amidst fraught and irreconcilable realities. It falls to them 'to show us how such suffering may be transformed into redemption' (ibid.: 33).

The recovery of diverse suppressed histories is an important task. Through the collection and dissemination of personal testimonies and narratives, oral history can bring to light and preserve experiences of individuals and communities which might otherwise remain completely neglected and hidden, on account of their inability in many instances to record their own past and inaccessibility of resources. Thereby, it can critically recast 'many accepted truths' (Portelli 1991: viii). Drawing attention to the democratising potential ascribed to oral history, and the exposure that it can offer to stifled and marginalised voices, Thompson writes:

> Reality is complex and many-sided; and it is a primary merit of oral history that to a much greater extent than most sources it allows the

> original multiplicity of stand-points to be recreated … witnesses can now also be called from the under-classes, the unprivileged, and the defeated. It provides a more realistic and fair reconstruction of the past, a challenge to the established account. (Thompson 2006: 28)

The resurgence of these suppressed experiences and recollections often clearly challenges the sanitised official versions of history, in addition to calling for the realisation of a more just and equitable society (McEwan 2003). However, a caveat must be made here: while analysing oral narratives, it needs to be remembered that memory—both individual and collective—is in itself not fixed and unchanging, one monolithic conception of the past. A contested arena, it is perpetually evolving, incorporating certain strands while discarding others. Memory always remains in a flux, being open to debate and newer interpretations. Explaining how memory is worked and reworked, shaped and reshaped, Portelli observes:

> Memory is not a passive depository of facts, but an active process of creation of meanings. Thus, the specific utility of oral sources for the historian lies, not so much in their ability to preserve the past, as in the very changes wrought by memory. These changes reveal the narrators' effort to make sense of the past and to give a form to their lives, and set the interview and the narrative in their historical context. (Portelli 2006: 37–38)

Oral history, thus, presents a host of contending narratives and worldviews which can be stitched together, juxtaposed or contrasted for excavating a clear picture of the past. In the present chapter, I have employed oral history techniques to study the 1984 pogrom and its after-effects. My fieldwork, lasting for about two years, centred on Delhi and its adjoining areas, from where most of my respondents were chosen and oral testimonies documented.[4]

Narrating the Historical Context

The 1984 anti-Sikh pogrom was inextricably linked to events in the north Indian state of Punjab. This violent blaze erupted following the assassination of India's then Prime Minister Indira Gandhi, who had authorised an army action inside the Golden Temple complex, code named Operation Blue Star. *Harmandir Sahib*, popularly known as Golden Temple, situated in the city of Amritsar in Punjab, is regarded by Sikhs (both in India and abroad) as their most important shrine. The storming of the temple complex in early June 1984 by the army was intended to flush out militants who had taken refuge there over the preceding months. In the face of a lackadaisical and delayed state response, these militants had firmly lodged themselves within the premises of the Temple. Gradually, arms had also been stocked there, with nothing being done to check their entry. This sordid state of affairs was in itself a culmination of the political machinations and manoeuvres of the Congress, led by Indira Gandhi (Gill and Singhal 1984).

The Congress was, for the most part, the ruling force at the Centre in those years, and a major contender for power in the state of Punjab. The ongoing political struggle in that state between the Congress and the Akali Dal acquired religious overtones in the 1970s with the rise of the charismatic figure of Jarnail Singh Bhindranwale.[5] Initially, he was propelled to prominence by the Congress itself. But soon, the situation started getting out of hand, with his followers resorting to violence against the dissenters. Following his brief arrest and then release, Bhindranwale moved into the Golden Temple complex for sanctuary. By then, Punjab was transformed into a field of pitched battles between security forces, who maintained a heavy presence there, and militant organisations whose activities were often supported as well as funded by diaspora Sikhs from Europe and North America (Gayer 2000).

The state, thus, continued to be on the boil. This chain of events ultimately culminated in the ruthless army action targeting the Golden Temple and a series of other brutal combing operations carried out in different parts of Punjab (Kaur 2006; Gupta 1985). The desecration of their holiest shrine sparked off a deep sense of hurt and rage within the members of the Sikh community (Chopra 2010), and exacerbated the prevailing apprehensions and insecurity. However, the anguish and betrayal that the Sikhs experienced were regarded as misplaced and even dangerous.

In the wake of Operation Blue Star, an uncanny atmosphere of incompleteness had been created. It was as if some sort of sequel to it had been expected (Das 2006). A sense of panic was being fostered by exaggerated and misleading press reports. Several state agencies and media houses precipitated the already strained situation with their campaign of misinformation and disinformation (Major 1987). Wide sections of the media—official as well as unofficial—played a divisive role throughout this episode.

Following the storming of the Golden Temple by the Indian army and in the face of growing state oppression in Punjab, the Sikh community was advised to recognise the larger national interest, and not to 'act in anger and haste',[6] while the Central government and the army were lauded for exercising restraint. The Sikhs were repeatedly asked 'to come out into the open'[7] and express their support for the government's actions. The grief and anger that large sections of the community were experiencing, at the desecration of their holiest shrine, were regarded to be unjustified and reprehensible, while the pressing fear and anxiety that they were grappling with, in view of escalating violence in Punjab, got dismissed as baseless and imaginary. Though repeated appeals were made to the government to prevent the situation from deteriorating further and provide 'a healing touch',[8] they remained, for the most part, unheeded. No steps were taken to assuage the growing feelings of unease and insecurity. These sentiments were, in fact, allowed to simmer and mature.

It was in this volatile climate that Indira Gandhi, who had given orders for the army action in Punjab, was assassinated by her Sikh security guards—Satwant Singh and Beant Singh—on 31 October 1984 (Kaur 2006). Following her assassination, systematic and organised attacks were carried out against members of the Sikh community in different parts of India. Persons of the community and were subjected to selective and vicious targeting. This calculated campaign of violence and destruction assumed frightening proportions in Delhi under the patronage of the Central government.

1984 Pogrom: An Overview

Violence raged all across the national capital, with marauding mobs holding the city to ransom for days on end. The newly created resettlement colonies situated on Delhi's outskirts, where mostly daily wage labourers and other impoverished sections were housed, counted among the worst-hit areas. Congress functionaries at different levels, ranging from Central ministers to metropolitan councillors, toured the city, inciting locals in various parts to attack Sikhs. They 'mobilized networks of people who identified Sikh homes, procured kerosene and set them on fire' (Basu 2000: 280). The police personnel, who at times accompanied these leaders, merely stood by and watched the unfolding events (People's Union for Democratic Rights [PUDR] and People's Union for Civil Liberties [PUCL] 1984). On other occasions, they joined hands with the attackers, actively facilitating the looting and killing spree (Das 2006).

The account given by one of my respondents S. D.—who resides in Sunder Nagri, a resettlement colony in Delhi—stressed how wide sections of the police force proved to be clearly partisan, their complicity with the perpetrators of violence becoming plain to the public at large. She recounted how violence began in her locality—when she saw that a ferocious mob was attacking Sikh residents, she appealed to her husband to inform the police. In response to her frantic appeals, her husband observed: 'police ismein ab kya karegi?' (What will the police do now?).[9] At the outset, it was expected that the police would intervene to rein in the gathering mobs, indulging in wanton destruction. But, when nothing was done to bring the rapidly deteriorating situation under control, these naive hopes were buried. The involvement of the police in the ongoing rampage may well have served as a signal to many, especially in the poorer localities, to freely target Sikhs and loot their property.

Although in some neighbourhoods, local residents, overwhelmingly men, did constitute tentative peace committees to keep a watch and guard against the possibility of an attack (Kishwar 1984), in many others, they became fairly active in fuelling anti-Sikh violence and according popular legitimacy to it. Sikhs were often hounded and harmed, with a view to even personal scores in petty localised disputes, long overdue and rooted firmly in the proximate everyday context. The prime minister's assassination, thus, served as a fitting occasion for giving vent to and decisively settling drawn-out mutual hostilities.[10] Such involvement of local neighbourhood communities—expressed either through implicit approval of or explicit participation in episodes of targeted collective violence—may lead to a considerable shrinkage, if not complete fracturing, of the 'space of safety, the moral zone of trust' (Robinson 2005: 54). Disconcertingly, those residents who spontaneously stepped forward to take stock of the prevailing situation and organise some sort of relief effort recalled that they found a pronounced anti-Sikh sentiment that pervaded among large sections of society as well as state agencies.

A variegated set of social workers, academics, journalists, lawyers and other concerned individuals, who attempted to raise their voice against this campaign of unbridled destruction and murder, encountered widespread callousness and connivance on the ground. For instance, a respondent J. J. told me: 'It was blatantly obvious that the attack was well-planned and well-organised. Everywhere, the police personnel were shoving us on. They said, "you are not a *Sardar*, why are you worried? Drive on." I faced this kind of thing myself.'[11] Detailed accounts document that some of the worst-hit localities, such as Block 32 Trilokpuri, were literally taken over by assailants baying for blood, and the police 'through their apathy and severe dereliction of duty' (PUDR and PUCL 1984: 36) facilitated the perpetration of ghastly attacks.

In several areas across the city, local neighbourhood communities condoned the violence and at times were actively involved in it. Large sections of the bureaucracy remained brazenly complicit with the attackers and chose to act as silent onlookers. The report prepared by Citizens for Democracy (1985: 32) notes that for the entire period of violence, only three FIRs were lodged at the Mongolpuri Police Station which saw some of the worst excesses and brutalities. Wide sections of the administration as well as Delhi citizenry approved of and acceded to what was going on, otherwise such savagery would not have been possible.

The 1984 survivors in Delhi whom I interviewed exhibited a clear awareness of and forcefully contested the misplaced logic of collective guilt that was deployed to justify violent attacks against them. One of them, S. S., bitterly commented:

> *Hum toh apne gharo mein baithe the. Humnein kisi ka ghar nahi jalaya, humnein kisi ko nahi mara. Hum toh mehnat karne wale log the. Hum mehnat karke apne parivaron ko chalate the ... humnein kya galat kiya tha? Jinhone kuch galat kiya, unhe toh saza mil gyi. Par humare saath jo kuch bhi hua—sarkar ne tab sikhon ko maarne ki khuli chuth de rakhi thi* (We [the Sikhs] were just sitting in our homes. We did not go out and burn anyone's house, we did not kill anyone. We were ordinary hardworking people. We laboured to support our families ... What wrong did we do? Those who did wrong [Indira Gandhi's assassination] were punished. But the kind of treatment which was meted out to us—the government had given a free rein to kill Sikhs then).[12]

Uma Chakravarti discusses how the 1984 survivors steadfastly refused to accept the flawed premise, resting on the principles of 'substitutability of guilt' (Chakravarti 1994: 2722) and attribution of collective responsibility, that was put in place to warrant the violence and, at a later stage, blot out calls for justice. They were alive to the bitter reality that the culpability of two individuals for the act of the prime minister's assassination had arbitrarily been shifted to the entire Sikh community, following which it became possible to talk of, act upon and legitimise the need to teach its members a lesson. This took the form of a fully planned pogrom, involving high levels of complicity of different wings of the government as well as undisguised sanction and support from many quarters of society (Banerjee 2002; Rao 1984).

Over four decades on, the survivor narratives are still punctuated by a keen sense of hurt and betrayal at the selective campaign of targeting and slaughter which was systematically unleashed against the members of their community. Inordinate delays in legal proceedings and blatant subversion of justice in repeated instances have bred continuing despair and discontent (Chakravarti 2005). Hope for some form of resolution wears thin, as years morph into decades. The mistaken assumption that 'reconciliation can come about without justice' (Gupta 2011: 105) only contributes to the deflection of accountability from culpable individuals and agencies, leaving little room for recovery. As a survivor P. K. painfully stated, '*humein 30 saal ke baad bhi insaaf nahin mila. Aisa lagta hai ki humein insaaf milne ka koi tareeka hi nahi hai. Phir hum kahan jaaye?*' (We have not got any justice, even after 30 years. It seems that there is no system of justice for us. Where should we go then?).[13]

Martyrdom: A Powerful and Recurring Motif

Most of my respondents could remember exactly when and how they got the news of the prime minister's assassination, wherever they were placed then and the manner in which they encountered the sweeping tide of violence on the evening of 31 October itself or on 1 November 1984. On the streets and in the bylanes, they saw columns of smoke rising in the distance and observed, with rising trepidation, the assembled mobs, going about their business in an unperturbed and unhurried fashion. For the legal and social activists with whom I spoke, the 1984 pogrom signalled a definite breach. 'There was a fracturing of innocence. This was a serious bloodying of a generation.'[14]

As far as the survivors were concerned, they had no inkling that pre-planned and premeditated violence would be unleashed against them, lasting for days on end. In their retellings of what had happened, they were often at pains to emphasise that they had no clue about the affairs in Punjab. Most of them were daily wage-earners, trying to provide for their families, and had nothing to do with how politics played out. In this vein, a survivor D. K. poignantly remarked: '*Humne kisi ka kuch nahi bigada, humne kuch galat nahi kiya. Phir bhi hamein maara gaya*' (We did not offend anyone, we did not commit any wrong. Even then, we [the Sikhs] were targeted).[15]

As it turned out, the boundaries between 'victims' and 'aggressors' (Das 2006: 127) came to be transgressed and, in fact, reversed in Delhi in the first week of November 1984. The Sikh community, which was at the receiving end of the violence, was chastised for antagonising 'the Indian people' and disrupting peace. The community as a whole was deemed liable to strictures, such as:

> Unfortunately some of the so-called Sikh leaders have chosen to add fuel to the fire … the Indian people could have forgotten and forgiven all this if saner council had prevailed especially among the Sikh intelligentsia at least after Operation Blue Star. Instead they continued to preach hatred of the government … the popular feeling of outrage has to be assuaged and it can be assuaged only if the Sikhs are seen to be willing to heed appeals to reason and patriotism … if a breach has opened between the Sikhs and the rest of India, the Sikh leaders and their intelligentsia are largely to blame. The Akalis and the head priests need to contribute to the process of restoring normalcy if the government's efforts are to succeed … a soft headed approach is not going to convince those who need to be convinced that the Sikhs are willing to live as peaceful and law abiding citizens of the country.[16]

Forty years on, the survivors still feel resentful and hurt at being othered as threats or disruptors. They grieve at the manner in which this hate-filled rhetoric, actively perpetuated by large sections of the government and media, acquired widespread currency and played havoc with their lives. But, at the heart of their persisting resentment lies the disconcerting realisation that at the immediate moment of violence, Sikh lives had come to be regarded as dispensable, with the state—which was represented before them by the police and local administration—as well as a sizeable segment of their neighbours turning against them (Chakravarti 1994). An activist J. S. recalled many women survivors poignantly telling her that food had not been cooked in their homes on the night of 31 October, after the news of Mrs Gandhi's assassination became known, as they were in mourning.[17] The fact that many of those who were killed in 1984, as a way of seeking retribution for the prime minister's demise, had not eaten, since they were themselves grieving over the tragedy, gets highlighted as symbolising the ultimate betrayal (Saluja 2015). The death of a loved one without taking a meal, thus, represents a powerful sense of rupture in the consciousness of trauma survivors, particularly women.[18]

Members of the Sikh community were taken aback by the force and ferocity of the attacks that were launched against them, and the popular sanction that these attacks came to enjoy. A survivor P. K. bitterly recounted that despite repeated pleas for help, nobody came to the rescue of desperate Sikhs, amidst wanton killing and destruction underway in the locality of Trilokpuri.[19] The grief and anguish of the victim families were compounded further by the absence of a dignified send-off to their loved ones who were killed in this wave of senseless violence, unleashed in Indira Gandhi's name. In some instances, my respondents referred to the symbolic function that the exhibition of Mrs Gandhi's corpse performed. The display of the late prime minister's dead body, as it lay in state[20] at Teen Murti Bhavan (House)[21] in Delhi for three days till the funeral on 3 November 1984 and its constant telecast on Doordarshan (the state-owned national television network) served to justify the killing of Sikhs on streets, running trains and in neighbourhoods as a macabre form of national mourning. Sociologist Veena Das, who saw the violence in Delhi unfolding at close quarters, pointed out how a sorry contrast emerged between the dead body of Indira Gandhi, which lay in state, and the bodies of thousands of innocent Sikhs who were butchered, lying strewn about in a state of utter neglect (Das 2006).

In their narratives, the 1984 survivors resolutely compare their own sufferings to the trials and travails endured by Sikh *gurus* (supreme teachers) and other eminent figures, dominating the religion's, not too long, history. The profound anguish that the survivors felt on seeing their family members being killed and their houses looted, the hardships that they endured as they ran frantically from pillar to post, in order to save themselves, the apprehensions that they continued to harbour, in the wake of the violence, and the strenuous struggle that they have persistently waged for negotiating everyday existence are narrated against the backdrop of Sikh history and mythology. The harrowing experiences that they have been through are stitched onto the recapitulations—historical as well as legendary—of Sikh sacrifice, courage and fortitude. For instance, one of my respondents N. K. spoke of the indomitable resolve and valour of Arjan Dev, the fifth guru of the Sikhs. She emphasised that his ennobling sacrifice in standing by and upholding his faith counts among those heroic deeds which act as a source of strength for the victim families, providing them inspiration and sustenance.[22]

Martyrdom, thus, emerges as a key theme, exercising a powerful sway over survivor narratives. Their near and dear ones, who lost their lives in the 1984 violence, are referred to as martyrs by the victim families. By placing their slain kin within the framework of martyrology, they seek to make sense of and work through the painful realisation that Sikh lives had been rendered expendable and 'ungrievable' (Butler 2009) then. The survivors and activists, whom I interviewed, lamented the denial of last rites to a multitude of helpless citizens, who were degraded, humiliated and brutally killed. But, even after being wronged so egregiously by the state, their families are not willing to let it walk away from its responsibilities. Instead of giving up, they continue to engage with the state, which they hold accountable for the hardships they have endured, and make their citizenship claims on it. Their language of martyrology embodies 'a discourse of resistance' (Ahluwalia 2010), whereby they demand an acknowledgement of the grievous failure of state institutions at varying levels, while simultaneously reclaiming spaces to legitimately moan the loss of their loved ones.

This reclamation assumes salience and needs to be explicated. In the immediate aftermath of the pogrom, the Sikh community felt deeply shaken. The survivors experienced acute fear and insecurity. The threat of further intimidation and attacks loomed large. Given these pressing anxieties and vulnerabilities, mourning became a very precarious exercise. Forced to flee their homes, many survivors could not give a proper send off to their deceased family members or lament their loss by performing prescribed death rituals. Further, in the immediate hustle and bustle of securing relief supplies and finding refuge, the excruciating pain and trauma of losing loved ones were suppressed temporarily, only to confront them later with grating intensity. Even the act of openly grieving the victims claimed by the 1984 violence seemed fraught with trepidation and danger in the initial stage, yet with time, annual commemorative traditions for mourning and memorialising this grave loss have emerged and crystallised.

Most survivors attribute the status of martyrs to their loved ones who were cruelly snatched away in those turbulent days. Even the gurdwara in Tilak Vihar[23] is known as the Shaheed Ganj Gurdwara, *shaheed* being the Hindi/Punjabi term for martyr. Every year, specific commemorative rituals, including *Akhand Paath*,[24] are performed at the Tilak Vihar Gurdwara, starting from 31 October. These rituals are intended to memorialise the violence endured by the community as a whole, together with the agony and indignity borne by its hapless victims. This annual commemoration, thereby, doubles as a space for both 'personal and collective mourning' (Chopra 2011: 33).

Martyrdom recurs as a dominant motif in Sikh history and mythology. It remains a potent trope, exercising marked influence over wide sections of the community. Critically, by remembering and referring to their slain family members as martyrs, the 1984 survivors attempt to impart a sense of dignity to their otherwise meaningless, and mostly violent, deaths, in addition to trying to achieve a degree of solace for themselves. As Ahluwalia observes, 'the very remembering of the lives lost in 1984 renders those lives meaningful' (2010: 109).

Herein, a specific issue that demands one's attention: How are these remembrances and recapitulations shaped and contextualised? While reading through survivor narratives and interpreting multiple layers embedded within them, it becomes vital to take note of major talking points as well as the fractures that emerge. We need to be sensitive to the concerns and considerations which are impressed upon in their narratives and those that get silenced or erased. As Indira Chowdhury points out, 'memory does not function merely as a storehouse of past events but rather becomes a permanent search for meaning' (2014: 41).

Bringing Displacement into the Dialogue

For most of the interviewed survivors, who had resided at that time in resettlement colonies on Delhi's fringes, the loss of their family members and the burning down of their homes in the pogrom constituted the hardest blows. Their homes represented to them the promise of a relatively stable and secure life, especially since permanent entitlements to land had been obtained in particular cases. Starting from the 1940s, these families had seen repeated displacements. In several cases, they trace their roots to Sindh, a province in present-day Pakistan. Initially, they had migrated from Sindh to the Indian state of Rajasthan due to escalating tensions and hostility on the eve of Partition. Some of them still have kin and connections in Rajasthan. For instance, the life trajectory of one of my respondents J. A., who owns a stretch of agricultural land and has relatives back there, becomes illustrative in this sense.[25]

The chief reason as to why these new settlers again felt induced to relocate elsewhere, before long, is not far to see. Increasingly, they found it difficult to make ends meet, given their material hardships. So, in many cases, the men migrated to Delhi in search of livelihood opportunities. In the capital, they got absorbed into the steadily expanding mass of petty workers, becoming carpenters, rickshaw pullers, construction labourers and the like. Typically, their families also came over after some lag and they started living in makeshift tenements there. During the emergency years of 1975–76, these migrants were uprooted yet again from disparate parts of the city and were forcibly transferred to its periphery,[26] where they found themselves on empty plots of land, even devoid of a roof over their heads. Over time, through their own efforts, they erected new houses in the outlying resettlement colonies. When their existence, along with these new homes, was tragically and abruptly rent asunder by the blazing violence of 1984, they felt extremely vulnerable.

Even now, their narratives are coloured by a deep-seated sense of hurt and loss, 'for there are too many memories that are difficult to forget' (Gupta 2011: 108). They speak nostalgically of their lives prior to the pogrom. The anguish of being left rootless and rudderless emerges through the retellings of these survivors who have seen and been through successive displacements. One of them, M. S. reminisced about what his life was like before the 1984 violence disfigured it. He lost his two brothers in the brutal onslaught and came to be burdened with the responsibility of providing for a large extended family. He sorrowfully told me: '*Chaurasi se pehle hum bahut khush the. Hum teeno bhaiyon ke apne-apne ghar the. Hum mehnat karke kamate, khate the*' (We were quite content prior to 1984. We were three brothers, each had his own house. We worked hard and earned our daily bread).[27]

For those Sikhs who came to Delhi from western Punjab in the late 1940s, battered by the country's Partition, that moment holds continued relevance, being recalled and reconstructed in multiple ways. The accompanying violence and dislocation[28] are widely recounted in their narratives. Brass (2003) discusses the dynamics through which genocidal violence was structured and engendered across the Punjab, in the face of Partition. This becomes a critical frame of reference that is often brought into play by Sikh residents of Delhi for outlining a comparison with the 1984 pogrom. For many, the two events get interlinked, their memories repeatedly intersecting and converging.

Significantly, for the poor low-caste Sikhs, who were the worst-hit victims in 1984, the said link holds limited appeal, pointing to a marked divergence. Their narratives draw parallels not so much with the tragic events of Partition, but are stitched, in fact, around the axis of displacement that has explicitly impinged upon their lives.[29] These victim families are keenly alive to a sense of displacement, since in different instances they have experienced a string of migrations and dislocations, often against their own will.

They harbour a profound sense of alienation, given that their existence in Tilak Vihar has been far from congenial. The quest for justice has been exhausting, breeding widespread frustration, while periodic interactions with state agencies, gurdwara committees and a range of activist groups—both from India and abroad—have remained inconsistent and laboured. The trauma of losing loved ones, of not getting justice and of being betrayed by the state as well as their fellow citizens continues to fester, casting its dark shadow over the lives of succeeding generations of survivors.

Conclusion

Finding an outlet to articulate and express traumatic memories is critical as a healing technique. For victims and survivors of incidents of large-scale violence and bloodshed, sharing their fraught experiences with empathetic listeners is an important means to come to terms with their feelings of loss and despair. With regard to the 1984 pogrom, a similar need for unflinching and informed engagement with the past, rather than its suppression or refutation, is seen to be imperative, for it can sensitively recover painful memories and bring about a degree of consolation in the present.

In this context, initiatives like oral history and memory projects—whether in the form of books, films or conceptualised through any other means—can assume special significance by providing avenues to trauma survivors to relate their past experiences and 'at least reach a symbolic emotional closure' (Field 2006: 34). As Sean Field puts it, oral history can 'offer subtle support to interviewees' efforts to recompose their sense of self and regenerate agency' (2006: 31). But finding spaces for retelling traumatic experiences and listeners for recapitulating hurtful memories is far from easy. Arlene Stein flags this when she writes: 'To tell a story, in addition to needing a storyteller and an intelligible narrative framework, a way of telling a story, one also needs an audience. But in the aftermath of trauma, potential storytellers are often hesitant and the audiences ambivalent, at best' (2009: 47).

Due to such constraints, the horrors and sufferings endured by survivors of targeted collective violence remain, for the most part, unacknowledged and unaddressed. These may get pushed into the margins of collective consciousness over time, yet they continue to shape individual memories in specific ways. Steady bids to downplay and deny this altered reality are undertaken and encouraged by many quarters,[30] but as Chatterji and Mehta (2007) have observed, the normalcy which gets reconstituted following an episode of collective violence is vastly different from the one which preceded it. Thereupon, new modes of perceiving, engaging and inhabiting have to be evolved and worked out.

Once the shared fabric of life gets ruptured, the resumption and recovery of everyday patterns of living and intercommunity dialogue can begin only gradually, if at all. Experiences of such violence inevitably impinge upon abiding frames of contact and coexistence, reshaping and reformulating mutual relationships in a variety of complex ways. Those whose lives have been torn apart by large-scale violence can never return to an earlier state of normalcy. As Gupta pertinently reminds us, 'after the earlier established relations between communities in the old normal have been severely disrupted, it is no longer possible to quietly slip back to status quo ante' (2011: 142). Indeed, he suggests that 'this fond and utopian hope needs to be buried. Instead, one should pay attention to the modalities by which one contested normal can give way to another' (ibid.: 100). Thus, the attempts intended to resuscitate the everyday, in the aftermath of intergroup confrontation or scripted violence, directed against particular segments of society, 'must necessarily be processes that remain fragile and always unfinished' (Robinson 2005: 146).

Instead of making deliberate efforts to stem a discussion of the past, trauma survivors need to be provided avenues to relate their disquieting impressions and recollections which should then be integrated within the broader collective memory. Their voices have to be retrieved and listened to, while the emerging gaps and silences in their narratives—whether resulting from compulsion or volition—have to be discerned. 'The simultaneous engagement of political and judicial institutions, as well as families and local communities' (Das and Kleinman 2001: 4) can be a welcome step in this direction, for it can help the survivors to work through their losses and, thereby, 'refashion a sense of self' (Stein 2009: 44). In that event, we can begin eventually to think of and hope for some level of recovery and restitution for the targeted groups and individuals.

For developing a viable resistance mechanism to guard against such targeting in the first place, sustained attempts aimed at forging/reforging varied forms of social dialogue, bringing together past experiences, present concerns and future aspirations of different people and communities, assume considerable salience. Day-to-day local interactions and alliances, geared towards achieving common ends, become especially efficacious in this context. 'Doing everyday things together' (Gupta 2011: 124) is the key to evolving durable sites and spheres of cross-community interface. It has both preventive and regenerative potential. It can be instrumental in checking the outbreak of conflict and violence at the outset. Further, it can also signal a degree of rapprochement and help to initiate a gradual process of coping in the aftermath of such conflagrations.

Notes

1. This is how Amitav Ghosh describes the sight that he encountered in Delhi on the morning of 1 November 1984 (Ghosh 1995).

2. Deliberate dereliction of duty by a large section of the police force in Delhi and its complicity with the perpetrators of violence have been documented by a number of concerned citizens' reports that were released in its immediate aftermath. These include 'Who Are the Guilty?' (People's Union for Democratic Rights and People's Union for Civil Liberties 1984), 'Truth about Delhi Violence' (Citizens for Democracy 1985) and 'Report of the Citizens' Commission' (Citizens' Commission 1985).

3. These two categories need not be strictly separated and compartmentalised. The figures of the survivor and the witness can and often do overlap. And it is left to them to wage the long-drawn arduous battle to establish accountability and secure a modicum of justice.

4. These testimonies, which are at times reproduced in the course of the chapter, have been translated into English by the author. In order to safeguard the identity of the respondents and to ensure their privacy, their actual names have not been revealed. Instead, their initials have been used.

5. Jarnail Singh Bhindranwale (1947–84) was a religious preacher. From 1977 to 1984, he was the head of a religious seminary called the Damdami Taksal, lying on the outskirts of Amritsar in Punjab. In the late 1970s, Bhindranwale was supported by the Congress Party, in a calculated bid to weaken its Akali rivals in the state's politics. He advocated the idea of establishing the theocratic Sikh state of Khalistan. However, in his conception of creation of an independent Sikh land, a clear primacy was accorded to the dominant *Khalsa* tradition, while other contending streams and strands within Sikhism came to be excluded. Gradually, his following increased among the youth in Punjab. But, his band of followers soon took up arms. They unleashed widespread violence, targeting those Sikhs as well as Hindus who opposed their actions. From the beginning of the 1980s, Sikh militants and state security forces became engaged in a fierce standoff, involving a series of attacks and counter-attacks. In 1981, Bhindranwale was briefly arrested by the state government for the murder of Lala Jagat Narain, the founder and editor of

a popular Hindi daily, *Punjab Kesari*. However, he was dramatically released soon after. Following this, his charisma grew rapidly, as did violence in the state. Fearing another arrest, Bhindranwale, along with his followers, took shelter within the precincts of the Golden Temple. In 1983, he moved into the *Akal Takht* within the complex which is viewed as the prime seat of spiritual and temporal power in Sikh history and mythology. Finally, in Operation Blue Star, conducted by the Indian army during 4–6 June 1984, Bhindranwale was killed. His body, riddled with bullet marks, was recovered from the Temple premises on the morning of 6 June 1984.

6. *The Times of India*, 7 June 1984, The Nehru Memorial Museum and Library, Delhi, microfilm.

7. *Hindustan Times*, 12 June 1984, The Nehru Memorial Museum and Library, Delhi, microfilm.

8. *The Tribune*, 8 June 1984, The Nehru Memorial Museum and Library, Delhi, microfilm.

9. Interview with S. D. on 27 September 2013 at 12 PM at her residence in Sunder Nagri, a resettlement colony in north-east Delhi. She was a witness to the violent onslaught launched against Sikhs in November 1984, and saw widespread arson and bloodshed in her own neighbourhood. She was then employed at a non-profit social welfare organisation and worked as a volunteer at the Nanaksar relief camp, set up in the immediate aftermath of the pogrom.

10. Veena Das has shown that a conflation of the event with the everyday and of the national with the local can spell tragic possibilities at specific moments. She has illustrated how the 1984 pogrom provided a convenient opportunity and a rightful justification for definitively settling long-standing personal scores with members of the Sikh community. The national event of Mrs Gandhi's assassination acquired particular salience in the local context of Sultanpuri, a resettlement colony in Delhi, as it got intertwined with the ongoing tussle between the Sikh and Scheduled Caste *pradhans* (chiefs) of the two resident groups residing there. At a time when widespread anti-Sikh violence was raging, this intertwining, this overlap signalled disastrous consequences for the Sikh pradhan and his family (Das 2005).

11. Interview with J. J. on 14 April 2013 at 4 PM in Nizamuddin colony, Delhi. She was the coordinator of Farash Bazar relief camp which was among the largest to be set up in the city, immediately following the 1984 pogrom. She is a social activist and writer who has been involved in Indian politics.

12. Interview with S. S. on 8 December 2013 at 11 AM at his shop in Tilak Vihar, Delhi. In 1984, he resided in the resettlement colony of Madangir. In the violence, he lost many of his relatives, including his grandfather, uncle and brothers-in-law. After that, he, along with many other survivors, was allotted housing in Tilak Vihar, where he continues to live and work.

13. Interview with P. K. on 30 October 2013 at 11 AM at her residence in Tilak Vihar, Delhi. In 1984, her family resided in Trilokpuri, a locality in east Delhi, where Sikh homes and even entire lanes were subjected to vicious assaults. She lost

10 members of her family, including her father and elder brother, in the violence. She was barely 15 then. Decades on, she continues to participate in protests and other gatherings, held periodically to raise survivor concerns and demand the delivery of justice.

14. Interview with H. S. on 23 September 2013 at 10:30 AM at his office in Delhi. He participated in the relief effort organised in the immediate aftermath of the 1984 pogrom. A journalist and writer, he helped in editing and bringing out a volume which documented the moment of violence, together with the dismay and horror that stemmed from it.

15. Interview with D. K. on 26 October 2013 at 3 PM at her residence in Raghubir Nagar, Delhi. In 1984, she was a resident of Trilokpuri and lost 12 members of her family, including her husband, in the horrendous anti-Sikh violence that lasted for days together. A lower-grade employee in a government hospital, she struggles to support a large family with her limited earnings.

16. *The Times of India*, 2 November 1984, The Nehru Memorial Museum and Library, Delhi, microfilm.

17. Interview with J. S. on 12 August 2013 at 11 AM at her residence in Gurugram (formerly Gurgaon) which functions as one of Delhi's satellite towns, while falling in the neighbouring state of Haryana. In the immediate aftermath of the 1984 pogrom, J. S. coordinated the relief camp set up at Nanaksar Gurdwara. She is a social activist.

18. Ross (2001) demonstrates how this constitutes a deeply troubling memory, drawing upon her encounters with black women who, along with their families, bore the brunt of violations and atrocities, committed by the Apartheid regime in South Africa.

19. Interview with P. K. on 30 October 2013 at 11 AM at her residence in Tilak Vihar, Delhi.

20. Lying in state refers to the ritual of last viewing of the mortal remains of a prominent national figure. The body of the departed personage is placed usually in a prime government building for the general public to pay their respects, before the final ceremonial send-off.

21. Teen Murti Bhavan served as the residence of India's first prime minister and Indira Gandhi's father, Jawaharlal Nehru, who stayed there till his death in 1964. Following his demise, it was converted into Nehru Memorial Museum and Library.

22. Interview with N. K. on 29 October 2013 at 12 PM in Tilak Vihar, Delhi. In 1984, she was a resident of Trilokpuri. A young girl of about 15 then, she lost 11 members of her family, including her father, in the violence. Like many other survivors, she resides in Tilak Vihar now, and still takes part in protest rallies and demonstrations, voicing survivor grievances.

23. Tilak Vihar is a locality in west Delhi, where families of survivors of the 1984 pogrom are housed. They live in small tenements that stand closely packed

together. They were allocated alternate housing there by the government, in the wake of the violence. The neighbourhood was established in 1985, but the issue of permanent ownership of houses still remains in a tangle. With most residents lacking permanent land entitlements, it is far from being resolved. Tilak Vihar counts among Delhi's multiple impoverished neighbourhoods, grappling with widespread neglect, decay and disrepair. It is bogged down by problems such as depression, high suicide rates, and heavy addiction to drugs and alcohol. Most of the workforce there is either engaged in low-paying jobs or unemployed. The need for providing educational and livelihood avenues to younger generations of the victim families, residing in Tilak Vihar, has been highlighted by most of my interviewees.

24. *Akhand Paath* refers to a complete and uninterrupted recital of the *Guru Granth Sahib*, the supreme religious text of the Sikhs, continuing over three days. The Paath is performed to mark key moments in the lives of adherents of the Sikh faith, including birth, death, marriage and the like, within the family and extended community network.

25. Interview with J. A. on 6 October 2013 at 10:30 AM at his home in Tilak Vihar, Delhi. His family had migrated to the national capital years ago from their village in Rajasthan in search of livelihood opportunities. He still has some kin and connections there. In 1984, he was a resident of Trilokpuri, and lost his father and elder brothers in the violence. Subsequently, he managed to secure alternate housing for his bereft family in Tilak Vihar. At present, he works at a reputed city hotel, where he is a junior staff member. Due to his relatively better economic and educational status, he is regularly approached by families of other survivors from the area for advice and assistance in negotiating official documentary procedures and wearisome bureaucratic channels.

26. Emma Tarlo (2000) discusses how such forced clearances are carried out and resettlement colonies develop.

27. Interview with M. S. on 2 March 2014 at 11 AM at his residence in Tilak Vihar, Delhi. In 1984, he lived in Block 32, Trilokpuri, which saw relentless savagery. He was fortunate to escape and counted among the few male survivors from that area.

28. The overwhelming strain and anxiety that Partition spelt, the sudden exodus it triggered across newly created borders, and the continuing trauma it generated have been studied by a number of scholars (Bhasin and Menon 1993; Butalia 1993).

29. Most of the 1984 survivors whom I interviewed in Tilak Vihar happened to be Labana Sikhs. This caste group falls on the lower rungs of the Sikh social ladder, and their life-worlds and language reflect a pronounced affinity with the cultural ethos of Rajasthan rather than that of Punjab.

30. Desai explains how this process of repackaging and reimaging was at work in the state of Gujarat in western India, following the 2002 tide of violence. The state was sought to be recalibrated and refurbished in local, national and global

imaginings. However, the attitudes and experiences of poor sections of society as well as of Muslim residents across class lines were accorded no place in these overzealous and glossy reconstructions (Desai 2012).

References

Ahluwalia, Pal. 2010. 'The Politics of Intimacy: (Re)Thinking 1984'. *Sikh Formations: Religion, Culture, Theory* 6 (2): 105–17.

Banerjee, Sumanta. 2002. 'When the "Silent Majority" Backs a Violent Minority'. *Economic & Political Weekly* 37 (13): 1183–85.

Basu, Amrita. 2000. 'Engendering Communal Violence: Men as Victims, Women as Agents'. In *Invented Identities: The Interplay of Gender, Religion and Politics in India*, eds Julia Leslie and Mary McGee, 265–85. New Delhi: Oxford University Press.

Bhasin, Kamla, and Ritu Menon. 1993. 'Recovery, Rupture, Resistance: Indian State and Abduction of Women during Partition'. *Economic & Political Weekly* 28 (17): WS2–WS11.

Brass, Paul R. 2003. 'The Partition of India and Retributive Genocide in the Punjab, 1946–47: Means, Methods, and Purposes'. *Journal of Genocide Research* 5 (1): 71–101.

———. 2006. *Forms of Collective Violence: Riots, Pogroms and Genocide in Modern India*. Delhi: Three Essays Collective.

Butalia, Urvashi. 1993. 'Community, State and Gender: On Women's Agency during Partition'. *Economic & Political Weekly* 28 (17): WS13–WS24.

Butler, Judith. 2009. 'Frames of War: The Politics of Ungrievable Life'. Public lecture presented by the Humanities and Arts Research Centre of Royal Holloway, the School of Psychosocial Studies (Birkbeck) and the Birkbeck Institute for Social Research, London. Available at https://backdoorbroadcasting.net/2009/02/harc-frames-of-war-the-politics-of-ungrievable-life/ (accessed on 23 January 2017).

Chakravarti, Uma. 1994. 'Victims, "Neighbours", and "Watan": Survivors of Anti-Sikh Carnage of 1984'. *Economic & Political Weekly* 29 (42): 2722–26.

———. 2005. 'Long Road to Nowhere: Justice Nanavati on 1984'. *Economic & Political Weekly* 40 (35): 3790–95.

Chatterji, Roma, and Deepak Mehta. 2007. *Living with Violence: An Anthropology of Events and Everyday Life*. New Delhi: Routledge.

Chopra, Radhika. 2010. 'Commemorating Hurt: Memorializing Operation Bluestar'. *Sikh Formations: Religion, Culture, Theory* 6 (2): 119–52.

———. 2011. *Militant and Migrant: The Politics and Social History of Punjab*. New Delhi: Routledge.

Chowdhury, Indira. 2014. 'Speaking of the Past: Perspectives on Oral History'. *Economic & Political Weekly* 49 (30): 39–42.

Citizens' Commission. 1985. *Report of the Citizens' Commission: 31 October to 4 November 1984*. Delhi.

Citizens for Democracy. 1985. *Report to the Nation: Truth about Delhi Violence*. Delhi.

Das, Veena. 1990. 'Introduction: Communities, Riots, Survivors—The South Asian Experience'. In *Mirrors of Violence: Communities, Riots and Survivors in South Asia*, ed. Veena Das, 1–36. Delhi: Oxford University Press.

———. 2005. 'Privileging the Local: The 1984 Riots'. In *Religious Politics and Communal Violence*, ed. Steven Wilkinson, 91–100. New Delhi: Oxford University Press.

———. 2006. *Life and Words: Violence and the Descent into the Ordinary*. Berkeley: California University Press.

Das, Veena, and Arthur Kleinman. 2001. 'Introduction'. In *Remaking a World: Violence, Social Suffering, and Recovery*, eds Veena Das, Arthur Kleinman, Margaret M. Lock, Mamphela Ramphele and Pamela Reynolds, 1–30. New Delhi: Oxford University Press.

Desai, Renu. 2012. 'Entrepreneurial Urbanism in the Time of Hindutva: City Imagineering, Place Marketing, and Citizenship in Ahmedabad'. In *Urbanizing Citizenship: Contested Spaces in Indian Cities*, eds Renu Desai and Ramola Sanyal, 31–57. Delhi: Sage.

Field, Sean. 2006. 'Beyond "Healing": Trauma, Oral History and Regeneration'. *Oral History* 34 (1): 31–42.

Gayer, Laurent. 2000. 'The Globalization of Identity Politics: The Sikh Experience'. *International Journal of Punjab Studies* 7 (2): 223–62.

Ghosh, Amitav. 1995. 'The Ghosts of Mrs Gandhi'. *The New Yorker*, 17 July. Available at https://amitavghosh.com/other-works-contributions/essays-and-posts/the-ghosts-of-mrs-gandhi/ (accessed on 23 November 2024).

Gill, Sucha Singh, and K. C. Singhal. 1984. 'The Punjab Problem: Its Historical Roots'. *Economic & Political Weekly* 19 (14): 603–08.

Gupta, Dipankar. 1985. 'The Communalising of Punjab, 1980–1985'. *Economic & Political Weekly* 20 (28): 1185–90.

Gupta, Dipankar. 2011. *Justice Before Reconciliation: Negotiating a 'New Normal' in Post-riot Mumbai and Ahmedabad*. New Delhi: Routledge.

Kaur, Jaskaran. 2006. *Twenty Years of Impunity: The November 1984 Pogroms of Sikhs in India*. Portland: Ensaaf. Available at https://ensaaf.org/wp-content/uploads/2018/08/20years-2nd.pdf (accessed on 15 September 2018).

Kishwar, Madhu. 1984. 'Gangster Rule: The Massacre of the Sikhs'. *Manushi* 25: 10–37.

Major, Andrew. 1987. 'From Moderates to Secessionists: A Who's Who of the Punjab Crisis'. *Pacific Affairs* 60 (1): 42–58.

McEwan, Cheryl. 2003. 'Building a Postcolonial Archive? Gender, Collective Memory and Citizenship in Post-apartheid South Africa'. *Journal of Southern African Studies* 29 (3): 739–57.

People's Union for Democratic Rights and People's Union for Civil Liberties. 1984. 'Who Are the Guilty? Report of a Joint Inquiry into the Causes and Impact of the Riots in Delhi from 31 October to 10 November 1984'. Available at https://ia601600.us.archive.org/26/items/WhoAreTheGuilty_201502/Who%20Are%20The%20Guilty.pdf (accessed on 21 November 2024).

People's Union for Democratic Rights. 1992. '1984 Carnage in Delhi: A Report on the Aftermath'. Available at https://www.pudr.org/publicatiosn-files/1992-Nov-1984%20Carnage%20in%20Delhi.pdf (accessed on 21 November 2024).

Portelli, Alessandro. 1991. *The Death of Luigi Trastulli and Other Stories: Form and Meaning in Oral History*. Albany: State University of New York Press.

———. 2006. 'What makes Oral History Different'. In *The Oral History Reader*, eds Robert Perks and Alistair Thomson, 32–42. New York: Routledge.

Rao, Amiya. 1984. 'When Delhi Burnt'. *Economic & Political Weekly* 19 (49): 2066–69.

Robinson, Rowena. 2005. *Tremors of Violence: Muslim Survivors of Ethnic Strife in Western India*. New Delhi: Sage.

Ross, Fiona C. 2001. 'Speech and Silence: Women's Testimony in the First Five Weeks of Public Hearings of the South African Truth and Reconciliation Commission'. In *Remaking a World: Violence, Social Suffering, and Recovery*, eds Veena Das, Arthur Kleinman, Margaret M. Lock, Mamphela Ramphele and Pamela Reynolds, 250–79. New Delhi: Oxford University Press.

Saluja, Anshu. 2015. 'Engaging with Women's Words and Their Silences: Mapping 1984 and Its Aftermath'. *Sikh Formations: Religion, Culture, Theory* 11 (3): 343–65.

Stein, Arlene. 2009. '"As Far as They Knew I Came from France": Stigma, Passing, and Not Speaking about the Holocaust'. *Symbolic Interaction* 32 (1): 44–60.

Tarlo, Emma. 2000. 'Welcome to History: A Resettlement Colony in the Making'. In *Delhi: Urban Space and Human Destinies*, eds Veronique Dupont, Emma Tarlo and Denis Vidal, 51–69. Delhi: Manohar and Centre de Sciences Humaines.

Thompson, Paul. 2006. 'The Voice of the Past: Oral History'. In *The Oral History Reader*, eds Robert Perks and Alistair Thomson, 25–31. New York: Routledge.

four

The Politics of Possibility in the Commemoration of Trauma[1]

Anne Murphy

On 6 June 2009, the widespread violence against Sikhs in the wake of the assassination of Prime Minister Indira Gandhi in 1984 was commemorated in a public square to the north of the Vancouver Art Gallery in downtown Vancouver, British Columbia (Canada). Such commemorations have now taken place for more than two decades; in that year and several others since, the ceremony opened with invited speakers representing some of the First Nations of Canada. With these speakers, organisers placed events in 1984 within a larger transnational human rights discourse, situated locally. The creation of such equivalencies is by no means new. Indeed, as Giorgio Shani argued, 'like the … holocaust [for Jews], or the slave trade for African-Americans, it is this "chosen trauma" [of 1984] that has enabled a Sikh *diaspora* to be imagined' (2008: 98; emphasis in original). An example of this explicit choice is the internet TV station 'TV84', based in Long Island City, New York City, formed (according to its promotional emails) 'to bridge the gap between the Panjabi Diaspora and their homeland by serving as a link to reconnect with their roots'.

This move towards parallels with other traumas is not without controversy; as Ali Kazimi has pointed out, efforts to commemorate the violence of 1984 in relation to the history of Indigenous histories in Canada has brought about sometimes facile analogies between the two, evoking understandings of 'right' to a place. The work of artist Nep Sidhu, with valorising visual references to the movement for a Sikh state under the name of Khalistan, Kazimi (2019) argues, 'draws a false equivalency between very different struggles: the fight for an ethno-religious, theocratic state in South Asia and the ongoing struggle of the Indigenous peoples in Canada who are grappling with the legacies and ongoing processes of colonialism'. This has also led to inaccurate representations of Canadian history: meritorious efforts to build alliances among South Asian and Indigenous communities led in 2019 to the construction of a public mural in Vancouver; however, descriptions of the historical underpinnings for the mural at the mural's inauguration and on the website associated with it misrepresented the historical record to assert connections between Indigenous communities and South Asian settlers that are not borne out by the historical evidence (Kazimi et al. 2021).

Commemoration is, as these examples indicate, always marked by political and other interests. My goal in this short essay is to consider the commemoration of 1984 within a larger memorial imperative, articulated at diverse locations in the world. This allows us to consider the politics of possibility in remembrance as commemoration, and as reconciliation, for Sikhs in the present, with regard to 1984 and within a broadly museological mode. The essay, then, is about commemoration in more general terms, as well as with reference to the violence against Sikhs in 1984, and the promise and failures of the museum and other commemorative forms in this context.

Sikh Museological Practice

The museum form has become prominent within the Sikh cultural worlds in the last two decades (Murphy 2015). Indeed, recent years in particular have witnessed increased interest in Sikh material culture and art in diverse national contexts. In some of these, objects are considered 'art'—recent major exhibitions at mainstream institutions include 'Piety and Splendour' at the National Museum in Delhi, and 'I See No Stranger: Early Sikh Art and Devotion' at the Rubin Museum of Art in New York City in 2006. Affluent Sikh donors in the United States have made possible a permanent exhibition of Sikh objects at the San Francisco Asian Art Museum—which was significantly enhanced in 2017 in celebration of the fiftieth anniversary of the Sikh Foundation—and an eclectic exhibition at the Smithsonian Institution in Washington DC which opened in July 2004.[2] In a different mode, the Wing Luke Asian Museum in Seattle, Washington, held 'The Sikh Community: Over 100 Years in the Pacific Northwest' exhibition in 2006, focusing on the history and material culture of the Sikh community in the region. (Other recent exhibitions, such as the Royal British Columbia Museum's 'Pocket Gallery' at its entrance, 'Exploring the work of the

Royal British Columbia Museum' on the theme of 'Haq and History, *haq ate itihas*' [inaugurated in 2019] and the Museum of Surrey's 'Being Punjabi: Unfolding the Surrey Story' [on display from 2 October 2019 to 23 February 2020], focus on Punjabi culture, rather than Sikh culture and history. [Chung and Bains 2020]) The Sikh Heritage Museum at the Gur Sikh Temple in Abbotsford, British Columbia, Canada—which itself was declared a Canadian National Historic Site in 2002—explores aspects of Punjabi and Sikh culture in diverse forms, from art to Sikh Canadian history (Ashley 2014; Francis 2017; Khalsa Diwan Society n.d.[a], n.d.[b]).

Such museological projects are by no means a North American phenomenon: the Maharaja Duleep Singh Centenary Trust in England (a registered charity in the UK since 1993), among many other organisations as well as individuals in Britain, has been active in commemorating the lives and activities of Sikhs in Britain as, according to the organisation's Director Harbinder Singh Rana, 'loyal subjects of the crown'.[3] Aside from collecting objects and preserving sites related to Maharaja Duleep Singh, the organisation has constructed an 'Anglo Sikh Heritage Trail', in association with the United Kingdom Punjab Heritage Association, to highlight the history and achievements of the Sikhs in Britain.[4] This is one of many heritage projects related to the Sikhs in Britain, and those mentioned are only meant to suggest a wider range of related activities (Murphy 2015).

In India, the situation is still more complicated. The museum-form that dominates in India is the Sikh gurdwara museum, such as the most prominent such museum, the Central Sikh Museum, located along the perimeter of the Golden Temple/Harmandir Sahib/Darbar Sahib, but parallel institutions are found alongside most of the important *itihāsik* or historical gurdwaras, such as Sis Ganj in Delhi. Here, images of the Sikh gurus and heroes accompany the display of historical objects and portraits of Sikhs engaged in acts of service; paintings that portray the persecution of the Sikhs in the eighteenth century are joined by photographs that portray Sikhs who died in 1984. The Gurdwara Museum form is found in the West as well—the first official Sikh Museum of Britain, recognised by the British Museum Services, is in Leicester, in association with a gurdwara and with a roughly parallel collection on display. The ambivalent status for the image was demonstrated in a sign that hung in the Sis Ganj museum in 2002, instructing those in attendance on how to behave: 'the garlanding of the portraits of the Gurus, offering worship of touching the feet of the Guru as shown in the paintings is not allowed … To indulge in such practices is to go against the basic tenets of Sikhism'.

It is not surprising, given the dominance of the integrated museum/ gurdwara form, that commemoration of 1984 violence first emerged in this domain, as we see with the Central Sikh Museum's portrayal of the torture victim, and victims of the 1984 attack on the Golden Temple. The Gurdwara Museum is indeed probably the primary articulation point of the Sikh commemorative imperative, a part of a broader means by which, in Brian Axel's words, 'many Sikhs have established a set of practices that remake the private scene of national torture into a transnational spectacle of subjectification' (2001: 139). The Central Sikh Museum in Amritsar is only one such example. As Kamal Arora's (2017) thought-provoking work has explored, the violence of 1984 is commemorated and enacted multiple ways in the 'Widow's Colony', founded for the rehabilitation of the women who lost their husbands in the pogrom of 1984, and their families. This includes both public expression of grief, often performed on the anniversary of the violence and sought out by journalists, and the constellation of images of those who were killed within the Shahidganj or Martyrs' Gurdwara (a name that also evokes a famous historical gurdwara in Lahore, and a smaller and more recent site in the Indian Punjab near Gurdwara Fatehgarh Sahib). In 2013, a memorial to victims of the 1984 Indian army attack at the Darbar Sahib/Golden Temple was inaugurated within the precinct of the Darbar Sahib itself (Burke 2012; Chopra 2013). Representations of the victims of the violence associated with 1984 and its aftermath in the period of police repression in Indian Punjab are common in diasporic locations in a broader museological, public exhibition mode, through the related form of the parade and related public exhibition, as well as in the gurdwara.[5]

This is therefore an incredibly productive cultural form; one might even argue that the museum (and the related temporary exhibition) is a primary articulation point for Sikh public postcolonial representation today. As Brian Axel has observed, the internet offers a more generally available representational space, but the institutionality of the museum and its ability therefore to make and take place (in literal as well as figurative terms) within the public sphere offers a considerable weight to the representational practices located there. And, again, not only are violence and trauma represented: victims of violence are represented alongside other portrayals of the Sikh past and Sikh being; this both highlights violence, and includes it in a larger narrative.

These are all commemoration projects, in different registers, building on the museum form. The form itself deserves consideration.[6] The modern Indian museum is born of the British colonial drive to categorise, rationalise and display the Indian past and present for the 'greater' good of control; as Cohn (alongside others) has argued, 'the major interpretive strategy by which India was to become known to Europeans in the seventeenth and eighteenth centuries was through a construction of a history for India' (1996: 78), and objects were 'discovered, collected, and classified' (and later displayed) as a primary means to serve this agenda (ibid.: 77).[7] As Kavita Singh puts it: 'The museum-as-microcosm [enacted by the British] was part of the imperial fantasy of being able to create a complete and comprehensive archive of the empire, in which a correctly classified and labelled array of samples could adequately represent the imperial domain' (2003: 187). The first museums in India were the product of colonial construction, such as the famed *Ajaibghar* or 'Wonder-house' in Lahore, immortalised in Rudyard Kipling's *Kim*. The Lahore museum was modelled after London's 'India Museum' and was first begun upon the order of the financial commissioner of Punjab, to serve utilitarian ends, 'with a view to the development of the resources of the country' (quoted in Qureshi 1997: 72; see also Prakash 1999: 37 ff.; Guha-Thakurta 1992; Davis 1997: 171). It was later merged with the contents of the Punjab Exhibition of 1864, which itself was part of a larger phenomenon of public fairs or exhibitions that, according to Breckenridge, worked to situate 'metropole and colony within a single analytic field' that was global, while simultaneously re-inscribing difference and the primacy of the nation-state (1989: 197). This dynamic also demonstrated the fundamental orientation of the colonial modern as a world-as-exhibition: the world ordered into representation and represented, organised and consumed by the modern metropole subject (and with unconventional, alternative readings by South Asian colonial subjects, as Gyan Prakash and Guha-Thakurta have shown) (Mitchell 1991 [1988]; Guha-Thakurta 2004: 45, 79–81; Prakash 1999). In general, the museum, according to Anderson, acted along with the census and the map to shape 'the way in which the colonial state imagined its dominion—the nature of the human beings it ruled, the geography of its domain, and the legitimacy of its ancestry', serving the very political purpose of justifying British rule (1991 [1983]: 164). This was accomplished in different ways within the metropole and colony, whereby the imperial museum in the metropole constructed a comprehensive vision of the imperial object, and the colonial museum, as Tapati Guha-Thakurta among others has noted, presented a local, utilitarian vision of the colony that would focus on 'local knowledge that was specific to the needs and context of the Indian empire' (Guha-Thakurta 2004: 43).

The museum can thus be seen as a form of colonial representation, like the exhibition: introduced into the colony and appropriated and transformed (although not always entirely) within the postcolonial state. Tony Bennett has argued that the growth of the museum in Europe exemplified a 'new "governmental" relation to culture in which works of high culture were treated as instruments that could be enlisted in new ways for new tasks of social management' (1995: 6). The museum thus constructed 'man' as both subject and object of knowledge—in radically different ways, of course, depending upon one's race and nationality (as well as gender), with a tension between the theoretical universality of representation and its limited realities. Today, this contradiction continues to haunt, as many museums in North America and Europe try to reach a diverse public, which remains largely under-represented, or un-represented, or is present only as 'other' within museum walls—and, at the same time, individuals and groups vie for representation within these institutions (Karp et al. 1992). Sikh museological representations take their place in relation to these forms of 'museumising', political and otherwise, a part of a larger phenomenon of the 'post-museum' form identified by Eilean Cooper-Greenhill (Sandell 2007: 5, 9). In the words of theorists Corinne Kratz and Ivan Karp, this creates museums as 'temples of civilization, sites for the creation of citizens, forums for debate, settings for cultural interchange and negotiation of values, engines of economic renewal and revenue generation, imposed colonialist enterprises, havens of elitist distinction and discrimination and places of empowerment and recognition' (2006: 1). The museum, thus, acts as not only an institution of public culture, but also as a social technology—a means by which a set of social processes and transformations are engaged by which publics are created and voiced. In this way, 'global theatres of real consequence' are created, with reference to principles of multiculturalism and pluralism (ibid.: 4).

Remembrance in Transnational Terms

The Sikh museological, and the museum form in general, thus exceeds colonial foundations as a particularly modern, postcolonial and hybrid form of representation that is being configured today in relation to a broader commemorative imperative within a larger field, both in specifically Sikh and global terms. In this way, it is in keeping with broader transformations: the museum form is used today for a wide range of commemorative practices that go beyond the form's imperial underpinnings. Today, in Andreas Huyssen's words, we suffer from a 'hypertrophy of memory, not history' (2003: 3). Although the surfeit in memory in the present does manifest aspects of an excess of marketing and commodification, 'the call simply to move on risks forfeiting what the recent convulsions of memory discourse have generated ... and it fails to give us a plausible explanation for the obsession with memory itself as a significant symptom of our cultural present' (ibid.: 3). Sikh engagements with the museological—from the Gurdwara Museum to the exhibition at the Smithsonian—parallel the developments Huyssen identifies more generally, around the world, from Buenos Aires to Berlin, where the 'focus has shifted from present futures to present pasts' since the 1980s; he argues that 'this shift in the experience and sensibility of time needs to be explained historically and phenomenologically' (ibid.: 10). Such institutions must also be seen within a larger context of tourism and the culture trade, as recent initiatives in Pakistan demonstrate (Appadurai and Breckenridge 1999); we can indeed see the recent opening of the 'Kartarpur corridor', giving access to pilgrims from India to the site founded by Guru Nanak in what is now Pakistan, along such lines (BBC 2019). Such practices both exceed and cannot be reduced to the form of the museum itself, as there is a long history of Sikh memorial practice that is reflected in the recognition of the itihāsik or historical gurdwara and objects that represented the Sikh past, before and alongside the Western museum form coming to the fore (Murphy 2012a).

An additional frame for understanding specifically the Sikh museological—in keeping with global concerns—is within a transnational phenomenon of remembrance of trauma. In this, Sikh memory-making in museum form is inherently modern and transnational, typical of a wider field of cultural production that is articulated from South Africa to Northern Ireland to the United States (Huyssen 2003: 15). There is, therefore, no coincidence in the fact that outside the Leicester Sikh Museum—the first officially registered Sikh Museum with the British Museum Service—is a Sikh Human Rights Centre; these two projects are fundamentally tied. Remembrance in such institutions takes place in relation to a series of traumas, even when a triumphalist tale about Sikh sovereignty and/or minority success is invoked, such as with the Anglo-Sikh Heritage Trail.[8] This mode of remembrance is one that is articulated in diverse global locations through the expressive form of the museum, and the bringing of the past into the present through the museum as a technology of remembrance. As we recognise the participation of Sikh forms of remembrance within larger transnational modes, we must also consider the alternative models that exist for such commemoration to take place. This will enable us to see why and how the Sikh museological has taken the form it has, and where it may go.

One of these models is the commemoration of trauma offered by the museological and other forms of memorialisation of the Holocaust. There are specific ways such a narrative is invoked in the Sikh case, such as, most obviously, the choice of Moshe Safdie & Associates for the design of the Khalsa Heritage Complex. This firm was involved, most famously, in the expansion of the Holocaust memorial in Jerusalem, and indeed the project was inspired by Chief Minister Prakash Singh Badal's 1997 visit to Israel and his viewing of Yad Vashem, and particularly Safdie's Children's Holocaust Museum (Launois [Sat Kaur] 2003: 135, 138 ff.) In this example, the project of recollection is an end in itself (although, in the case of the Khalsa Heritage Complex, as of the time of writing this essay, the creation of Pakistan and the loss of Sikh sites there is commemorated, but the trials of the last 50 years are left unaddressed, while in the gurdwara museum this is a powerful presence). The other model that we can consider in relation to the Sikh case is the reconciliation model, exemplified by South Africa's Truth and Reconciliation Commission and associated memorial projects (many in museum-form), and parallel processes inspired by it, such as the 'Healing Through Remembering' initiative in Northern Ireland, whereby the commemoration of trauma provides a politics of possibility for communities and nations alike: in the words of the 'Healing Through Remembering' project report in 2002, 'what we remember is what we are' and remembering must occur so 'that healing can take place for all people affected by the conflict in and about Northern Ireland' (Healing Through Remembering 2002: 1). Pradip Datta, along these lines, has advocated for a 'truth and reconciliation' approach to the past in South Asia, noting recent work on Partition that has, for example, sought to 'dismantle the strategies of forgetting that had hidden the public memory of partition and to recover the traumas of partition along with the identities that it produced' (2005: 317). The Partition Museum in Amritsar can be seen as one step in that direction (Mahn and Murphy 2018). What is of interest, in the end, is how the differences between these two modes—commemoration and reconciliation—can inform our understanding of

Sikh forms of remembrance, and what is required in the politics of the present for a politics of possibility, through reconciliation, to exist within remembrance.

Remembrance itself has its dangers. As Pradip Datta notes, the same imperative to 'remember' that feeds recuperative strategies for addressing Partition and 1984 also animates the rhetoric of those who seek to avenge perceived past wrongs committed against Hindus, where, quoting him here, 'The national trauma of Hindus seeks not simply to memorialize the past, but also to use this to reverse and overcome the trauma of the past' (Datta 2005: 318). This has been performed as a weapon against minoritised communities in India. A preoccupation with trauma can also unduly limit memory itself, over-determine its valences and denude it of real politics—the politics, for example, of real struggles for rights in the present, as Huyssen (2003: 8–9) notes. But it is imperative that we also remember that this need not be the case. This is the importance of the invocation of the experience of First Nations communities in Canada at an event remembering 1984, and the inclusion of exhibitions on contemporary human rights conflicts in the world (for example) within the confines of the Anne Frank House in Holland, which commemorates one Jewish child's experience of the Holocaust. A larger politics is invoked with such connections, and connections are made to struggles of different kinds, today and now. There is, therefore, responsible remembering, a remembering that lives in the present and draws connections, not only distinctions.

The concept of reconciliation beyond and through remembrance offers an important alternative here. The *working through* and *questioning* of absolute truths are key to the political possibilities that reconciliation offers over remembrance. Remembrance, in itself, does not guarantee such. A reconciliation approach, which focuses on working through opposing positions, and coming to terms with difficult truths that at times cannot be resolved, takes the political possibility of remembrance one step further. It is the means by which, in the South Africa case, those 'imprisoned in history', in the words of one involved in the Truth and Reconciliation Commission hearings, can 'walk through' it together (Ericson 2001: 259–260). On a personal level, given extreme levels of dispossession and violence, forgiveness may be impossible—but a hearing allows remembering to occur: in the words of another, with the TRC Commission hearings, 'a gigantic mirror [was] put in front of the country' (ibid.: 339). Story-sharing was the key principle behind the project and the memorial projects that grew from it, informing Northern Irish efforts along similar lines. The recent five-year-long Truth and Reconciliation process in Canada, as a response to the violence and cultural genocide committed within residential schools for members of the Indigenous people of the country, also embraced this model, which led to the development of concrete recommendations that are crucial to moving past the Truth and Reconciliation Commission process into a changed future (Truth and Reconciliation Commission of Canada n.d.). It remains to be seen, however, how much reconciliation will influence real life practices and choices, particularly when the interests of business and government may not converge with those of Indigenous peoples.[9] This is where the real test lies.

The project of reconciliation, however, requires a set of circumstances that have not yet been arrived at, in the case before us, to bring about a new and broader museal form for the remembrance of Sikh trauma. The political possibility of reconciliation requires acknowledgement, and a broader context within which the injustices of the past are *not* those of the present. Thus, the Truth and Reconciliation Commission in South Africa was a function of the dismantlement of apartheid, it did not bring it about (nor can it ameliorate the effects of it in material terms). In Northern Ireland, remembrance and dialogue could begin during the height of violence as a shared experience of violence, but more extensive remembrance in Northern Ireland could only begin to take place—although still in a fractured way—within a fragile peace that is now at risk again, as this essay moves into print, by the politics of Brexit. In Canada, the Truth and Reconciliation process proceeded only after the official state apology for residential schools delivered by then Prime Minister Stephen Harper, in Parliament, in 2008 (this followed a 1998 'Statement of Reconciliation' delivered by a federal minister, but not in Parliament) (CBC Archives 2018). In these cases, state agencies or actors were a part of the process, which followed from political recognition. This is the problem of remembrance within the politics of the present, in the Sikh case: the Sikh community has led in commemoration efforts, in diverse forms; these efforts towards remembrance in Sikh terms must be balanced by both *recognition* and external *institutional support*, which together can provide the conditions of possibility for reconciliation. As Gyanendra Pandey has noted, in discussion of the politics of tolerance: 'It is only those in power who are in a position to practice [tolerance] … [for] tolerance and coexistence is not a luxury permitted to the marginalized and subordinated, except in the obvious sense that they often have no choice' (2006: 159). Remembrance must, therefore, be *dialogical*. If monological, and memories do not find a hearing and grounds for recognition, then there is no basis for the creation of what Ericson (2001) has called a 'shared moral landscape' within remembrance.[10] Reconciliation cannot occur as an effect and product of memory, until the possibility of such sharing exists.

What is needed, then, is for official and *multi-vocal* memory-making processes to proceed alongside those described in brief here. This would allow for a fuller accounting of memory, recognition of the memory work that has been done and needs to be done, and the telling of stories from diverse perspectives that challenge but need to be heard. It is for this reason that the politics of the present have not yet made possible alternatives to partial and shattered memory-making. This is what makes the narratives articulated in the religious and private locations referred to here so multiple and marked as controversial. As Anokh Singh (2016) has pointed out in a recent essay, within gurdwara memory-making as a whole in greater Vancouver, the Canadian Sikh diaspora still struggles to represent the range of positions that exist with reference to the violence associated with 1984.[11] In this, they reveal the political present. In the end, to achieve the difficult possibility of reconciliation, it is not the Sikh community that needs to engage in remembrance, but instead others. Sikhs have done much to remember and reflect on the significance of the violence of 1984, through the kinds of commemorative projects mentioned here. Individuals and non-governmental groups have also done their part to document and remember the violence of 1984: for example, the violence was first and well documented by left and progressive organisations, such as the early report completed jointly by the People's Union for Democratic Rights and the People's Union for Civil Liberties (1984). The Indian state and other non-state institutions and actors, however, have overall failed to provide recognition and redress. A coordinated effort of individuals and institutions beyond, in collaboration with individuals within the Sikh community, is needed to engage in the careful and difficult work of remembering.

Closing

The musealised form of representation in Sikh contexts today cannot be seen as a mere 'derivative' of the Western form, and reflects the confluence of colonial and postcolonial regimes of meaning, with the particular politics of the present (Appadurai and Breckenridge 1999: 405).[12] Sikh gurdwara-based museological constructions of the past locate themselves less explicitly in relation to multicultural transnational and national discourses, and more explicitly to the construction of a particular version of Sikh history and the definition of the religious community centred around important individuals and events. Trauma is a central feature of these memorial projects, enacted in and enlivening Vaisakhi parades, exhibitions and gurdwaras around the world. National and regional forms of museological engagement differ in orientation, with more attention to state interests, while transnational, diasporic mainstream Sikh museological interests vie for a place at the cultural table, in broad terms. Sikh museological interests are thus notations in a global script of remembering and recognition, within a larger concern for representation within the museum form, in relation to diverse interests—just as in the case of South Africa, commemoration is torn by competing interests, those of the market and the state, and of tourists versus South Africans (Kirshenblatt-Gimblett 2006: 39). No commemorative project, museum or not, is free of these tensions.

To remember is to own, but no one person owns all of memory. Memorial work must be multi-vocal, and complex, if it is to represent the diversity of people's experiences. Only through the complexity of these stories—and their articulation by and for diverse communities, and in conversation with diverse parallels—can memory lead to something more. As Launois (2003) has noted in her work on the Khalsa Heritage Complex, we can return to the idea of negotiated truth in a more general way here: that the museum in general *must* be this, negotiated and contested. It must foster debate *within* the Sikh community, and within other communities, while also making a demand of a larger public sphere to recognise these histories. There are conditions of possibility in the articulation of 'plural memory', as Launois (2003) puts it, towards the achievement of a negotiated truth through the difficult project of reconciliation that other societies have faced. True reconciliation requires this kind of messiness: to bring multiple voices and perspectives to the conversation, and reveal the complexity of memories that cannot and should not be contained. But it requires the participation, and recognition, of those in power: without this, there is no reconciliation.

Notes

1. This essay contains material, extended in a new direction, previously published in Murphy (2015), and presented publicly as Murphy (2009).

2. On the Delhi exhibition, see Goswamy (2000). On the US museum projects, see Allen-Agostini (2001: C08) and Sohrabji (2017). See also Stronge (1999).

3. Interview undertaken in July 2002 in Birmingham. See also discussion of this organisation in Axel (2001).

4. In an organisation pamphlet, it is noted that 'the V&A's 1999 "Arts of the Sikh Kingdoms" exhibition and other nationwide events marking the tercentenary of the Khalsa (Sikh commonwealth) acted as a significant catalyst for a renaissance in Sikh heritage in the UK'.

5. See discussion in CBC News (2008, 2010); Bolan (2011).

6. This discussion of the museum form draws on Murphy (2015).

7. See also Prakash (1999: 21–22, and *passim*).

8. On issues related to the 'success narrative', see a recent unpublished essay by Gill (2016).

9. This is visible in the controversies over a large-scale pipeline project in Canada, where there is significant debate and many, but not all, Indigenous groups oppose the project. See Cecco (2019); Kane (2020); Smyth (2020).

10. This refers to the title of her book. See Ericson (2001).

11. See also discussion in Murphy (2012b).

12. On the notion of derivation, see Chatterjee (1993); Appadurai and Breckenridge (1995).

References

Allen-Agostini, Lisa. 2001. 'In the Sikh Spirit at the Smithsonian'. *The Washington Post*, Monday, 13 August, C08.

Anderson, Benedict. 1991 [1983]. *Imagined Communities: Reflections on the Origin and Spread of Nationalism*. London, New York: Verso.

Appadurai, Arjun, and Carol A. Breckenridge. 1995. 'Public Modernity in India'. In *Consuming Modernity: Public Culture in a South Asian World*, ed. Carol Breckenridge, 1–20. Minneapolis/London: University of Minnesota Press.

_____. 1999. 'Museums are Good to Think'. In *Representing the Nation: A Reader; Heritage and Museums*, eds David Boswell and Jessica Evans, 404–20. New York: Routledge.

Arora, Kamal. 2017. 'Legacies of Violence: Sikh Women in Delhi's 'Widow Colony'. Ph.D. diss., University of British Columbia.

Ashley, Susan L. T. 2014. 'Re-Telling, Re-Cognition, Re-Stitution: Sikh Heritagization in Canada'. *Cultura* (Iași, Romania) 11 (2): 39–58.

Axel, Keith. 2001. *The Nation's Tortured Body: Violence, Representation, and the Formation of a Sikh 'Diaspora'*. Durham, NC: Duke University Press.

BBC. 2019. 'Kartarpur Corridor: India Pilgrims in Historic Visit to Pakistan Temple'. BBC.com, 9 November. Available at https://www.bbc.com/news/world-asia-india-50342319 (accessed on 19 January 2020).

Bennett, Tony. 1995. *The Birth of the Museum: History, Theory, Politics*. London and New York: Routledge.

Bolan, Kim. 2011. 'Surrey Vaisakhi and Sikh "Martyrs"'. *The Vancouver Sun*, 24 April. Available at http://vancouversun.com/news/staff-blogs/surrey-vaisakhi-and-sikh-martyrs (accessed on 8 September 2018).

Breckenridge, Carol. 1989. 'The Aesthetics and Politics of Colonial Collecting: India at World Fairs'. *Comparative Studies in History and Society* 31 (2): 195–216.

Burke, Jason. 2012. 'Sikh Golden Temple Memorial Reopens Old Wounds in India'. *The Guardian*, 2 October. Available at https://www.theguardian.com/world/2012/oct/02/sikh-golden-temple-memorial-india (accessed on 21 January 2020).

CBC News. 2008. 'Controversial Photos Displayed at Surrey's Vaisakhi Parade'. 12 April. Available at http://www.cbc.ca/news/canada/british-columbia/controversial-photos-displayed-at-surrey-s-vaisakhi-parade-1.729743 (accessed on 8 September 2018).

CBC News. 2010. 'Surrey Sikh Parade's Martyrs Float Angers Mayor'. 18 April. Available at http://www.cbc.ca/news/canada/british-columbia/surrey-sikh-parade-s-martyrs-float-angers-mayor-1.889362 (accessed on 8 September 2018).

CBC Archives. 2018. 'Government Apologizes for Residential Schools in 2008'. 25 June. Available at https://www.cbc.ca/archives/government-apologizes-for-residential-schools-in-2008-1.4666041 (accessed on 5 February 2025).

Cecco, Leyland. 2019. 'Pipeline Battle Puts Focus on Canada's Disputed Right to Use Indigenous [sic] Land'. *The Guardian*, 11 January. Available at https://www.theguardian.com/world/2019/jan/11/canada-pipeline-indigenous-trudeau-treaty (accessed on 19 January 2020).

Chatterjee, Partha. 1993. *The Nation and Its Fragments: Colonial and Postcolonial Histories*. Princeton, NJ: Princeton University Press.

Chopra, Radhika. 2013. 'A Museum, a Memorial, and a Martyr: Politics of Memory in the Sikh Golden Temple'. *Sikh Formations: Religion, Culture, Theory* 9 (2): 97–114.

Chung, Tzu-I and Satwinder Bains. 2020. 'The Punjabi Canadian Legacy Project: Possibilities and Limitations of Institutional Heritagisation from Below'. *International Journal of Heritage Studies* (IJHS) 26 (3): 221–236.

Cohn, Bernard S. 1996. *Colonialism and Its Forms of Knowledge: The British in India*. Princeton: Princeton University Press.

Datta, Pradip. 2005. 'Historic Trauma and the Politics of the Present in India'. *Interventions* 7 (3): 316–20.

Davis, Richard. 1997. *Lives of Indian Images*. Princeton, NJ: Princeton University Press.

Ericson, Maria. 2001. *Reconciliation and the Search for a Shared Moral Landscape: An Exploration Based Upon a Study of Northern Ireland and South Africa*. Frankfurt am Main: Peter Lang.

Francis, Matthew. 2017. 'Community-led Museums Exploring Religious Life in Canada: Abbotsford's Sikh Heritage Museum and Mennonite Heritage Museum'. In *Religion in Museums: Global and Multidisciplinary Perspectives*, eds Gretchen Buggeln, Crispin Paine and S. Brent Plate, 129–34. London: Bloomsbury Academic.

Gill, Sukhwinder Singh. 2016. 'Challenging the Hero Plotline: A Continued Sikh Disaspora Struggle' (unpublished essay).

Goswamy, B. N. 2000. 'About the Making of a Throne'. *The Tribune*, 9 July. Available at http://www.tribuneindia.com/2000/20000709/spectrum/art.htm (accessed on 8 September 2018).

Guha-Thakurta, Tapati. 1992. *The Making of a New 'Indian' Art: Artists, Aesthetics, and Nationalism in Bengal, c. 1850–1920*. Cambridge: Cambridge University Press.

———. 2004. *Monuments, Objects, Histories: Institutions of Art in Colonial and Postcolonial India*. New Delhi: Permanent Black.

Healing Through Remembering. 2002. 'Healing Through Remembering: The Report of the Healing Through Remembering Project'. Available at http://healingthroughremembering.org/resources/reports/core-htr-reports/ (accessed on 7 January 2017).

Huyssen, Andreas. 2003. *Present Pasts: Urban Palimpsests and the Politics of Memory*. Stanford, CA: Stanford University Press.

Kane, Laura. 2020. 'Work Must Stop on TransMountain, Site C, LNG Pipeline until First Nations Approval, UN Committee Says'. 7 January. Available at https://www.cbc.ca/news/canada/british-columbia/un-racism-committee-trans-mountain-site-c-coastal-gaslink-pipeline-1.5417343 (accessed on 19 January 2020).

Karp, Ivan, Christine Mullen Kreamer, and Steven D. Lavine, eds. 1992. *Museums and Communities: The Politics of Public Culture*. Washington: Smithsonian Institution Press.

Kazimi, Ali. 2019. 'Nep Sidhu's Art Stirs Controversy about the History of Sikh Separatism'. 25 June. Available at http://theconversation.com/nep-sidhus-art-stirs-controversy-about-the-history-of-sikh-separatism-118590 (accessed on 19 January 2020).

Kazimi, Ali, Hugh Johnston, and Anne Murphy. 2021. 'True Both to History, and to Solidarity'. *Rungh Magazine* 8 (3) (April). Available at https://rungh.org/true-both-to-history-and-to-solidarity/ (accessed on 5 February 2025).

Khalsa Diwan Society. n.d.(a). 'Current Exhibition'. Available at http://canadiansikhheritage.ca/exhibitions/ (accessed on 9 December 2024).

———. n.d.(b). 'History'. Available at http://canadiansikhheritage.ca/gur-sikh-temple/history/ (accessed on 9 December 2024).

Kirshenblatt-Gimblett, Barbara. 2006. 'Exhibitionary Complexes'. In *Museum Frictions: Public Cultures/Global Transformations*, eds Ivan Karp, Corinne A. Kratz, Lynn Szwaraja and Tomás Ybarra-Frausto, 35–45. Durham and London: Duke University Press.

Kratz, Corinne A., and Ivan Karp. 2006. 'Introduction'. In *Museum Frictions: Public Cultures/Global Transformations*, eds Ivan Karp, Corinne A. Kratz, Lynn Szwaraja and Tomás Ybarra-Frausto, 1–31. Durham and London: Duke University Press.

Launois (Sat Kaur), Anne-Colombe. 2003. 'The Khalsa Heritage Complex: A Museum for a Community?' In *New Insights into Sikh Art*, ed. Kavita Singh, 134–45. Mumbai: Marg Publications.

Mahn, Churnjeet, and Anne Murphy. 2018. 'Introduction'. In *Partition and the Practice of Memory*, eds Churnjeet Mahn and Anne Murphy, 1–14. London: Palgrave UK.

Mitchell, Timothy. 1991 [1988]. *Colonising Egypt*. Berkeley/Los Angeles/London: University of California Press.

Murphy, Anne. 2009. 'The Politics of Possibility and the Commemoration of Trauma'. Unpublished paper presented at the *After 1984?* Conference organised by Arvind S. Mandair (University of Michigan). 12–13 September, at the University of California, Berkeley.

———. 2012a. *The Materiality of the Past: History and Representation in Sikh Tradition*. New York: Oxford University Press.

———. 2012b. 'The Specter of Violence in Sikh Pasts'. In *Teaching Religion and Violence*, ed. Brian Pennington, 149–63. New York: Oxford University Press and the American Academy of Religion.

———. 2015. 'Sikh Museuming'. In *Sacred Objects in Secular Spaces: Exhibiting Asian Religions in Museums*, ed. Bruce Sullivan, 49–64, 157. London: Bloomsbury Academic.

Pandey, Gyanendra. 2006. *Routine Violence: Nations, Fragments, Histories*. Stanford: Stanford University Press.

People's Union for Democratic Rights and People's Union for Civil Liberties. 1984. *Who Are the Guilty? Report of a Joint Inquiry into the Causes and Impact of the Riots in Delhi from 31 October to 10 November 1984*. New Delhi: People's Union for Democratic Rights and People's Union for Civil Liberties.

Prakash, Gyan. 1999. *Another Reason: Science and the Imagination of Modern India*. Princeton, NJ: Princeton University Press.

Qureshi, M. Naeem. 1997. 'A Museum for British Lahore'. *History Today* 47 (9): 71–74.

Sandell, Richard. 2007. *Museums, Prejudice and the Reframing of Difference*. London and New York: Routledge.

Shani, Giorgio. 2008. *Sikh Nationalism and Identity in a Global Age*. London and New York: Routledge.

Singh, Anokh. 2016. 'The Politics of Memory' (unpublished essay).

Singh, Kavita. 2003. 'The Museum is National'. In *India: A National Culture?* ed. Geeti Sen, 176–96. New Delhi: Sage Publications and India International Centre.

Smyth, Mike. 2020. 'Opinion: As Hereditary Chiefs Block a Key Pipeline, and the UN Calls for Project Shutdowns, an Indigenous Leader Speaks up for Jobs and Development'. 9 January. Available at https://theprovince.com/news/bc-politics/mike-smyth-not-all-indigenous-leaders-back-un-call-to-stop-b-c-projects (accessed on 19 January 2020).

Sohrabji, Sunita. 2017. 'Sikh Foundation Celebrates 50th Anniversary with Exhibit at Asian Art Museum'. 16 February. Available at https://www.indiawest.com/news/global_indian/sikh-foundation-celebrates-th-anniversary-with-exhibit-at-asian-art/article_3942de84-f46c-11e6-bbae-9fb6e3687a60.html (accessed on 8 September 2018).

Stronge, Susan. 1999. *The Arts of the Sikh Kingdoms*. New York: Weatherhill.

Truth and Reconciliation Commission of Canada/National Centre for Truth and Reconciliation. n.d. Website of the National Centre for Truth and Reconciliation, https://nctr.ca/ (accessed on 5 February 2025).

III

Literary Imaginaries and Cinematic Representation

five

Demonising the Dear

Identity and Violence in Vaasanthi's *The Silent Storm*

Amutha Charu Sheela

> What makes a fanatic? A fundamentalist?
> What makes communities that have lived together for years
> Suddenly discover a latent hatred for each other?
>
> – Githa Hariharan (2009: 67)

At the turn of the twentieth century, a new vision towards religion and politics started emerging rapidly around the globe. Religion and politics began to interact with each other. The erstwhile colonies that emerged as new nation-states after the retreat of colonial powers tried to forge an alliance between religion and nationalism. The attempt to accommodate religion in national politics is always fraught with dangers. Many religious activists see this as an attempt to marginalise religion. They also fear that the nation-state may compromise due to its allegiance to secular nationalism. They feel that the modern nation-state should be constructed on religious nationalism rather than secular nationalism.

In India too, after independence, nationalists tried to merge the absolutism of nationalism with absolutism of religion by proclaiming India as a secular nation. As both nationalism and religion are strong and respected, efforts to strike a balance became a subject of controversy within both religious and secular circles. The religious leaders thought religion may lose its exclusivity and its essential aspects in the new social order. They feared losing their autonomy. The upsurge of many religious movements and their anti-governmental activities warrant some of those fears.

The power struggle between these two ideologies—secular nationalism and religious nationalism—in the public space has unleashed violence.

In the 1980s, the whole of Punjab was engulfed in violence and Sikh militancy was on the ascendency. The fallout of the Punjab violence was felt in the national capital too when the Sikhs were mindlessly massacred after the assassination of the then Prime Minister Indira Gandhi. Though violence is condemned by everybody, people took sides. Some of them blamed the militants for their anti-social activities and some people held the Indian state responsible for inciting violence in Punjab. Both camps condemned each other for perpetrating violence. The present study analyses the purpose of violence, its effect on the local communities and how it has been justified by both the groups.

Foucault observed that every relationship of power contains a potential strategy of struggle. This struggle is concerned with the questions of who we are. It identifies the individuality of people, categorises them and attaches them to their identity. The ideologies of two opposing camps, the Indian state and the Sikh militants, suggest a form of power that subjugates and constitutes individuals 'as subject to someone else by control and dependence and tied to their own identity by a conscience or self-knowledge' (Foucault 1982: 212). Hence, they are in double bind. This new form of struggle is to combat subjection, forms of subjectivity and submission. To Foucault, investment in identity appears as one of the principal vehicles of subjection in the modern period. The novel chosen for this study, *The Silent Storm*, reiterates the fact that the illusion of a singular identity nurtures violence and generates the articulation of fear and hatred towards the other and their claim on the nation. Amartya Sen asserts that, 'The world is frequently taken to be a collection of religions (or of civilizations or culture) ignoring the other identities that people have and value, involving class, gender, profession, language, science, morals and politics' (Sen 2006: xvi).

The novel *The Silent Storm* is the English translation of a Tamil novel *Mauna Puyal* by Vaasanthi. Vaasanthi is a writer, journalist and columnist, and has written over 40 books including novels and short stories. She served as the chief editor of the Tamil edition of *India Today* for nine years. She has received many awards which include the Uttar Pradesh Sahitya Sanstham award, the Gyana Bharathi award and the best novel of the year award for her novel *Ammani*. She received Punjab government's Sahithya Academy Award for *Mouna Puyal*. The 1984 Sikh massacre prompted Vaasanthi to write this novel, which vividly portrays the cataclysmic events right from the rise of terrorism, the entry of armed forces into the Golden Temple, the assassination of Mrs Gandhi and its aftermath in the form of brutal killings of Sikhs in Delhi pogrom. She explores a macrocosm of public history within the microcosm of private history. By dredging and excavating the horrific memories and experiences of the common man, the novelist re-inscribes the effective histories of the subaltern into the national narrative. The novel describes in detail how the pogrom in Delhi wreaked havoc on the close relationship between two communities that had coexisted peacefully for centuries together. The story unfolds through the eyes of Ranjani, a Tamil journalist, who is in love with Manmohan Singh, a Sikh.

The novel opens with Ranjani watching television, which suddenly breaks news of an important announcement. This is followed by Prime Minister Indira Gandhi's address to the nation, which explains and justifies the actions she will undertake in the future in order to protect and safeguard the unity and integrity of the nation—she is left with no choice as it is being openly challenged. Though the announcement is vague, Ranjani senses an impending disaster. The next morning when all the newspaper headlines screamed, 'Army enters Golden temple' (Vaasanthi 1989: 8), Ranjani's fears multiply as she thinks of the enormity and repercussion of that action. She immediately thinks about her Punjabi friends Ruma and Manmohan Singh. She goes to Ruma's house which she finds unusually quiet. It is very much obvious that an ordinary Sikh family could not bear the news. Ruma is very much confused over the developments. Her comments, 'I don't think I've thought seriously about my religion or my community till yesterday … His anguish and my father's silent anger has made me realise something. I now knew that this is a very serious matter for us' (ibid.: 13) clearly imply that a rift has been created in the minds of the people and the difference is very much felt.

Manmohan Singh, who has leanings towards leftist philosophies and who claims himself as an atheist, is very deeply troubled by this news. He feels this as a suicidal move by the government as it hurts the sentiments of every Sikh who shares intimate ties with the Golden Temple, which cannot be easily understood by non-Sikhs. On his way back home by bus, he finds another Sikh passenger with his family. On seeing these two *sardarji*s, the crowd talks loudly, in order to be heard, supporting the prime minister's decision and criticising sardarjis, calling all of them 'henchmen' because consider a murderer Bhindranwale as their religious leader—hence the words, 'No sardarji can be trusted, if you ask me' (ibid.: 17). The novel underscores the fact that ethnic and religious minorities have to undergo this test of nationalism. 'Modern nationalism grants its religious and ethnic minorities either to assimilate into the dominant nationalist culture or to be charged with the familiar accusation of treachery or disloyalty' (Kumar 2008: 111). Suddenly, Manmohan Singh feels that he and his fellow Sikh family have become aliens and outsiders. Vaasanthi provides another evocative instance which shows how a house is divided against itself because of the army's entry inside the Golden temple. Ranjani's friend Kishore tells Ranjani that a wall has sprung up within his house between his Sikh mother, who has not eaten anything since she heard the news, and his Hindu father who feels the government has acted rightly though he has not uttered anything openly.

Even people who are least affected by all these happenings are forced to take sides. Rupa, wife of writer Trilok Singh, warns him not to forget his Sikh identity when he gives an interview to the press. He muses:

> Don't forget the fact that you are a Sikh. That was a three hundred year-old constraint—the constraint of the five K's. The need of the tributary to assert its differences, its separateness from its parent river. But Rupa was right. Not to assert that difference may mean a threat to your life. The Government has made a fool of every Sikh now. Humiliating me within my own house, a well planned move. (Vaasanthi 1989: 21)

Suddenly, religious identity seemed to take precedence over all other identities. Trilok Singh finds himself believing that when the whole world wants a clear identity, a neutral position will not work. He desires a singular identity to safeguard and protect him, and identifying with a particular sect can provide this much-needed security. Though identity strengthens the confidence of people, communal identity is always fraught with dangers. Amartya Sen says, 'Identity can also kill and kill with abandon' (2006: 1). Ranjani, who interviewed him, is very shocked to find him supporting religious fundamentalists instead of giving solutions to reduce the tension. He also defended piling up arms inside a place of worship using the rationale that Sikhs are a martial race who always carry and worship arms. 'This obsession with the identity uses past to legitimise the political requirements of the present' (Hariharan 2003: 132).

April 1984

The focus of narration shifts from Delhi to Punjab—which had become a boiling cauldron in the past few months. Vaasanthi uses fiction to explore the events of historical significance of this event that tore the secular fabric of India, fusing chronicles with accounts of the events that lead to the entry of troops into the Golden temple.

The symbiotic and syncretic nature of Punjab's civilisation and its grim present spectre are seen through the eyes of Gurucharan Singh, a theatre person who surveys the street in Amritsar at 6.40 AM, a few months before the army's action in the Golden Temple.

> It never used to be so dull and sad on this street. The noise and bustle of devotees heading for the temple would wake even the soundest of sleepers by four o'clock. But now a fanatic had his seat inside the temple, people had become wary of their devotion. The Golden Temple had been a common bond between Hindus and Sikhs, they shared a natural devotion born of a common culture. Intermarriage between the communities was quite common. Hindu families would sometimes dedicate their eldest sons to the gurudwara by converting them into Sikhs … . But now this bigot was bent on destroying the glorious heritage of Punjab. Hindus and Sikhs alike, anyone who opposed him had been made to taste the limits of terror. The Akalis were keeping quiet. And the Government seemed merely to be watching the fun. (Vaasanthi 1989: 29)

Bhindranwale was accused of spreading of terror in the name of religion, killing anyone who spoke against him. Akali Dal leader Sant Longowal says in his anguish, 'One does not know whose turn it will be next. All Punjab has become a slaughter house' (ibid.: 37).

The violence that erupted in the 1980s had its roots in earlier movements for Sikh autonomy and a separate state. There was a clash between a group of Sikhs and the Nirankari, a breakaway sect from the Sikh tradition that Bhindranwale, a young rural preacher, considered inappropriate as they worshipped a living guru. He was arrested for the alleged murder of the publisher of a chain of Hindu newspapers in Punjab. At the same time, militancy grew in the state. The violence had begun to engulf Punjab. He was scared that Sikhs would lose their identity. The notion of 'minority' in the hands of jingoists and religious zealots can be used as a deadly weapon to control or manipulate, and such labelling becomes a means of differentiation and exclusion. It feeds on misunderstandings and prejudice. Violence is the corollary of sharply disparate identities. To D. E. Smith, the term '[c]ommunalism as it is used in India today refers to the functioning of religious communities or organisations which claim to represent them in a way which is detrimental to the interests of other groups or of the nation as a whole' (quoted in Ludden 2005: 242). A strong sense of belonging to one particular group, spawns the carnage. Other identifications such as Indian, sub-continental, members of the human race give way to newly detected belligerent identities. Nobel laureate Amartya Sen is of the view that neglecting various identities of people makes the world more flammable. He warns, 'violence is fomented by the imposition of singular and belligerent identities on gullible people, championed by proficient artisans of terror' (Sen 2006: 2).

At the same time, Bhindranwale, the Sikh leader, tried to establish strong religious identity which would pare people to a single dimension, a religious identity, thus excluding all their other identities about them. He proclaims, 'I was born to redeem our religion. It happened one Baisakhi's day six years ago when there was that fight between our people and the Nirankaris. Sixteen of our people were killed that day—I felt a changed man then and saw my path—a different path—clearly before me' (Vaasanthi 1989: 43).

When Gurucharan Singh accused him of spreading terror by inflaming communal speeches, which prove no good to Punjab, Bhindranwale justified the reasons for possessing arms. He firmly stated, as quoted by Vaasanthi:

> It is every Sikh's birth-right to possess arms. How dare they prevent [us] from doing so? My weapons are not just to protect myself but to protect my faith. Remember what Guru Gobind said: 'The best death is that which comes while protecting onc's rcligion' (Vaasanthi 1989: 39 40).

Religion legitimises violence which is empowering. In the context of Algeria's war of independence, French philosopher Frantz Fanon in his *The Wretched of the Earth* argues, 'even a small display of violence can have immense symbolic power by jolting the masses into an awareness of their own potency' (quoted in Juergensmeyer 1994: 170). Most of the social revolutions in the world are rooted in violence and seem to have been inspired by violence. It has its analogue in Islamic, Jewish, Sinhalese and many other traditions. The marginalised, who were powerless earlier, feel empowered with the use of violence. Bhindranwale's call to fight and defend the faith jolted the whole of Punjab. Sikhs, who are socially marginalised, especially village people, who have not tasted power, developed a sense of belonging to Bhindranwale. By resorting to violence cloaked within a garb of morality, the young religious radicals challenge the state and 'claims power on behalf of those who previously had been impotent and ignored by those in power' (Juergensmeyer 1994: 170).

In the novel, Vaasanthi deftly portrays people's religiosity through various incidents. Gurucharan Singh, who warns of these fiery religious speeches, is rather pained at the thought that 'these simpletons will listen only to the absurdities blaring out of the Manji Sahib (assembly hall) inside the temple' (Vaasanthi 1989: 30).

The conversation between Manmohan Singh and Saint Longowal that '[o]ur village folks, they cannot be approached except through the Gurudwaras' (ibid.: 36) underscores the fact that the villagers are completely beholden to gurdwaras. The reason behind large numbers of village folks identifying themselves with Bhindranwale is that he struck the right chord—religion—to consolidate his strong base among the villagers. He chose the right place—temple—to reach out to the masses. Through his sermons he implored his young radicals to defend the religion—Sikhism—to protect the oppressed. He was not only against Hindus; but he is also against atheists, Marxists and secularists. When his aide Amrik Singh gives him the details about Gurucharan Singh, an atheist and Marxist, Bhindranwale comments, 'It is the growth of this sort of people that weakens our religion. Every change in our appearances, every change in our ideas, spells danger for us. Any Sikh who does not follow Guru Gobind Singh's instruction is unfit to be called a Sikh' (ibid.: 46). With anguish Vaasanthi observes that the two intertwined and intermarrying communities have suddenly become estranged because of all these extremist positions. But the driver of Gurucharan Singh's van expresses hope that people will not support violence and that not all the people were carried by the evil wind that was blowing. He shares a poignant instance that 'three Hindu families who had been living there for forty years fled after hearing about massacre of Hindus in other places. But the Sikh elders of the village brought them back, assuring them they would not be harmed' (ibid.: 31). Gurucharan Singh trails off doubtfully that such things would have happened earlier, but people might change in future. Vaasanthi opines that words can incite violence, make people turn against one another, thus alienating them. By constantly telling the devotees that, 'Some groups are inferior, evil, satanic or condemned by god, religions encourage the demonising of others and their social death, making their slaughter seem inconsequential, justified or even required' (Jones 2008: 157).

Most of the terror tentacles were also spread by the state authorities themselves. The police's troubling of the masses, especially the young boys, sparked a conflict between the common people and state-led institutions, thereby leading to the rise to of extreme positions. Eventually, Bhindranwale was projected as someone so dangerously powerful that Prime Minister Indira Gandhi decided to send troops—'Operation Bluestar'—to flush out militants from the Golden Temple. The Golden Temple is the most respected seat for the Sikhs who are emotionally attached to it. The military operation killed many people, including innocent worshippers as well as Bhindranwale. Much against the Sikh sentiments, this incident led to distrust among the Sikh community that was horrified at the act of army stomping upon their holy places. The entire Sikh community, including moderate and impartial persons like Manmohan Singh and Gurucharan Singh, condemn the army action. All the Sikhs feel humiliated and insulted by the army's entry, their presence inside the temple and the damage caused to it. Ranjani is terribly shocked when her Punjabi friend Ruma's grandfather declares that he has decided to wear a black turban until the shame is wiped off.

Manmohan Singh is scared of the massive repercussions that this move would bring in. Gurucharan Singh opines that 'this is not tragedy of Punjab, beti, but it is an Indian tragedy' (Vaasanthi 1989: 74) James W. Jones, when he talks about the psychology of religious violence in his *Blood That Cries Out from the Earth*, opines:

> Religion also strengthens feelings of shame and humiliation and the longing for revenge ... Such psychological process as shame and humiliation, splitting and seeing the world in Black and White terms, along with the inability to tolcrate ambivalence and the dynamics of projection and demonising the other all contribute to violence. (2008: 17)

Operation Blue Star, as Manmohan Singh feared, widened the rift between the two communities. Though not all were fanatics and in a murderous frenzy, they expected a reaction which would avenge this act. Their worst fear came true with the assassination of Prime Minister Indira Gandhi by her own bodyguards, an outcome of collective fury.

As Trilok Singh rambled:

> The ordinary Sikh is not politically aware. But Operation Blue Star was interpreted as an assault on every Sikh home. Sikhs then began to think of themselves as a different community. They are not likely to listen to any justification for that assault. And once they had pinned the responsibility for the assault on somebody, no power in the world could have saved that individual. Their anger needed an outlet ... In far off times, men and animals used to be sacrificed to appease the anger of the gods. But now it is a community that has demanded a sacrifice to appease its collective anger. (Vaasanthi 1989: 123–124)

This collective fury was also projected as turning the lonely lady Mrs Gandhi into a scapegoat. The scapegoat mechanism assumes that the victim is the root cause of all evils, a virus that contaminates the system and potential source of conflict which should be removed to cleanse the system. Jones contends that this theology of purification is a falsehood as it turns a blind eye to the actual cause of violence, that is, desire and rivalry. Jones comments that

> this sense of purification as the elimination of the supposed source of the problem—the core of the scapegoating mechanism—is at the heart of religiously motivated terrorism because it is central to many of theologies of purification found in the world's religions. Such theologies of purification easily slide into justification for genocide and terrorism and are a major way religion contributes to terrorism. (2008: 151)

As soon as the news spread, people started abusing and agitating against the Sikhs. Ranjani sensed the brewing trouble, the worst communal violence. The people were bewildered, tense and afraid. Mob violence broke out. Sardars were targeted. Houses and shops of Sikhs had been plundered. Charred vehicles had become a common sight. Shyam Kishore, photographer of the magazine in which Ranjani was working, recollected the ghastly events that happened before his eyes. '"I still can't believe it," he continued, "wherever the train stopped, they got in pulled out the Sardarjis and..." He stared ahead, trying to come to terms with his own shock. "Beat them, cut off their beards knocked off their turbans and burnt them...' (Vaasanthi 1989: 90).

Radhakrishnan, the editor on his way to commissioner's office to report on the massive violence in Mongolpuri and Kalyanpuri areas, saw a few people being burnt alive. Manmohan Singh, who spent three sleepless nights, 'was prey to an amalgam of fear, grief and other nameless emotions ... His parents—not only his parents, all Sikhs—had reached the limits of fear—the fear of death' (Vaasanthi 1989: 95). One of the purposes of violence unleashed against innocent individuals who were members of a group deemed to be the rival was to threaten the entire group and not let them assume that they would live in peace there. Many of Manmohan Singh's relatives are killed, their houses looted and their beards shaved off. Manmohan too decides to cut his hair and shave his beard so that he will not be identified as a Sikh when he goes out. Manmohan's decision to shed his religious identity exposes the failure of the secular policies and law which were framed by the elite nationalists at the time of independence to ensure a safe and secure future of its citizens.

One of the main reasons for the incidence of the communal violence is the political advantage to be gained. Jones observes that the scapegoat mechanism, by fixing the victim as the guilty, turns a blind eye to 'the actual cause of violence—desire and rivalry' (Jones 2008: 151). In the beginning, the communal violence appeared as the natural outcome of people's anger against the assassination. After careful analysis, the Sikhs felt that this orgy of violence was a calculated move to wipe out their community. Manmohan Singh feels that the savage brutalities seem to be the handiwork of experienced professional marauders who tried to exploit the confused situation. He accuses the politicians of instigating and perpetrating violence for their personal gains. It highlights the painful fact that the political leaders are very safe, without getting affected by the violence, whereas common innocent civilians are highly unsafe and become the scapegoats for the political leaders' wrongdoings. Vaasanthi's lines—'we are the ones to pay the price for our leaders' sins. Not even the tip of their finger nails would be chipped off. Don't ask why scape goats have always been an essential feature of human society' (1989: 104)—imply the scapegoat has deep psychological roots. Splitting or creating a rift seems to be at work behind the dance of destruction. Jones clarifies that:

> A person or community weighed down by guilt, shame or humiliation can come to feel pure and purposeful by scapegoating another, expelling those feelings by projecting them onto another and finally being rid of the feelings by getting rid of the scapegoats in acts of terror and genocide. (2008: 152)

Violence is the upshot of these disparate identities which try to assert their supremacy over the other.

Violence in the name of religion has claimed many innocent lives. Home and state are spaces where violence exists. It is a repulsive force that exists around religious, linguistic and ethnic identities, as Ludden comments:

> Communalism is alive in everyday politics that invokes community identity—in the streets, courts, media, election, religious and cultural institutions schools, academic research and intimate conversations—anywhere that people can be influenced to form their identities and public opinions around oppositional, ethnic or religious categories. Its most dramatic moments are massively organised public spectacles and

> elections which in India engage society widely and directly and which animate competitions for power in Indian Constitutional democracy. (2005: 13)

Manmohan bemoans the fact that violence has grown deep roots in every sphere of society, thus eroding social values. With profound despair, he speaks of how the society has become so immune to various forms of violence that have permeated our society.

> We are accustomed to living with violence. After all, this is a society that had accepted untouchability as normal. This is a society that turns blind eye to the atrocities committed against women; to the criminal acts of the police and to countless other things. Violence has become a necessary weapon needed in day-to-day life. (Vaasanthi 1989: 104)

Violence has not only occupied the public space but has also intruded the personal space. Rupa's fiancée, Arim was brutally burnt alive inside his car. When she tells her close friend Ranjani that she would not say a single word against Hindus and would not let them down as she was also a Hindu, Ranjani feels aghast and she does not know how to condole her. Ranjani is even advised by her friends to end her relationship with Manmohan Singh as they believe Sikhs are not to be trusted. Ranjit, Ranjani's friend who has married a Sikh, too expresses his fear that 'walls have risen between them now. Nobody dares to extend a hand across the wall. It has happened in my house, Manmohan. I may end up with a divorce, I am afraid' (Vaasanthi 1989: 72). At the end, Manmohan Singh too rejects Ranjani's marriage proposal, stating that he wants to work for the state till a peaceful atmosphere is restored.

Gurucharan Singh, who went to Golden Temple, saw no life or laughter there. 'It was evident that the November riots in Delhi had made Hindus and Sikhs enemies' (Vaasanthi 1989: 133). The rift runs too deep. Amartya Sen feels violence can be instigated by reducing individuals to the single status of religion.

> A great many person's identities as Indians, as sub continentals, as Asians or as members of the human race, seemed to give way—quite suddenly—to sectarian identification with Hindu, Muslim or Sikh communities. The carnage that followed had much to do with elementary herd behaviour by which people were made to discover these newly detected belligerent identities, without the process to critical examination. The same people were suddenly different. (Sen 2006: 10)

These comments by Sen demonstrate the transformation at the personal, social and political levels. The centrality of identity gains prominence depending on the issue at stake. But at present, religious identity is projected as the dominant identity.

The state is also blamed for inciting violence in civil society. Whenever the state uses its brutal force to suppress civil unrest, it resorts to violence. In Weber's view, 'the monopoly over legitimate violence in a society is the very definition of a state' (quoted in Juergensmeyer 1994: 33). The state's inability to maintain its neutrality also triggers violence. The allegations that the state is under the control of rival communities also incite violence. When Radhakrishnan and Shyamkrishnan went to the police station to report the anti-Sikh violence in Trilokpuri, the sub-inspector calmly replied that he had not received any such reports and he refused to send a police team as he did not have enough police personnel. When Radhakrishnan went to the commissioner's office to report on the emergency situation, the commissioner was not available and the policeman who was there curtly refused, saying he was on leave. These kinds of situations enhance the feeling among the public that there is a nexus between the police and the mobsters during these massacres, and the state's corrupt force cannot be trusted. It emphasises that the state has failed to give protection to the minorities, which is guaranteed to them by law.

Vaasanthi does not stop with merely registering the events, she goes one step ahead and tries to find the epicentre of this hatred towards each other. The reasons are numerous, but Partition could be the founding trauma for crimes against humanity in the name of religion. The cinders of the divide-and-rule policy among various religions promoted by the British rulers, which culminated in the partition of India along religious lines, remains responsible for many communal flare-ups. It was thought that such divisions would never recur and they had become a thing of the past. But the mass violence that sparked off after Operation Blue Star and the November pogrom after the assassination of Indira Gandhi made people acutely aware of the ghostly presence of Partition, which looms large even today. As critic Priya Kumar observes, 'Memories of Partition violence have inevitably seeped into their consciousness, shaping and informing their self-definition and ways of being in the world especially for the population of those regions that were directly impacted by the event' (2008: 94).

The communal carnage at Delhi compelled Trilok Singh, the writer, to recall the dark days of Partition that he had experienced 37 years prior. 'Once again, he experienced the fear, the sorrow and the despair of partition, when he had to leave Lahore just because he was a Sikh ... When his Sikh friends now talked of another partition, those thirty-seven-year old memories returned to haunt him' (Vaasanthi 1989: 121). Manmohan feared that communal carnage against Sikhs in the national capital would force them to migrate to Punjab in search of security and they would demand autonomy—another spectre of partition. Both Hindus and Sikhs struggled and suffered together at the time of Partition. But now the pogrom against Sikhs in the national capital made them move away from Hindus. When Manmohan Singh told his friend Bhaskar that two of his cousins were killed when they were waiting for an army truck to take them to the army-run refugee camps, Bhaskar sympathised with Sikhs for 'becoming refugees in one's own country' (Vaasanthi 1989: 106). Vaasanthi's description of ghettoisation points out a growing sense of alienation and insecurity among Sikhs due to religious intolerance. Thus, Vaasanthi exposes the failure of the administration in its treatment of the citizens of independent India and the hypocrisy of secular religious freedom practised in the country.

Another factor she analyses is the historical reason that led to such violence. She traces its roots to thoughts rooted in religious conditioning, which have strands of violence. As Trilok Singh says, 'thoughts sow the seeds of action. The thoughts of violence, then the cult of violence' (Vaasanthi 1989: 124). He adds that though Buddhism condemns ritual sacrifice, animal sacrifice is still in existence in a different form, 'a goat would be made out of dough and then cut ritually! The point is not whether you cut a live goat or a dough-goat, but what led you to the act of killing in the first instance. There lies the basic impulse of cruelty ...' (Vaasanthi 1989: 124). A spate of studies attests to the fact that most significant religious events like crucifixion of Jesus, epic battles in Mahabharata and Ramayana in Hinduism, religious wars described in the Sinhalese Buddhist Pali chronicles, the sacrifice of Guru Teghbahadar in Sikhism, martyrdom of Hussain in Islam are stained with blood and clearly indicate that violence occupies the central space of religion, which greatly influences the thinking of human race.

Another most important reason the author cites is failure of the people to condemn the violence when it is inflicted on others. When Manmohan

Singh's mother saw his short hair, she broke down in tears, questioning why innocent people were being tortured. He replied in an exasperated voice, 'Those who killed Hindus in Punjab were the terrorists of our community, why don't you feel ashamed of that? He who had taken an oath to safeguard her life has taken it away—all in the name of your religion why don't you grieve for that?' (Vaasanthi 1989: 97). Trilok Singh blamed himself for this state of affairs. He felt, 'Every Sikh who remained silent when he ought to have spoken was to blame, though on one including himself would be prepared to admit it openly. He had to don a mask of indifference in order to protect himself from his own herd (Vaasanthi 1989: 121).

Vaasanthi tries to prove that 'Violence breeds violence' (1989: 102). Though many radical religious movements advocate the use of violence to establish identity, many members of those movements who share the same ideals do not resort to violence, instead they are committed to democratic means of achieving things. In the novel, the characters of Manmohan Singh and Gurucharan Singh hold proof to the fact that still many people repose their faith in the government machinery, educated elite and achieving things through peaceful means.

Arun Shourie, an eminent Indian journalist and politician, also insists that people should focus on the commonalities among them rather than the features which differentiate them from one another. He says Gandhi and Nehru focused on the common attributes among the people to unite India whereas Jinnah believed that since there are differences people cannot live together peacefully. He bemoans:

> In one type of politics, the whole is the focus in the other parts are – to the point that the 'reality', the very existence of the whole is denied, the very notion that it exists is denounced as a device which has been fabricated to crush the parts one by one. Our politics since Jinnah's time, and even more so since the passing of Panditji has been of the latter kind. (Shourie 1997: 23)

The novel poignantly picturises the wounded psyche of Sikhs, their rage and their sadness. The narration demonstrates that violence, which is highly destructive, has spread its tentacles to all spheres of society. Its presence is felt at home, in the public place and in politics. In their struggle to identify their place in society, both majority and minority communities have not attacked the respective leaders; instead, common people have become the victims. The clash between the religious identity and national identity has proved destructive and disturbed the equilibrium. Violence in the name of religion has always dichotomised society and demonised the other. In developing nations which are multi-religious, where globalisation and modernisation are operating, religion still serves as a site for identity struggle.

Vaasanthi's novel also underscores the idea how the people of Punjab and people in the national capital want to put an end to terrorism. They welcomed the Punjab accord, the treaty signed between the Centre and the state. 'In the next few days it was evident that, in Delhi, the people supported the Punjab accord wholeheartedly. Ranjani's father called it the greatest achievement since independence' (Vaasanthi 1989: 151). The people of Punjab considered this accord as a victory for the Akalis and they believed that terrorism would slowly recede. It is very important to identify ourselves with others in various possible ways for a peaceful living. In a parliamentary debate about the mass violence against Sikhs after Mrs Gandhi's assassination by her Sikh bodyguards, the then Indian Prime Minister Manmohan Singh told Parliament, 'I have no hesitation in apologising not only to the Sikh community but to the whole Indian nation because what took place in 1984 is the negation of the concept of nationhood and what is enshrined in our constitution' (quoted in Sen 2006: 168). Here Manmohan Singh's multiple identities—as prime minister of India, leader of the Congress party, member of the Sikh community and citizen of India—are very much in prominence. There are many identities other than religious identity that are crucial for a person's relationship with other people who belong to different backgrounds in a pluralistic country like India. As Sen rightly says, 'The prospects of peace in the contemporary world may well lie in the use of reasoning as common inhabitants of a wide world, rather than making us into inmates rigidly incarcerated in little container' (2006: xvii).

References

Foucault, Michel. 1982. 'The Subject and Power'. In *Beyond Structuralism and Hermeneutics*, eds H. Drefus and P. Rainbow, 208–26. Chicago: University of Chicago Press.

Hariharan, Githa. 2003. *In Times of Siege*. New Delhi: Penguin.

———. 2009. *Fugitive Histories*. New Delhi: Penguin.

Jones, James W. 2008. *Blood That Cries Out from the Earth: The Psychology of Religious Terrorism*. New York: Oxford University Press.

Juergensmeyer, Mark. 1994. *Religious Nationalism Confronts the Secular State*. Delhi: Oxford University Press.

Kumar, Priya. 2008. *Limiting Secularism: The Ethics of Coexistence in Indian Literature and Films*. Minnesota: The University of Minnesota Press.

Ludden, David E. 2005. *Making India Hindu*. Oxford University Press: The University of Michigan.

Sen, Amartya. 2006. *Identity and Violence: The Illusion of Destiny*. London: Penguin Group.

Shourie, Arun.1997. *A Secular Agenda: For Saving Our Country, for Welding It*. New Delhi: HarperCollins.

Vaasanthi. 1989. *The Silent Storm*, tr. Gomathi Narayanan. Madras: Affiliated East-West Press Pvt. Ltd.

six

It was a Dog's Life

Evocation in Gurvinder Singh's Movie *Chauthi Koot*

Jasmine Anand

In Punjab, 1984 was a year of curfew, religious extremism, trouble, Sikh militancy, religio-political movement led by Sant Jarnail Singh Bhindranwale and his killing in Operation Blue Star, a four-day military operation by the then Prime Minister Indira Gandhi, culminating in her death five months later. It was an eclipsed time when all lines of communication were severed and transportation in and out of Punjab came to a halt. The press was censored and Punjab grew isolated not only from India but rest of the world too. The turn of events led to deaths of numerous militants and soldiers, consequent rounding up and killing of innocent Sikhs, and the ensuing anti-Sikh riots in Delhi and various other parts of India.

In Punjab, this was another period of death and destruction after the catastrophe of India's Partition and Independence in 1947. Following the assassination of Indira Gandhi, bearded and turbaned Sikhs were savagely and ferociously attacked by Hindus in Punjab and surrounding areas. The *New York Times* reported:

> Soldiers were ordered to shoot rioters on sight in New Delhi and five other cities … Curfews were also imposed in 30 cities … More than 150 people have been killed and 1,000 hurt since Wednesday … Most of the deaths and injuries were believed to have resulted from attacks by the majority Hindus on Sikhs in revenge for the slaying of Mrs. Gandhi. (Stevens 1984)

After Operation Blue Star, the Khalistani Sikhs undertook their militant activities under the wings of scared and fearsome Sikhs who were traumatised to give their consent to support and shelter these militants.

Mark Tully in his 'Note to Readers', appended to his book *Amritsar: Mrs. Gandhi's Last Battle*, co-authored with Satish Jacob, writes:

> Amritsar, Mrs Gandhi's last battle, was not a battle against the Sikhs, a community Mrs Gandhi always regarded with great affection. It was a battle in which infantry, armour and artillery were used against a small group of Sikhs who had fortified the Golden Temple complex and used it as a base from which to defy the authority of the Indian government. The tragedy is that many Sikhs do not accept this definition. (2011: ix)

This version of history looks quite neutral and orientalist in appeal. It operates as an apparatus of the state's ideological machinery, obscuring complexities and suppressing dissenting voices to construct an illusion of seamless coherence and unquestionable authority. The language used—particularly the phrase 'a battle in which infantry, armour and artillery were used against a small group of Sikhs'—places the focus on the state's military response without interrogating the larger political, historical and ideological structures that led to the confrontation. The phrase 'a small group of Sikhs' depoliticises the insurgents by presenting them as a minor faction rather than engaging with their ideological or socio-political grievances. The assertion that 'Mrs. Gandhi always regarded [the Sikh community] with great affection' functions as a rhetorical strategy that distances her actions from communal antagonism, thereby obscuring the broader context of Sikh political aspirations and state repression. Furthermore, the statement that 'many Sikhs do not accept this definition' acknowledges the existence of alternative perspectives but does not engage with them critically. From an orientalist standpoint, this can be seen as an implicit othering of Sikh narratives, positioning them as reactionary or subjective in contrast to the ostensibly objective state narrative. More than the tragedy of definition, the ensuing communal violence led to enormous humiliation, frustration, rage, a sense of betrayal, suffering, looting, rapes, murders and arson; thus creating an environment of silence, mutation, mistrust, anxiety, fear and paranoia in Sikhs as well as Hindus.

Here, an alternative reference to history by Joyce Pettigrew mentioned in the book *The Sikhs of the Punjab: Unheard Voices of State and Guerrilla Violence* catches one's attention:

> The army went into Darbar Sahib not to eliminate a political figure or a political movement but to suppress the culture of a people, to attack their heart, to strike a blow at their spirit and self-confidence. (1995: 8)

It reveals how a religious minority was viewed as a threat to the Indian nationhood and Sikhs were equated with 'anti-nationals'. Not denying the fact that to create a moderate Hindu nation the Congress tried to plant Bhindranwale who would defeat Akali Dal, who aimed for a sovereign Sikh state (Khalistan); this was a risk to the secularity or to the moderate appeal of India as a nation.

Jarnail Singh Bhindranwale remains a deeply polarising figure in Punjab's history, viewed by some as a defender of Sikh principles and by others as a symbol of extremism. Politically, he was initially supported by the Congress to counter the Akali Dal in electoral battles. His ideological stance, rooted in a strict interpretation of Sikh values, led him and his followers to resist any perceived threats to religious identity, and their actions eventually escalated to militant activity. These actions were increasingly framed by the state as targeting Punjabi Hindus during the early 1980s, contributing to heightened communal tensions. Paradoxically, the very political forces that once fostered his rise later perceived him as a threat, ultimately resulting in widespread unrest across Punjab and triggering a broader national crisis. To crush him, the Indian army on the instructions of the Central government attacked him inside the Golden Temple, where he was residing and propagating anti-Hindu speeches in June 1984, which led to both sacrilege and massacre inside the pious complex. This episode greatly accentuated Hindu–Sikh tensions within Punjab during that time. The followers of Bhindranwale were called *Khalistani*s or *Amritdhari*s.[1]

In contrast, Bhindranwale was also seen a 'saviour and a saint' for the women and children of Punjab as he saved the 'Sikh peasantry from the rack and ruin' coming with the success of the Green Revolution and its resultant intoxication (Singh 2003: 44). To quote Khushwant Singh's *The End of India*:

> The Bhindranwale chapter in Indian history is a perfect illustration of the disastrous results of not keeping politics separate from religion. Bhindranwale was a creation of the Congress and the Akalis. Indira Gandhi was advised by Zail Singh that this small-time kattar (hardline) Sikh preacher should be built up as a leader to counter the ruling Akalis in Punjab. Later, the Akalis tried to woo Bhindranwale away from their rivals and propped him up. Sant Longowal once described him as saadda danda (our stick) to beat the Congress government with. … Believe it or not, one main reason for the rise of Bhindranwale was the prosperity that came to Punjab with the Green Revolution. With prosperity came sudden

> changes, Western influences, a crisis of identity, and degeneration—alcoholism, smoking, drug addiction, gambling, blue films, fornication. … On this scene came Bhindranwale preaching against these evils and carried on a vigorous campaign of 'Amritprachar'. [Sikhs] did not break their oath. Money previously squandered was saved. Time previously wasted in drink and drugs was now spent on more careful tillage—bringing more money. (2003: 43–44)

This short introductory section sets the tone of 'it was a dog's life' (pun intended) with the hard times of the year 1984. The parallel between the unpleasant and difficult life of humans and a dog (a significant character in the movie *Chauthi Koot*) metaphorically become synonymous with the grind of the 1980s. The fragmentary appeal of the movie and doddering assimilation of the narrative echo the implied narrative and the evocative technique used by Gurvinder Singh in his movie *Chauthi Koot*. The various paths of turbulence and gorging repression and terror have found their factual and figurative accounts through oral story-telling, reportage and fictional accounts of gruesome brutality. But *Chauthi Koot* (The Fourth Direction), a '[combination of] two short stories ["The Fourth Direction" or *Chauthi Koot*, and "I'm Feeling Fine Now" or *Main hun theek thak haan*] by the Sahitya Akademi Award–winning author and co-scriptwriter Waryam Singh Sandhu, is an insightful and artfully restrained study of the psychology of fear, and the violence and poisonous suspicion [unleashing] within households and communities [during the period of 1984 in Punjab]' (Kappal 2016). The movie quietly narrates the veiled times of Punjab's insurgency with its forgotten silence and gestures of very local, insignificant mortals *sans* overt violence and bloodshed. The movie, using non-actors and few theatre artists, without being judgemental or biased, being evocative than direct, presents alternate narrative of Punjab without the clichés of *bhangra*[2] and spectacle. It was screened at the Un Certain Regard section at the 2015 Cannes Film Festival and won the Golden Gateway of India Trophy at MAMI Film Festival in Bombay. It was also felicitated as the 'Best Asian Feature Film' at Singapore International Film Festival. In 2016, the movie won the National Award for the best feature in Punjabi language.

Cinema is an audio-visual and spatio-temporal medium of exploration of movement. Conventionally, making a movie means recording of moving images and sounds. Less frequently, some thought is given to recording the non-kinetic expression of stillness and silence—this is what *Chauthi Koot* is all about. The phrase 'stillness in motion' used by film historian Walter

Kerr (1979) can be associated with Gurvinder Singh's endeavour. As the movie progresses, we encounter the sharp stillness, the mystery of silence and sombre dark notes with a marked absence of overacted rhetoric. Gurvinder proves Luis Bunuel dictum, 'Mystery, the essential element of any work of art, is for the most part lacking in films' (Campbell 2017). The cinematic poetry of mystery comes to the surface in the movie and shows itself, according to Dibakar Banerjee, 'Without any excess and with masterful restraint… Villain *nahi hai*. Yet *tension hai* [There is no villain, yet there is tension]'; it turns this 'tragedy' into a 'thriller' (Chatterjee 2016). There is no overt use of menace or violence; rather, it is subtly done in a Hitchcockian[3] style where fear has to rise from the mind and not through actions. The movie is not formulaic but non-linear. Gurvinder fuses two stories along with flashback technique to create his canvas. For him, 'Diversifying the narrative sheds dominance of characters and the result is a multiplicity of emotions and perspectives' (Sahi 2016). For references to the storyline and to evoke certain emotive cadences, the English subtitles of the film have been quoted in this chapter.

The film is based around a specific time period; hence, it deliberately plays with many extended shots and its pace is slow. Eschewing the usual 50mm lens, cinematographer Satya Rai Nagpaul employed 28mm and 35mm long lenses to create his eloquent images and capture an introspective material atmosphere. When we use a 28mm lens, it is as much about the subject that we are shooting as it is their background, their surroundings and their context. In this we cannot use 'bokeh', that is, soft out of focus background; hence, we will be careful with the frame and can capture a larger narrative in a frame. It artistically leads the eye of the viewer while focusing on the subject. It captures a frame within a frame and works well with angles to create a great composition. On the other hand, the 35mm lens lends a crisp view of the subject as it captures a tighter angle of view, making the subject more precise and immediate. It helps in capturing the whole story without any distortion and can also use bokeh to centre-spot the subject or image. Where 50mm will focus just on 'who' in the story, 35mm helps in answering all the 5Ws and 1H (what, why, when, where, who, and how), allowing for a more holistic narrative and thus adding more to the evocative element of the film.

The movie encompasses three journeys that are levied with fear—the train journey; flashbacks to the journey of Jugal along with his wife and daughter one night; and the rite of passage of Joginder Singh, his family and pet dog Tommy. The movie begins with a notification regarding the storming of the Golden Temple and assassination of Indira Gandhi. In addition, the portrayal of Khalistani Sikh militants, mention of the city of Amritsar and the radio news within the movie situates the movie within the time frame of 1984. Apart from this, the darkness of the 1980s looms large in the worried faces of the travellers as they stare into oblivion and sneak shifty glances at their co-passengers.

The impending apocalypse foreshadows itself at the outset with the irony of a romantic Punjabi folk song playing in the bus, the stern and sullen faces of the people travelling, and the front windscreen of the bus with blurred outer images in mist contrasting with a clear picture of Guru Nanak Sahib inside the bus. The fog-like image symbolises the era unaccounted for with blurred understanding of people regarding religion and their mistrust of each other. One is alarmed to see very few women in the bus and lack of communication among fellow passengers resonating the fear-ridden age.

The two Hindu men, Jugal and Raj, travel on a rickety bus in Punjab in order to land at the railway station of Ferozpur Cantt. We see them running, and then struggling to catch their breath, confused at having missed their train to Amritsar. This is then followed by the cadence of steps of marching policemen wearing tall black boots, armed with rifles, hinting at state interference and security check. The danger lurking around and blood in the air manifests through the red glittering reflection of the train in the background of the policemen. The first eight minutes have no distinct dialogue but diegetic sounds of a dog barking, noise of shoes rubbing, chanting of Sikh *mool mantra*[4] by a monk, and the horn of an arriving train with its piston slapping. At the ninth minute, we see Jugal hesitantly asking people around him (snipping his fingers and clearing his throat) whether the train would leave for Amritsar. With a negation from every side, he sits back in dejection, and is then approached by a Sikh gentleman who also wants to leave for Amritsar.

The Sikh gentleman reveals that the train is definitely bound for Amritsar but shall leave empty. The policemen get onto the train, going from compartment to compartment, closing the windows. The metal shutters fall with staccato sounds akin to gunfire shots. The long shot of secluded platform turns into mid close shot of despair, when the three of them ask for help from an elderly Sikh policeman who refuses and says, 'How do I know who you are? How can anyone be trusted. There are strict orders that the train should go empty.' Raj again asks him to help them. They are then told to contact the guard of the train. The guard in turn tells

Jugal, 'I understand your problem. But how can I take responsibility given the prevailing situation? Who wants to risk one's job … or even one's life? Sorry, I cannot help you.' Jugal forces his way into the moving train and appeals to the guard that they were his Hindu brothers and he must help them. Jugal, Raj and the Sikh gentleman reach the guard's compartment to find two more Sikh youths sitting in silence there. The Sikh youths tell one of them to sit with them and rest of the two on a metal trunk as it was two-and-a-half-hour journey. The compartment is drenched in anxiety and mutual suspicion. Jugal tells the Sikh gentleman to sit with the Sikh youths, exemplifying the stark binary opposition because of Hindu–Sikh tensions during that time. The helplessness and the difficult times they belong to are clearly etched on all the passengers' faces. The camera lingers uncomfortably on each face. The compartment becomes an essential sequence, displaying the microcosm of clandestine atmosphere of fear and tension in Punjab at that time.

The film is rife with close-up shots that lend emotional content without resorting to melodrama. The passengers' costumes consist of sweaters and muffler, again suggestive of the months of November or December of 1984. A comment from the guard's assistant in a mocking vein, 'See that you do not damage the trunk', lends comic relief to the stressed environment. All the guard's dialogues reiterate the seriousness and his unease, 'If I am caught allowing you on the train, I could end up losing my job. Also, these are difficult times …Who can know someone's intentions? What if something untoward were to happen? To whom will I turn for help?' It is crucial to notice how Gurvinder creates a fascinating mix of minimal dialogues, restricted motion, persistence of vision, along with sculptural moments. The moments are 'sculptural' in the manner of art historian Philip Rawson uses the term to denote 'structured shapes of space as well as in space' (1997: 5). The placement and the play of characters and space both independently as well as with each other reveal the *mise en scene* of stillness which is not peaceful but cold enough that it trails throughout the movie.

The camera pans from Jugal and Raj to a glass window with waning train horn and passing rail tracks, taking us to a flashback of a different nighttime journey for Jugal and his jitters a few months ago. The dew-laden field welcomes one to the next journey. The spider weaving its web or trying to clutch at the last strand, the ugly croaking and jumping of a frog in front of Jugal, his wife's footsteps and an eventual twisting of her foot in the mud, all very serenely set the strain of the times in the delightful imagery. The signs of monsoon point to the months of July and August, a month or so after Operation Blue Star. The chapter may go to the extent of close reading or symbolisation for critical perusal as well as to understand the coldness, irate madness and the violence of 1984. Interestingly, for the director, his reaction to the space and the atmosphere while shooting was a matter of chance than a planned execution. He mentions, 'We shot the film during the monsoons … The thunderstorm became a sequence by itself which was not in the script. Nature will give you what you can never plan. You have to remain open to accidents which bring their own vitality to the story' (D'Souza 2016). In this context, it is important to understand 'that even though art contains symbols, it is not symbolic. Rather, it is a presentiment which leads us to the symbolic' (Bradley 1981: 33). Hence, it can be said that for the director Gurvinder, his reserve of constant consciousness about the spacial time and its due evocation of emotions kept him moving towards the metaphysics of the symbolic life of the shots in his movie.

The 360-degree pan shot gives a total view of nothing in reach at night. The rear shot of the characters fills the scene with dread and doubt. The shot stills at a house with blue smoke, giving some direction and hope to the couple who has lost the sense of direction in the darkness of the night. Soon they realise that it is not the appropriate place to ask for help or find the way. Walking again, they reach a house that has animal stock and Jugal musters up the courage to call at the door for help. A farmer named Joginder comes out of his house and looks at both of them with eyes of suspicion. Joginder's mother, on learning their connection with Rampur, calls them in. Even amid fear, we notice some positive receptivity between both the sides. Notably, the flow of fear in this frame is very aesthetically dealt with. A frame which shows Joginder's wife pouring in milk in two glasses for Jugal and his wife is accompanied with Joginder's mother's account of the horrors of living in that village. She remarks:

> We shifted here from the village [Rampur] hoping for a better life. Farming would be easier. So would looking after the cattle. How could we have known the circumstances would change. Sometimes we spend all night in fear. You never know who might land up at odd hours … You should not be out and about so late. You know the prevailing situation. Who knows who might be out there in the night.

Joginder helps them at night to find the way towards their village. The background non-diegetic sound of the marriage ritual music sets a positive tune of camaraderie and support scarcely achieved from the fraternity or the community during that time.

The third journey focuses on Joginder and his family, who find themselves caught between religious extremism and state oppression. Their rite of passage unfolds through the trials they face, navigating challenges that extend beyond ordinary expectations. Central to their ordeal is addressing the issue of a barking dog and the accompanying threats that characterised those turbulent times. This transitional or liminal phase of terror in the soul creates confusion as well as retrogresses into chaos and guilt. The slow burn narrative explores the inner conflict of Joginder and his family as they are agonised over the decision to kill their pet dog Tommy, whose barking hinders the movement of militants at night. The family makes half-hearted attempts to get rid of their beloved pet. Other times, they reassure themselves, perhaps futilely, that they will protect him. Courage mixes with terror, and danger constantly lurks in the shadows.

After Joginder comes back home, the frame shifts to a quiet night, clouds thundering, Tommy panting and his sudden barking. The night seems unnerving and its silence is undercut only by these sounds, and then a knock on Joginder's bedroom door. His mother cautions him about Tommy's barking and the presence of militants around. The stressful night and angst for his dog make Joginder remark, 'This dog will doom the entire family.' Joginder's close shot is full of tension and his contemplative gaze in the air steers the inevitable disquieting situation. He hears a gunshot and combatively goes out to quieten Tommy. His family is in the midst of a stew. Beside himself in anger, Joginder abuses and hits Tommy with his slippers to silence him. In the dark of the night he hears some men talking near the back door and opens it to them. He addresses the group of men as *Khalsaji*[5] and calls them in, telling them not to fear the dog. The crude dialogues of one of the fanatic Khalistani militant from the group—'Do you really think we are scared of the dog? We live by the edge of the sword. You, however, seem to have lost fear. You know our orders, why haven't you killed the dog yet?'—are awe-inspiring. Joginder is pushed inside his house and is beaten up by the militant Sikh. The people who come in are five in number, which symbolically represents *panj pyare*[6] in the Sikh religion. They are supposedly the Guru's beloved who will celebrate His love in kindness in all the times, but here we see their separatist rage. No direct violence is shown on screen; we only hear the wailing of Joginder's mother and his wife, pleading with them to free him. Joginder's mid close shot in the darkness, the moment he is pushed to the cot with a pointed rifle reveals the dark, horrendous, helpless times of that age and ushers out the trauma of the times. Suddenly the light is switched on and we see Joginder's eyes popping out in fear. His sobbing mother inquires as to what his crime was. His wife bids them to think of her as their sister and leave her husband. But the Sikh militant up in arms asks Joginder in a raised voice, 'Should I waste a bullet now?' The other comrade barges in and tells him to sit on the cot. With fixed eyes and a surreal smile on his face, the militant exclaims, 'You are standing as if accused!'

The next frame shows tea boiling along with the brewing of the story of Joginder's contrived efforts to get rid of Tommy. This scene presages the storm seething the next morning, both literally and metaphorically, in form of paramilitary men coming to look for the terrorists. Then, Joginder's mother explains to Khalsaji:

> Samma and Joginder took Tommy on their cycles to the mazaar of Baba Budha Sahib. They even tricked him into getting lost in the crowd… When they returned, Tommy, wagging his tail, was already waiting on the threshold … Joginder took Tommy to Sheikh Fatta. They tied the dog with a chain to a peg in the ground and instructed the volunteer not to untie it till the next morning … We were sure we had got rid of Tommy … But on the 6th day, Sukhdev started jumping with joy on the terrace. He came running down the steps, shouting, Tommy is back … Tommy is back … You tell us what should we do?

The frame then shifts to a complete lull inside the room. The image of a burning *chullah* without any vessel on it mirrors the fire within the hearts of militants.

One of the militants is once again enraged and asks Joginder if he cares for his life. Another intervenes, alluding their ordeal, 'For the sake of the community we have left our homes. Security forces are pursuing us like dogs. Thirsty for our blood. We have to move around at night at odd hours … If you keep dogs, they will bark and betray us … And the security forces certainly don't spare people like you.' These dialogues shed new light on the plight not only of the common man but also militant Sikhs. In those days it was a dog's life—beyond the usual allusions to the harassed point-blank deaths of many innocent Sikh youths, who were treated akin to the poor stray dogs, here it is the innocent pet Tommy that drives the symbolism. The madness of the storm or the madness of barking Tommy provide enough metaphors for the invested and authored madness of the crowds during that time which included militant/Khalistani Sikhs, police, 'antisocial elements, dacoits, and even the Pradhans of other castes to teach the Sikh community a lesson as a retaliation against their aggression towards the leader of the nation' (Das 1996: 160).

Joginder's mother affirms and promises the group of Khalistani Sikhs at her place that they would do as they were asked. She blesses them as they were sacrificing their lives for Sikhs' sake and the cause of the religious order. She cries remembering her martyred nephew Sukhwant who had died the previous year, around the time of Operation Blue Star. Only her voice is heard and the frame consists of rear and side profiles of characters, including her. The aim is not to portray her emotions, but to convey the information regarding young Punjabi men killed in fake police encounters. She mentions how the

> hordes of security forces came striding forth that night. The family was rudely woken up, made to stand in a line and asked, 'Who is Sukhwant amongst you?' Sukhwant came out so that family members would be spared … Before [his mother's] eyes her son's leg was broken, and he was bundled into a van and taken away. For many days villagers made innumerable rounds trying to find him. Police kept saying they knew nothing. They denied arresting any boy named Sukhwant. And then brother after fifteen days there was a report in the paper … saying Sukhwant had been killed in some encounter.

The militant asks her to be brave like Mai Bhago[7] and not to cry over a martyr's death. They reassure Joginder that they have undertaken to guard the community and that his family should not fear thefts now and must inform in case of any threat. Hence, they are advised to 'kill the dogs and keep the lights switched off'. They are also told that some people use the name of Khalistan to indulge in crime or to blackmail people. The frame leaves Joginder in deep thought and a sleepless night evoked by tense music.

The frame shifts to the vigorous mixing of poison with curd and sugar for Tommy the next morning. The camera pans abruptly to the gathering of relatives, both women and men, in the courtyard of the house. They, along with Joginder, share the helplessness and anxiety of the moment. There is great unease in the air, with Joginder overfeeding the poisonous curd to Tommy, which he does not eat. Sukhdev, Joginder's son, gets shaky and melts down upon seeing Tommy. Sukhdev is rebuked both by his father and mother and told to leave the place.

Hukamnama[8] is heard from a distant gurdwara[9] in the background. Meanwhile, amidst this action of feeding Tommy, police vehicles arrive.

The family's morning eclipsed by darkness reminiscent of the previous night. They get scorched between the state forces in the morning and religious state apparatuses at night. 'Operation Blue Star' was followed by 'Operation Woodrose' in which the army, supported by the paramilitary forces and the police, invaded the villages of Punjab to remove anti-social elements, that is, Khalistani Sikhs/Amritdharis of Damdami Taksaal[10] who were supposedly the followers of Bhindranwale. In this direction, Sandhu highlights how all the Sikhs initiated into the faith were thought to be extremists and how the government gave orders to abduct and kill them during that period:

> Instructions given to the troops at that time stated: 'Some of our innocent countrymen were administered oath in the name of religion to support extremists and actively participate in the act of terrorism. These people wear a miniature kirpan round their neck and are called Amritdhari ... Any knowledge of the "Amritdharis" who are dangerous people and pledged to commit murders, arson and acts of terrorism should immediately be brought to the notice of the authorities. These people may appear harmless from outside but they are basically committed to terrorism. In the interest of all of us their identity and whereabouts must always be disclosed.' These instructions constituted unmistakably clear orders for genocide of all Sikhs formally initiated into their faith. (1997: 1)

Thousands disappeared in Punjab around the beginning of the operation. Cordoning a house or a whole village by the army or the police to search was quite common. The enforcement agencies in Punjab were ruthless while following the said orders and led to a large number of cases of torture, rape, disappearances and murder of Sikhs, which was all later ascribed to the violence perpetrated by the so-called Sikh terrorists/militants. In the film, a policeman comes and interrogates Joginder about who comes and stays at night at their place. He is then blamed of conspiring with the militants. His whole house is ransacked and searched thoroughly by the policemen. Joginder is badly hurt by the policemen. The metallic non-diegetic music and a strain of pulsating drums creates an atmosphere of caution, fear and doubt around the house as the interiors are investigated. The policemen gingerly scrutinise the house adn its environs. The rustling of leaves, combined with a 180 degree panning shot, creates suspense and anticipation of an action. The still camera's gaze on characters, uncanny faces of policemen, Joginder, and his relatives, their pose in the courtyard or speechless children within the frame of a window—these unmoving images amid chaos have the quality that Yvette Biro perceptively calls 'ironic serenity' (2008: 196). The dark secret nights or obscured inner pain of people in the daytime in those times are captured not only through lingering musical notes but also through objects or through the silence of characters that slip away like musical notes in the movie.

Joginder's mother confides to the head of the police that they were already troubled and scared as the militants had visited the previous night, fired a gunshot, threatened them and left. They had no clue about any of them. This conversation is interrupted by Tommy's barking as he comes running out of the lush green paddy fields. The policemen get alert. The police head commands to shoot the dog. There is a loud thud and utter silence. Everyone jumps to see the plight of Tommy. Apart from the dialogue, 'Let it be,' there is no evidence as to what happened to the dog and the lurking tragedy turns into a dilemma.

Fear assimilates in the viewers as there is no rhetoric or melodrama. The picture, in keeping with the old saying, is worth a thousand words. The movement of the landscape and space speaks directly to the viewers and gives them time to think and immerse themselves in remembrance or the feel of an un-called for anxiety and unbearable tension. In this context, as film scholar Martin Lefebvre writes, we learn to develop a kind of 'landscape gaze' that 'mentally arrests the unfolding of the film and internally holds the space for contemplation until returning to the narrative mode' (2006: 52). The screen is taken over by overcasting of clouds, dust storm, rustling paddy, thunder and rain. The accompanying sound of flapping paddy, fluttering and rustling leaves, splurging storm, water ripples, pounding rain, swishing trees, rumbling thunder, and whirring, scratching, squeaking, grating underlying metallic creepy music by Sushmit Bob Nath, Bruno Tarriere and Marc Marder add on to the whole effect of dread and doubt. The archetypal rain metaphor might symbolise regeneration, inevitability of something or equilibrium. The chaos of the stormy night sets the stage for Tommy's arrival, marked by the open gates of Joginder's house the following morning. The atmosphere and the space in the movie are inspired by Abbas Kiarostami's films,[11] *Once upon a Time in Anatolia* by Nuri Bilge Ceylan[12] and *The Forsaken Land* by Vimukthi Jayasundara.[13]

The evocative or the poetical aspect in the movie is created through music, landscape and camera compositions. Hence, the aesthetic attitude of feeling of evocation is embodied in the 'form'. This lends a metaphorical centre that is alive and compelling to this story. It is not a story of conflict and resolution. In the end, the meaning becomes more complex and more lyrical than simply the plot the story, which is not that significant and memorable aspect of this kind of a cinema. There is another kind of rhythm, a pulse that subverts the melodic line, where the fragments re-organise into a more intricate set of sounds going beyond the lexical and denotative content in the movie. It touches viewers not by the intellect but through their imagination. It is forged of emotions that take thought and recreate it into a textured experience, essentially composed of the feelings evoked more by the sound and images that they cast than by the words or dialogues. There is a simultaneous rite of passage for the audience as they engage in the transformation emotionally. The ultimate meaning of the story thus becomes emotive. The movie becomes a ritualistic experience, the objective of which is to move the members of the audience into the metaphorical centre that is an aesthetic blend or poem in the movie. In an interview with Ananya Ghosh (2015), Gurvinder mentions:

> Literature is descriptive, whereas cinema is the instance suggested through images and associated sounds ... Unlike literature, here you can haunt the memory of the viewer, as there is no escape for them. The transformation from the imaginary to concrete imagery is exciting and challenging ... In 'Chauthi Koot', though both the stories were complete in themselves, they evoked a similar feeling of fear through a public space and a personal space under siege between the warring sides. My idea was to evoke this sense of insecurity, which permeates spaces and minds in such troubled times.

That night the whole extended family gets together at Joginder's house for support. The expressionless faces eloquently convey their suppressed emotions. The environment gets complaisant when Joginder offers a piece of bread to Tommy. Joginder's cousin hates the life of dread and threat and wants to join the militants. The trope of dog is used very evidently in their conversation. His father rebukes him and comments, 'Don't talk rubbish. Stop howling like a dog. Stay level-headed.' Aggression among the youth rises because of the tyranny of the police in uniform over innocent people. Joginer's cousin, thus, thinks that it is time for them to take up weapons. This depicts how many young Sikhs in those times took to militancy because of open and hidden reign of terror around them. In their discussion, another relative remarks that 'dogs are more loyal than humans'. He quotes Baba Bulleh Shah[14] and says, 'Oh Bulleh Shah, invoke the blessings of the Master. Look, even the dogs have excelled over you.' This sets the analogy between dogs like Tommy and human beings—the latter are turncoats in comparison to the obedient and faithful dogs who alarm their masters of any hazard even at the cost of getting poisoned because of policemen and militants' warnings.

The next morning, the settling of the mist personifies Joginder's determination to get rid of Tommy and the Mukha's resolve not to kill any more dogs. The militants issued an order to eliminate barking dogs on farms as their barking revealed the militants' positions to security forces. In the village, Mukha was assigned the task of carrying out this directive. The scene shifts to a Punjabi newspaper *Ajeet* lying on a table with headlines 'Bomb blast in Pathankot, 2 dead' and 'Militants Strike Panipat: 13 Shot Dead at a Wedding'. Reading this news, Mukha exclaims, 'Waheguru! Waheguru! Bless humanity, Almighty. Let peace and harmony prevail. O supreme divine.' He is shattered by the news in Punjab and silently stares at the newspaper when asked by Joginder's cousin about his worry. Mukha is called inside the dispensary to agree to kill Tommy as he had been killing many dogs, but he objects and says, 'I have no fear. I will repeat what I've already said. Come what may, I will not kill the dogs ... I will not kill the voiceless innocent ... I will face the bullets. I'm not afraid.' Joginder's cousin again requests the doctor either to give them some poison to kill the dog or send someone to do it. The next frame is set at night-time when the whole family is enjoying dinner along with Tommy. The camera takes a close shot of Tommy eating bread and milk, enjoying the warmth of his family.

Early morning, Joginder's cousin tunes the transistor. The tilt shallow focus shot as he pulls the antenna out raises curiosity. The focus is on tuning the transistor and his anxious wait for the news with folded hands. The camera pans along with pauses on the set of people present around, all ears for the BBC News broadcast:

> Nearly 300 people have been killed as Indian troops stormed the Golden Temple in Amritsar held by Sikh militants. The army's attack was resisted with heavy firepower. Weapons captured included machine guns, anti-tank missiles and rocket launchers. Reports say 250 militants and 48 Indian soldiers have died in the battle. Around 450 Sikh militants have been captured. The storming of the temple, code named Operation Blue Star, followed weeks of growing tension between the government of Prime Minister Indira Gandhi and Sikhs in the northern state of Punjab. Indira Gandhi first moved forces in to surround the temple in early March. Before this, the temple was under the occupation of Sikh extremists led by Sant Jarnail Singh Bhindranwale. The religious risks of storming the shrine led to a tense stand-off. The security forces were

> hoping the militants would surrender, making a direct attack unnecessary. With the imposition of a 36-hour curfew on 3rd June, the speculation of an attack on the Sikh shrine increased ... The army's next task would be to wipe out militancy from the state of Punjab.

The camera captures a 360-degree panorama with abrupt stills focusing on villagers listening to the news.

Suddenly all the heads turn to an asynchronous chorus of voices from a procession coming from a distance. Soon a procession of tractor trolleys enters the scene, with people singing holy hymns and shouting slogans of '*Bole So Nihal, Sat Sri Akaal*'[15] as they travel to Sur Singh, a place in Amritsar district, after hearing about the Golden Temple massacre. Mukha, Joginder and his cousin, along with other villagers, join the procession to Sur Singh. The camera holds on to various group compositions of people singing hymns. The diegetic music of hymns is mixed with non-diegetic whirring and rusted metallic music when the *nihangs*[16] pass the tractor trolleys on horseback. The cinematic aerial shot of trolleys, to show procession and togetherness of people, has been crafted very intelligibly. This scene becomes the establishing shot of *Chauthi Koot*, that is, it represents how the way to Amritsar became the fourth or the forbidden direction in those days. After hearing about Operation Blue Star, Sikhs as a community wanted to go to the Golden Temple in Amritsar to protect its sanctity. At the same time, Amritsar became a place that was not safe, where people feared to go, where they were not free to go or from where there were minimal chances of return. In the film, Khalistani militants stop the procession and command, 'Everybody has been warned that it is prohibited to go ahead. If you continue to move ahead, there will be a baton charge.' A bullet is fired in the air and everybody rushes back.

The scene shifts to night-time. Joginder listens to Tommy's barking, and brings him inside to his room. The next morning, Joginder's mother is reading *Japji Sahib*.[17] The prayer is very significant at this hour as we hear second and third *pauri*[18] of the prayer. The 'second pauri imparts patience and stability. The third pauri turns insufficiency into sufficiency, depression into elevation, and transforms low self-esteem into self-confidence' which is the need of the hour (Sikh Dharma International 2024). At that very instance, Joginder's daughter and son both have doubts about Tommy's welfare and interrogate their mother: 'Are we going to kill our Tommy? ... Then, are we going to leave him somewhere?' That very night Tommy again barks incessantly. Joginder's frustration is apparent in his expression and in the dialogue, 'Why doesn't this bloody dog stop barking?' He goes out and whispers him to be quiet. He climbs down the stairs in anger and hits Tommy with a spade, breaking his back. The scene is captured very subtly. Martyred human beings were many during those times. It was a time of martyrdom or sacrifice in the name of religion or because you were a Sikh. But poor dogs like Tommy were sacrificed by their masters for the fear of their barking. Tommy becomes a vital character embodying the central theme of the film, as he actually travels in the 'fourth direction' and represents the voiceless—the silent witness and bearer of the suffering of 1984.

The director has used Tommy in similar vein to Robert Bresson's memorable donkey in the movie *Au Hasard Balthazar.*[19] Violence is not overtly expressed, but instead is implied on Joginder's face. There is a strain on the family members' faces, who are all silent apart from Sukhdev who wails in grief. The whole family has a sleepless night. Though Joginder resolves to get rid of Tommy, he still cares for him. Next morning, half-dead Tommy is put in a trolley and taken to a distant place. The panorama of fields blurs into grassy railway track and the frame shifts to the window of the train guard's compartment.

The story shifts from these flashbacks to the clandestine train journey to Amritsar in the present. Everyone in the train compartment looks at the other with suspicion. The train guard opens the door of the compartment and instructs, 'I cannot drop you at the station. You people will have to get off here … Make sure nobody sees you otherwise you will unnecessarily get caught.' All the passengers slowly get down. Jugal and Raj hasten their steps, but are stopped from behind. The two Sikh boys come running after them. They confess, 'We are scared [that] if the police spot us, they may fire at us thinking we are terrorists. Who asks questions these days before firing?' The elder Sikh gentleman comes running and expresses his anguish that they did not even wait for him when all of them were together. The five of them walk close together, leaving behind the rail track and darkness of the night and militancy. The tracking technique gives viewers a sense of involvement, with their hurried steps following all the characters. They move towards the opposite direction and not in the direction of station. It is pertinent that the 'fourth direction' here is the opposite direction; symbolically, a direction against not only the repressive and ideological state apparatuses but also the cinematographer's camera.

In the interim of Operation Blue Star and post Indira Gandhi's assassination, the anger of Sikhs was palpable over growing Hindu majoritarianism. It was directed at aggressors who wanted to 'teach Sikhs a lesson'. The failure of the state to protect all its citizens equally and its complicity in the killings had orphaned certain sections of it by denying them of a basic requirement—safety. *Chauthi Koot* explores this dichotomy of the state as being both a facilitator and a repressor at the same time. Feelings of anger, humiliation, insecurity, fear, anxiety and alienation turned the Sikhs, especially, as the marked 'others' in this period. In the year 1984, 'dark margins came to life and roamed at large, displacing national shock with private griefs, and bloodshed with a blood bath ... [it was a time when] the communal nation state was reconstituted amidst howls and arhythmic chants of "khoon ka badla khoon"' (Gupta 1985: 1185).

The three journeys in *Chauthi Koot* are intricately tied to fear, which initially appears vague and undefined. When the audience begins to move along the path of images recalled in the movie, they detect a union that was previously only dimly perceived, if it was perceived at all; the images begin to form new configurations. The images along with sound catch an experience and reshape it; images that have the capacity to do this become easily recalled memories of experience. The viewers, even if they had not witnessed the period of 1984, still become participants in the story. It is this developing ironic journey to sameness, a sensation of recognition, that contributes to much of the energy and the evocation created by the movie.

Notes

1. *Amritdhari* is a person who has been formally initiated into the Sikh faith through having taken *Khande da Pauh*. The ceremony is often referred to as taking Amrit/baptising by drinking sweet water from one vessel.

2. *Bhangra* is the folk dance of Punjab usually performed by men.

3. Alfred Hitchcock, the famous British director, was called a 'Master of Suspense'. He did not rely on dialogue but effectively used things, objects, music and camera direction to create suspense. He built up tension by emphasising details, bringing the audience closer and by breaking the action into puzzle pieces—he would then reveal the hidden psychological meanings behind what is perceived, evoking fear and anxiety within the audience.

4. *Mool mantra* is the root sacred-utterance composed by Guru Nanak that appears as the first composition in Guru Granth Sahib Ji.

5. *Khalsaji* is a term similar to *Amritdhari*, that is, the initiated Sikhs.

6. *Panj pyare* were the five beloved of Guru Gobind Singh who were ready to offer their heads to him.

7. Mai Bhago was also known as Mata Bhag Kaur, a revered, courageous and patient Sikh saint. She was known for rallying the 40 Sikhs (*Chali Mukte*) who had abandoned Guru Gobind Singh Ji at the siege of Anandpur Sahib and persuading them to return to the fight.

8. *Hukamnama* is the Sikh thought for the day from Guru Granth Sahib ji's daily reading.

9. Gurdwara is Sikh temple of worship.

10. *Taksaal* is a school for Sikh religious instruction.

11. Abbas Kiarostami, an Iranian filmmaker, largely used minimalism, natural landscapes, long shots, free spaces, darkness and silence. He is recognised as a 'poet of space' because of his perception of directions, natural light and the visual aesthetics of real spaces.

12. Nuri Bilge Ceylan, a Turkish filmmaker, is a practitioner of slow cinema. He uses the effect of painting while framing the scenes. In *Once upon a Time in Anatolia* (2011), the outcome is akin to a noir rendered in oil paints. It includes a handful of characters. He keeps the details scant and instead turns up the atmosphere with expressive images and lovely observational long takes. This movie has a three-part structure which has also influenced the structure of *Chauthi Koot*. Even their rhythm matches that is frustrating yet immersive at the same time.

13. Vimukthi Jayasundara is a Sri Lankan director who, in *The Forsaken Land* (2005), plays with haunting images that have a painterly quality. He does not glorify violence or highlight the thrill often associated with the adventure of it; instead, he portrays how characters endure and respond to its persistent presence. Jayasundara evokes an atmosphere that represents lack of trust, alienation and an inner emptiness. His film too is a non-linear, lyrical critique of war and modernity, focusing on the climate of fear in Sri Lanka and the suffering of the people, using the landscape to present the states of mind of his characters. He has also used sounds efficiently to create an atmosphere.

14. Bulleh Shah was a Mughal-era Islamic Punjabi philosopher and a Sufi poet.

15. '*Bole so Nihal, Sat Sri Akaal*' is a *jaikara* or a clarion call of Sikhs given by the tenth Guru, Guru Gobind Singh Ji, meaning whoever utters shall be fulfilled, eternal is the great timeless Lord.

16. *Nihang*, literally 'immortal', is a term for the armed Sikh warriors. They are believed to have originated from Sahebzada Fateh Singh Ji, the youngest son of Guru Gobind Singh Ji, and the attire he wore, or from the *miri* and *piri* started by the sixth Guru, Guru Hargobind Singh Ji.

17. *Japji Sahib*, written by Guru Nanak Dev Ji, is the Sikh morning prayer.

18. *Pauri* means stanza in a prayer written in verse form.

19. The main character of Robert Bresson's *Au Hasard Balthazar* (1966) is a donkey named Balthazar. While Balthazar is not exactly a main character in the sense of a protagonist, it is his existence and journey which drive the action of the

film. Through him, the interconnected lives unfold. It is the one connection that links all the characters together and laces through the story. Tommy, like Balthazar, can be interpreted minimally as a character of purity and innocence who is witness to the joys as well as the depredations of the world. There are times when characters blame Balthazar for their misfortune. In the end, Balthazar ultimately sacrifices himself for the wrongdoings of one of the film's characters.

References

Biro, Yvette. 2008. *Turbulence and Flow in Film: The Rhythmic Design*. Trans. Paul Salamon. Bloomington: Indiana University Press.

Bradley, William. 1981. 'Evocative Images'. *Studies in Art Education* 23 (1): 33–39.

Campbell, Christopher. 2017. '6 Filmmaking Tips from Luis Bunuel'. *Film School Rejects*, 23 August. Available at https://filmschoolrejects.com/filmmaking-tips-luis-bunuel/ (accessed on 23 January 2025).

Chatterjee, Suprateek. 2016. 'Exclusive: Dibakar Banerjee Raves about Award-winning Punjabi Film "Chauthi Koot" in Email'. *The Huffington Post*, 4 August. Available at https://www.huffingtonpost.in/2016/08/04/exclusive-dibakar-banerjee-raves-about-award-winning-punjabi-fi_a_21444881/ (accessed on 2 September 2016).

Chauthi Koot. 2015. Film. Directed by Gurvinder Singh, India.

Das, Veena. 1996. 'The Spataialization of Violence: Case Study of a "Communal Riot"'. In *Unravelling the Nation: Sectarian Conflict and India's Secular Identity*, eds Kaushik Basu and Sanjay Subrahmanyam, 157–203. India: Penguin Books.

D'Souza, Heena. 2016. 'Interview with Gurvinder Singh on *Chauthi Koot*'. *India Independent Films*, 6 November. Available at http://indiaindependentfilms.com/2015/11/06/interview-gurvinder-singh-chauthi-koot/ (accessed on 2 September 2016).

Ghosh, Ananya. 2015. 'Being an Artiste Has Become a Risky Occupation: Gurvinder Singh'. *Mid-day*, 10 May. Available at https://www.mid-day.com/articles/being-an-artiste-has-become-a-risky-occupation-gurvinder-singh/16199154 (accessed on 4 July 2016).

Gupta, Dipankar. 1985. 'The Communalising of Punjab, 1980–1985'. *Economic & Political Weekly* 20 (28): 1185–90.

Kappal, Bhanuj. 2016. 'Film Review: Chauthi Koot—Insurgency on the Punjab Plain'. *The National Arts & Life*, 24 August. Available at https://www.thenationalnews.com/arts/film-review-chauthi-koot-insurgency-on-the-punjab-plain-1.142137 (accessed on 22 December 2024).

Kerr, Walter. 1979. *The Silent Clowns*. New York: Knopf.

Lefebvre, Martin, ed. 2006. *Landscape and Film*. New York: Routledge.

Pettigrew, Joyce. 1995. *The Sikhs of the Punjab: Unheard Voices of State and Guerrilla Violence*. London: Zed Books Ltd.

Rawson, Philip. 1997. *Sculpture*. Philadelphia: University of Pennsylvania Press.

Sahi, Harjeet Inder Singh. 2016. 'Cinema Must Portray a Multiplicity of Emotions and Perspectives'. *Hindustan Times*, 15 January. Available at https://www.hindustantimes.com/punjab/cinema-must-portray-a-multiplicity-of-emotions-and-perspectives/story-ZdUA6KBHl7yx2LgDp9CqbK.html (accessed on 4 July 2016).

Sandhu, Ranbir S. 1997. *Sant Jarnail Singh Bhindranwale—Life, Mission and Martyrdom*. Ohio: Sikh Educational and Religious Foundation.

Sikh Dharma International. 2024. 'The Effects of the Paurees of Japji Sahib'. Available at https://www.sikhdharma.org/the-effects-of-paurees-of-japji-sahib/ (accessed on 26 December 2024).

Singh, Khushwant. 2003. *The End of India*. New Delhi: Penguin Books.

Stevens, William K. 1984. 'Indian Army Goes into 9 Cities as Anti-Sikh Battling Flares; Throngs File by Gandhi's Bier'. *The New York Times*, 2 November. Available at https://www.nytimes.com/1984/11/02/world/indian-army-goes-into-9-cities-anti-sikh-battling-flares-throngs-file-gandhi-s.html (accessed on 23 January 2025).

Tully, Mark, and Satish Jacob. 2011. *Amritsar: Mrs. Gandhi's Last Battle*. New Delhi: Rupa Publications.

seven

Trauma and Restitution, the Healing Power of Compassion

A Psychoanalytical and Cinematic Analysis of *Kaya Taran*

Diamond Oberoi Vahali

> 'Don't turn your head. Keep looking at the bandaged place. That's where the Light enters you.'
>
> – Rumi (n.d.)

Kaya Taran (*Chrysalis*), a 2004 Malayalam film directed by Sashi Kumar, and based on the Malayalam short story 'When Big Tree Falls' by N. S. Madhavan, is set in the backdrop of the 1984 violence against the Sikhs in Meerut. It depicts the face of humanity in a situation of mass violence, wherein a group of Christian nuns in a convent give protection to a Sikh woman Amerjeet Kaur and her young son Jagpreet, also called Jaggi (remarkably performed by Neelambari Bhattacharya), and Preet,[1] even at the risk of their own lives. *Kaya Taran* is a paradoxical study into the shining light of compassion which holds life intact at a time when the darker forces of communalism and vested interests are completely manifest. The film also takes us deep into the abyss of darkness emanating from a traumatic past which apparently Preet has forgotten but which nonetheless insidiously haunts his existence. It is the unmourned past and the force of the death instinct that determines Preet's existence until he unconsciously walks in the direction of understanding the almost erased parts of his self. His encounter with Sister Agatha, the benevolent light of his and his mother's existence, helps him to ultimately settle his trauma. Even more significantly, it is by embracing the darkness that he gradually emerges into light, the light which has the power to transform him in crucial ways, even if his trauma is not fully dealt with. Psychoanalyst Grotstein (2007) suggests that it is through darkness, and only through darkness, that an intense beam of light can begin to radiate in one's life. The suffusion of this light through darkness propels him into selfhood, an arrival into reclaiming a forcibly forsaken identity.

This chapter will focus both on the darker forces of communalism, violence and self-interest, as well as on the frozen traumatic darkness[2] within. It will depict the manner in which the darkness gradually wanes when an unconscious sojourn into benevolent memories of a dissociated past is undertaken in the presence of a protector who had once given up her self-interest to save an other, the then little boy Jaggi, the film's protagonist.

The film assumes a docu-fictional mode at its very beginning as it incorporates statements which are both factual as well as historical. In the beginning of the film, a grown-up Jagpreet interviews a journalist who had directly witnessed the anti-Sikh violence. The journalist informs Preet that in 1984 he was a reporter with the *Indian Express* and had covered the massacre in Trilokpuri. He reports:

> The riots occurred in Block 32, a resettlement camp for poorer Sikhs whose main occupation was making rope beds. It was around 7 in the evening and getting dark. We learnt that killings had been going on for the last 48 hours. Indira Gandhi had been shot on Wednesday and we were there on Thursday evening. We found the narrow street choked and blocked with bodies. Human limbs, hair, footwear, clothes were strewn all over and there was blood everywhere. It was so bad that we could not place a foot firmly on ground. We had to walk on the tips of our toes. We saw a young woman half paralysed, seated at the entrance of her door.

As the voice of the journalist continues to report, on the soundtrack we hear the sound of a child wailing. This sonsign[3] of a child's cry is significant as the film centralises the impact of violent killings on the psyche of children. Moreover, it is by juxtaposing dead bodies and the aftermath of violence with cries of children that a thematic of conflict between life and death forces is being suggested in the sequence. If the child's cry can still be heard amidst the debris of dead bodies, then some hope and faith in humanity can be retained, else all is lost for our collective future, the film obliquely suggests. The journalist continues:

> The child was lying in a small room which was also filled with bodies. In front of the room was a young Sikh man whose stomach had been slashed open, some eight to ten hours earlier. He was trying to bandage it with his turban cloth … and crying out for water. We lifted the child,

> woman and man.... By then a police van and a couple of policemen had reached the spot. We put them in the van. But what was most eerie and frightening was that there were thousands of people all around us but not a sound from anyone. The place was cast in silence. The police told us later that between 300 and 350 people were killed in this street. There was no doctor, no police, and no army. The police didn't do anything because they were hardly present. And although the army had been deployed they didn't know their way about, or where the riots were taking place.

As is evident from the reporting of the journalist, the 1984 violence did not merely have a communal angle to it but also a gender, class and a caste angle. It was the poor, mostly lower caste Sikhs who were killed and many women were raped. Most of these Sikhs lived in Sikh ghettos in Trilokpuri refugee colonies on 25 square yards of land. Incidentally, the violence in the refugee colonies takes us back to the partition of India and covertly to a history of multiple displacements and annihilations. The sequence also reveals the chilling indifference of the larger community, as we are told that no one came to the rescue of the victims. It further highlights the legitimacy that people get during mob violence to give vent to their most evil instincts and how easy it is to motivate people to loot and kill. Preet proceeds to interview the journalists, Joseph Malliakken from the *Indian Express* and Alok Tomar from the *Jansatta* who too had witnessed the mob violence. They inform him that it was an individual named Rahul Bedi who had pursued the case systematically. He had lodged complaints with the People's Union for Civil Liberties (PUCL) and the police commissioner. But nothing actually came from these complaints except the harassment of victims, who were brutally beaten and who have been summoned endlessly before commissions of enquiry. Ironically, none of these commissions resolved the issue. After speaking to the journalists, Preet visits a gurdwara. It is while he is returning from the gurdwara on his motorcycle that the film very subtly, for the first time, offers us a glimpse into his traumatic past.

Interweaving itself within the context of the Gujarat pogrom, *Kaya Taran* situates itself in 2002. In the aftermath of the Gujarat pogrom, in a press conference, a little boy gives his testimony. The journalist who is facilitating the young child's speech emphasises in his speech the violence that is meted out to children during mass violence. As the journalist informs about the impact of trauma on the psyche of children, at the visual level the scene shifts to a shot of Preet boarding a train. The testimony of the little boy is superimposed on Preet, travelling by train to Meerut to do a story on conversions. It is through this cinematic device that the film suggests that though it is the little boy from Gujarat who is giving his testimony, at a deeper level, it is Preet who must bear inner witness to his own traumatic past. In the context of holocaust survivors, Shoshana Felman and Dori Laub (1988) invoke the crucial role of the witness and the inner witness in oneself. Through extremely poignant case accounts of adults who had endured insurmountable losses in early childhood, including the killing of their parents, forcible displacement and a brutal annihilation of their Jewish identity, Felman and Laub trace the psychological roots of unnameable and unbearable trauma and losses and how these are eventually symbolised in human life. Their study highlights the deep rupture in the psyche and the interruption of the mind as a psychic container (Bion 1962) if a person is placed under inhuman conditions when self and being are brutally violated. Any reparative possibility in adult life remains contingent on rediscovering or finding a relationship in which the benevolent other can serve as a witness to one's unnameable dreads. This eventually allows for dreaming to take place, through which raw beta elements—the dark dreadful, horrors—can very gradually, in the presence of an inner witness—an other; a part of the self as situated in the loving, acknowledging and transforming other—be converted into digestible alpha elements (Bion 1962). In Preet's case, there is an inner witness, an aesthetic transformational experience (Bollas 1987) with Sister Agatha that he can eventually recover.

In his testimony, the child says, 'My mother and sister were there. The people got inside.' As the child states this on the soundtrack, we hear the sound of loud knocking, which almost transports the viewers to the site of the mass violence. This sound of loud knocking is a recurrent sonsign in the film. The child continues:

> They caught hold of mother and stabbed her with swords. She was cut from here. She tried to flee. She was hit on the head and fell unconscious. Then they poured petrol on her and set her on fire. I ran and climbed up a wall and jumped to the other side.

As the testimony comes to an end, we see Preet entering the convent in Meerut.

Preet's entire endeavour to research the 1984 anti-Sikh violence indicates the motif of quest in the film. This becomes obvious, especially when one of the journalists directly questions him, 'But why do you want to rake up all this again? Where were you then? How old are you?' Preet reveals that he is 25 years old. He was only 7 when he had witnessed the mass violence in 1984. In a revealing moment, he says to the journalist, '... the Gujarat violence dug up old memories. The more you want to forget the more you are forced to remember.' Similarly, the visit to the gurdwara after speaking to the journalists also signifies his deep-seated relationship with his past, the search for his lost self and identity; just as Preet's literal journey to Meerut to do a story on conversions reflects his unconscious quest to heal himself. The visit to the convent is actually an invitation to visit his past which, unbeknowst to him, in terms of its magnitude, continues to haunt him. The film suggests that for a person to live a complete existence, an encounter with one's own traumatic past is a must. In forgetting, the path to healing is blocked. Healing happens when we face up to our traumatic reality through mourning and embracing it. And mourning, as we know, is always a long and painful process. Emily Dickinson (1862) in her poem 'To be forgot by thee' pertinently states, 'The heart cannot forget unless it contemplates what it declines.'

Preet arrives in Meerut to do a story on conversions. As he enters the convent, once again on the soundtrack we hear the same traumatic sound that had occurred when Preet was exiting the gurdwara. At a conscious level, Preet has a few memories and is aware as to why he has come here, but at a deeper level he himself is unaware of the complete significance of his return. When Sister Agatha, who is in charge of the convent, refuses to speak on conversions and directs him to the Bishop's, suddenly Preet utters the word, 'But'. The word is extremely significant as it connotes the unconscious reason that has motivated Preet to return. After meeting the Bishop, Preet is compelled from within to return to the convent, and tries to tell Sister Agatha, 'I want to tell you why I came here.' As he utters these words, the past and the present fuse and all of a sudden we are transported to the moment of Sister Philomela's death, years ago in 1984. We see Sister Agatha praying, '... to be the salt of the earth'. The shot cuts to the camera tracking an open field in a haphazard manner. From the way the shot is constructed, it seems as if someone is running, followed by a mob shouting and chasing. We are told that Indira Gandhi, the then prime minister of India, has been shot by her Sikh bodyguards. As the news breaks, there is a deep sense of fear in the convent. The guard informs Sister Agatha that

> ... riots have broken out in the town and that the Sardars are being beaten; a lot of people have gathered near the clock tower, they have looted the shops of all the Sardars and are burning their cars and taxis. There are also a lot of bodies that are strewn on the road.

As we see the funeral procession of Indira Gandhi on the television, we witness a funeral procession here through the reporting of the guard. Night descends. Sister Agatha along with another Sister takes a walk in the veranda; on the soundtrack we hear the sound of loud knocking and a woman's voice crying, '… open the door, save my child in the name of God'. The nuns, with much trepidation, open the door and 'receive' Amarjeet Kaur and her son Jagpreet into the convent.

Through Amarjeet Kaur's elaborate narration, the film offers us details about the violence meted out to the Sikhs in 1984. Interestingly, Amarjeet Kaur's entire narration is repeated by Jaggi (little Jagpreet) as the camera cuts to his mid close-up, frontal image. Jaggi speaks in a monotonous, listless voice which soon becomes traumatic as he bears witness to the violence, speaking at a press conference, '… My name is Jagpreet Singh. We live in Model Town.' The flash of the camera clicks. Once again, the film assumes a docu-fictional mode, and we are transported to a moment in the past when Jagpreet, like the little boy survivor of the Gujarat pogrom, bears witness to his testimony and informs us what actually happened to him and his family in 1984 while they were living in Model Town in Meerut:

> So many people came into our colony, early in the morning. They began burning the shops because this year we did not celebrate Diwali. The police station is in front of our house. The people of the colony went there in the morning. My father too went with them. But the police sent them away. They said they can't help us. They don't have men. We then locked up the house and went to the gurdwara.

The scene shifts to a gurdwara as Jagpreet's voice continues on the soundtrack. '… There were Nihangs there in blue dress. They had long swords.' The camera takes a slow 360-degree turn. On the soundtrack we hear the sound of a *shabad* (Sikh religious prayers which are sung in gurdwaras) and the preaching in the gurdwara. The testimony continues:

> In the evening the police appeared on the road and we felt that everything was all right. People began returning to their homes and we went back to our house. That night when we were preparing to sleep those people came back and began attacking. They killed papa with a knife. They also killed Babloo.

As Jaggi says this, the camera cuts to a shot of Amarjeet Kaur howling, Jagpreet in a state of shock clinging to her. A man whom she later identifies as Ramji pulls her, but she bites his hand and escapes. Jagpreet continues,

'I pulled him from behind with all my strength. Then we ran away as fast as we could.' At the visual level, we see Jagpreet and Amarjeet Kaur run, it is night-time and there is fire all around. 'Then we ran away as fast as we could and kept running and running.' Jagpreet runs ahead of his mother as we see men on motorcycles chasing them, until they finally jump over the wall of the convent. On the soundtrack we hear hard knocks as Amarjeet Kaur in panic pleads for the door to be opened, '... open the door, is anyone listening.' In this shot, the film reveals the source of the sonsign of knocking which is so prevalent in the film and almost becomes a marker of Jagpreet's traumatised being.

The nuns give solace and shelter to the mother and the son. The next morning, still in a state of shock, Jaggi hides under a table. In a poignant shot framed in a mid close up, we see two hands coming closer as Jaggi joins his finger to Sister Agatha's outstretched finger. On the soundtrack, the soothing sound of bells is heard. Though Jaggi feels secure in the convent, the loss of his brother continues to haunt him. He hallucinates that his brother Babloo is standing next to a nun playing the piano. As the days pass, Jaggi becomes the cynosure of the convent. The nuns feel as if Jaggi has come like 'Adam in their garden'. After four days, when the curfew is lifted, the nuns help Amarjeet Kaur and Jaggi depart for Delhi, to their relative's place in Fatehpur Nagar camp, but again they are chased by the mob. They return to the convent. The camera traces a traumatised Jaggi once again hiding under a table, as Sister Agatha again offers her finger in a gesture of support and protection to him. The repetition of this sequence, of Sister Agatha offering her finger to Jaggi, is extremely crucial and poignant as a life theme in the film. The sequence suggests the transmission of faith and hope in a moment of utter despair. Once again, the film juxtaposes the interplay between life and death forces. The death instinct which wants to destroy by killing and annihilating, and the life affirming touch of the Sister, which re-instils a faith of goodness in life in the little boy, by spontaneously offering him the first symbol of human contact, 'touch', which sends alive sensations from finger to finger, body to body and being to being. Eventually this is what will inject his horror with hope. One is reminded of Erikson's (1964) formulation that if trust can be established in the first stages of life though the mother's touch, then hope as a companion can combat the fervent darkness of life's subsequent terrors.

Despite several threats by the goons, the nuns decide to stand by the mother and the son with the conviction that God alone will show them the way. The scene cuts to a long take of Sister Agatha along with several nuns praying desperately. The music turns surrealist as the camera positions itself into a top angle lens. We see a coffin in the middle of the room and Jaggi standing beside it, surrounded by the nuns. The nuns along with his mother, who too is dressed as a nun, hold him. In a state of utter despair, Jaggi cries to be rescued. Closing his eyes with their hands, they remove his *patka* and Sister Agatha cuts his hair. In an utter state of anguish, Jaggi screams, 'No, no Mummy, see what they are doing. Mummy, don't cut my hair. Let me go. Don't cut my hair.' Jaggi is then placed inside the coffin. On the soundtrack we hear the voice of Amarjeet Kaur crying and praying along with Jaggi, seeking forgiveness from *Waheguru* (God). The shot dissolves into a sequence which is almost surrealist. Encompassed within this sequence is an image of a grown-up man with long hair 'rising' from a coffin as several nuns surround him and nurture his hair tenderly with their fingers.

Eventually, Jaggi and Amarjeet Kaur, accompanied by the nuns, dupe the goons as Jaggi escapes hidden in the coffin. Through a long take in which the present and the past fuse, we see little Jaggi sitting in a train compartment. The camera continues to move and within the same shot we see Preet, now a grown-up man, sitting in another compartment in the same position framed next to a window where years back Jaggi was sitting. Sister Agatha runs to bid goodbye to Preet. In this deeply moving scene, she touches his hair and says, 'Now you don't feel upset when someone touches your hair.' In this moment of recognition, Preet smiles peacefully with gratitude as he acknowledges his identity not merely to Sister Agatha but also to his own self.

In the last sequence, Preet returns to his office wearing a turban. His colleagues look at him in amazement. There is serenity and peace on his face as he affirms, 'For your information, what I am wearing on my head is a *dastar* [turban] and it is my intention to keep it there, always.' As the film ends with an image of a smiling, peaceful Preet, on the soundtrack we hear a song connoting the impermanence of life.

In terms of its form, the film is extremely modernistic. It diffuses and collapses the boundaries between the past and the present. As Sister Agatha narrates incidents from the past, we see the same being fuse into the present. This fusion is so prevalent in the film that sometimes the viewers become completely fused and fail to comprehend whether the incidents on the screen belong to the present time zone or to a moment in the past. It is only after a few events are narrated that the viewers are able to identify the time zone of the events. Another interesting formal technique that the film adopts is the manner in which it operates across two time zones within a single shot. In many a sequence, while at the visual level the film situates itself in the present moment of time, at the level of sound it transports us into the time frame of 1984. Throughout the film, intermittently, we hear the traumatic sounds of violence and mutilation, of people screaming for help and wailing. Inferentially through its form, the film suggests that even though traumatic events may have happened in the past, they continue to haunt and determine one's present. It suggests that psychically trauma never becomes a thing of the past. The film thus reaffirms Lacan's (2014) formulation that we may forget traumatic events but these events never forget us.

Kaya Taran overtly informs us about the violence that Jagpreet and his mother faced, the manner in which they were thrown out of their house and how they became homeless in a moment. But the deeper trauma which is understated is the fact that Preet witnessed his own father and brother being brutally massacred in front of his eyes. Though Preet remains a well-functioning person, his life is deeply scarred by this trauma. The film goes deep into the impact of mass violence on the psyche of children, whether they are Muslim or Sikh children. At an unconscious level, Preet feels a deep sense of affinity with the Muslims post Godhra violence, for, like the Muslims, he too is the other of the majoritarian Hindu.

Another significant aspect that thc film achieves through this device of operating in two time zones, wherein the image refers to the present and the sound to the past, is to historicise and contextualise the 1984 mass violence within the context of mob-led violence in Gujarat. In terms of its time, the film situates itself in 2002, the year of the violence in Godhra in Gujarat. *Kaya Taran* opens in the canteen of an office where journalists are discussing the Gujarat violence. The discussion in the canteen revolves around a majoritarian discourse, which denounces the Muslims. In a dialogue reminiscent of M. S. Satyu's *Garam Hawa* (1973), one of the characters, while insulting the Muslims, says, 'Why don't they all return to Pakistan?' In a moment, the film reveals the fractured secularism of India as a nation, where the Hindu majority views all Muslims as a liability and as superfluous to their existence. It is in this sense that the film becomes all the more significant, as by situating itself within the Gujarat violence, it inferentially states that the real issue is not about killing Muslims or Sikhs but about the hegemony of Hindu majoritarianism which tends to eliminate anyone and everyone it perceives to be the other of itself. The majoritarian discourse is about othering and the need to annihilate the other. India witnessed such violence at the time of Partition, in the 1984 violence against the Sikhs, at the time of the demolition of the Babri Masjid in 1992, in Gujarat in 2002 and in the the mob lynching in Dadri in 2015, to name a few. This continuing violence against religious minorities, including the people of the North-East and the Dalits, is a manifestation of othering. Apparently, the minority can exist safely only as long as the dominant majority feels that they should be allowed to exist. But the moment the majority is displeased with them, they can be killed and massacred. But what is of specific importance in this case is the fact that after the death of India Gandhi, the anti-Sikh massacres that followed did not merely have a communal angle to them (though they did indicate a sense of vengeance) but were also a result of state-instigated violence which functioned as a designed programme to 'punish' the Sikhs.

The report *Who Are the Guilty?* published jointly by the People's Union for Democratic Rights (PUDR) and the PUCL (1984) clearly states:

> The attacks on members of the Sikh Community in Delhi and its suburbs during the period, far from being a spontaneous expression of 'madness' and of popular 'grief and anger' at Mrs. Gandhi's assassination as made out to be by the authorities, were the outcome of a well organized plan marked by acts of both deliberate commissions and omissions by important politicians of the Congress (I) at the top and by authorities in the administration. (PUDR/PUCL 1984)

Similarly, the report by Citizens for Democracy reiterates:

> We have shown in this report that several meetings were held all over Delhi—central, outer and trans Yamuna areas in the late hours of 31st October to give final touches, as it were, to the plans already prepared with meticulous care, with an eye to every minute detail that nothing was left out to successfully exterminate the Sikhs (Rao et al. 1985: x).

Veena Das in her chapter 'The Force of the Local', included in her book *Life and Words*, while summarising several people's reports on the riots, writes:

> ... that on the night of the 31st, meetings of Congress functionaries were held in different parts of Delhi in which every act was planned in meticulous detail. ... that on the morning of November 1st between 9 and 11 A.M., attacks would be launched on Sikhs simultaneously in various parts of the city. The attacks ..., came in four phases: first Gurudwaras were attacked, then Sikh houses were looted and set ablaze; next men

> were humiliated by shearing their hair and shaving off their beards, and then they were killed; finally women were molested and raped, and some were killed. The purpose of this carnage, according to the report, was to get the sympathy vote of Hindus to win upcoming elections. (2007: 141–142)

Analysing such forms of violence, Terry Eagleton states:

> The point is that most wickedness is institutional. It is the result of vested interests and anonymous processes, not of the malign acts of individuals. One should not, to be sure, underestimate the importance of such acts, just as one should not be so excessively sophisticated as to reject the idea of conspiracies. It is a fact that men and women with shady intentions gather from time to time in what these days are smoke free rooms to plot some moral outrage or other. For the most part, however, such outrages are the products of particular systems. (2012: 144–145)

Nevertheless, what is most difficult to accept, but nonetheless true, is the inherent evil in humans who so easily can be activated to participate in state-instigated communal violence. Eagleton offers deep psychoanalytical insights into the nature of evil when he says:

> There are those who feel uneasy about this way of viewing evil. ... it is here I think that psychoanalytical theory can ride to the rescue, allowing us to maintain that evil is a kind of deprivation while still acknowledging its formidable power. The power in question, as we have seen already, is essentially that of the death drive, turned outward so as to wreak its insatiable spitefulness on a fellow human being. Yet this furious violence involves a kind of lack—an unbearable sense of non-being, which must, so to speak, be taken out on the other. It is also oriented to another kind of absence: the nullity of death itself. Hence, then, terrifying force and utter vacuousness come together. (Ibid.: 127–128)

The film delves into this aspect when Amarjit Kaur reveals that one of the goons who killed her husband and son was their neighbour Ramji, who saw this as a good opportunity to take over their shop since it was next to his. This episode signifies the multiple vested interests of people in situations of mass violence. Similarly, the little boy's testimony in the film's opening shots and little Jaggi's testimony signify the untamed, incomprehensible dark forces in humans that can devour anyone in a state of frenzy instigated by a hegemonic communal order, as essentially there is a propensity to 'other' anyone and everyone who seems to be different from the self.

Despite depicting the inherent evil in humans, the film, on the other hand, offers us insights into the true meaning of religion, especially in the context of Sikhism and Christianity. In the sequence in which little Jaggi gives his testimony, on the soundtrack we hear the preachings in the gurdwara:

> God created the *Khalsa* for the well-being and protection of all. The ideal of the Khalsa was and is to cherish the well-being of all. It does not think bad of anyone. It asks for the entire world's well-being. O' lord the world is on fire, save it by showering your grace. This is the essential Sikh principle.

Similarly, the ending of the film through a song states, 'The world is the destination of the disappearing ... that alone is the certainty ... the angel of death holds me by the hair and yet unaware am I.' The song suggests the impermanence of life and hence the futility of violence and communal disharmony, which is especially embodied in the image of the stoning of the statue of the 'Lady of the Lourdes' by the goons when they were threatening the nuns. Within the Christian context, the film suggests that the true meaning of religion is 'To be the salt of the earth'.

The soundtrack continuously reinforces the sense of lived trauma that marked Jaggi's childhood, and which continues to haunt him. This is evident in the sequence when Preet is on his motorcycle after his visit to the gurdwara. In this sequence, Preet's past and present fuse as traumatic memories from the past return to him. On the soundtrack we hear the sound of the mob, a haunting sound that recurs in the film. At the visual level, we see children playing and shouting 'catch catch', but this shot is fused with the shot of a Sikh man on a scooter who is being lynched by a mob. The sequence once again highlights Preet's traumatic past. *Kaya Taran* thus is a remarkable study into trauma associated with mass violence and the lingering effect it has. The sequence once again highlights Preet's brutally interrupted past. Vahali (2009), analysing trauma, offers her insights along with Max Hernandez's insights:

> ... that at the time of trauma, its powerful impact creates in the ego a basic inability to annihilate it. In the unconscious its traces continue to exist as '*primitive agonies*' and come to pervade the present as a '*fear of breakdown*' that is yet to take place. For as long as trauma is not recognized and not assimilated, it cannot be accorded its place in the past. (Hernandez 1998: 134–44)

In a different context, Hernandez further states, 'There is nothing post about … trauma. In becoming the present it is happening all the time' (Hollander 1998: 208).

The film, in a very subtle manner, symbolises Preet's struggle through his relationship with his *kesh* (hair). At several instances in the film, especially when he is a little child, we see his deep sensitivity related to his hair. Even in the convent when he develops close bonds with the nuns, he is extremely resistant to any touch on his head. The most haunting sequence, as delineated earlier, is when the nuns cut his hair in order to protect him. Jaggi screams in anguish for he perceives the cutting of his hair as a complete violation and mutilation of his being. This is emphasised through the soundtrack when even after his hair have been chopped, he continues to howl to be rescued by the nuns. Later, when the nuns finally come to bid goodbye to him in the train, we see a distraught Jaggi touching his hair, still unable to come to terms with his amputated being. This basic angst of his existence is developed throughout the film through several nuanced details. In the sequence when Preet returns home after interviewing the journalists, we see him applying shaving cream on his face. As he picks the razor to shave, in the mirror he perceives the white foam of the cream as a beard. Looking at his bearded face, he stops himself from using the razor and instead washes his face. This particular sequence is a nuanced cinematic insert as it reflects his deep-seated anguish pertaining to his amputated identity as a Sikh. This insert finally acquires significance towards the end of the film, when Preet returns to his office wearing a turban, especially in the context of his insight when he reflects, 'Nothing happens suddenly. This *dastar* has being tied since childhood. And today it is done. Today it has been decorated.' The ending of the film signifies the culmination of his psychic journey.

It is the loss of hair and its restoration that forms the leitmotif in the film, and yet Preet has to consciously encounter this angel of death who is holding him by his hair, and has to accept the impermanence of existence that he had so early encountered in his life, in order to live a healthy life.

Kaya Taran focuses on the trauma of a Sikh child related to the killings of his father and brother and of cutting his hair which symbolically is the mutilation of his being. The restoration of Preet as a Sikh who decides to wear a turban at the end of the film, thereby consolidating and reinstating his Sikh identity, finally depicts his coming to terms with his inner journey of mutilation and violence and hence the self. The presence of a benevolent other in one's past, in this case Sister Agatha in Preet's past, however gory it may have been, instils seeds of healing and recovery. Such acts of benevolence, in even the most devastating massacres, can lead to healing, the film affirms. Albert Camus (1951) reminds us that our future depends not only on remembering the violence meted out to us but also and equally on the histories of compassion and friendships that we encounter in life.

In working through trauma, the film connects to acts of kindness and support that were given to people during mass violence and highlights their deep significance. It thus states that the power of goodness and kindness is greater than the power of massacres and destruction that can be partially held by acts of love. The theme of love and nurturance as binding forces of the life instinct is especially communicated through the sequence in which we witness the dance of the nuns as fantasied by Preet. The nuns symbolically touch with gentleness the now-adult Preet's hair, and thus his being, with tenderness. In the process, they repair and heal the mutilation of his being which was precipitated by the cutting of his hair. The chopping of his kesh had led to his spiritual death, which is signified through the coffin in which he was placed. The sequence marks the rebirth of little Jaggi and signifies his resurrection through the help and loving nurturance of the nuns in the convent. Jaggi, who had become disintegrated, is made whole again. Like Christ, Preet receives a second birth. The nuns' sense of responsibility and compassion is commendable. *Kaya Taran* revokes memories of the partition of the Indian subcontinent, but memories not only of violence and acts of inhumanity, but of compassion and restoration as well. Preet's encounter with his benevolent past restores his lost, wounded identity of being a Sikh, which he had earlier been compelled to give up.

Kaya Taran advocates a universe where if kindness and compassion reigned, the inherent evil in human nature could be counteracted. In the last chapter of their book *On Kindness*, Adam Phillips and Barbara Taylor write:

> Our resistance to Kindness is our resistance to encountering what kindness meets in us, and what we meet in other people by being kind to them. And, of course, our resistance to seeing the limits of what kindness can do for us. Kindness comes from what Freud calls—in a different context—'after education', that is a revised awareness of something that is already felt and known. And this after education, entails the recognition of kindness as a continual temptation in everyday life that we resist. Not a temptation to sacrifice ourselves, but to include ourselves with others. Not a temptation to renounce or ignore the aggressive aspects of ourselves,

> but to see kindness as being in solidarity with human need, and with the very paradoxical sense of powerlessness and power that human need induces. (Phillips and Taylor 2009: 117)

The title of the film can be set in contrast with Kafka's *Metamorphosis* (2016). The title 'Metamorphosis' becomes ironical as it suggests the loss of all loving forces and the eventual death of Gregor Samsa, who because of lack of love is transformed from a human into an insect, a non-being. On the contrary, the title of the film *Kaya Taran* (Chrysalis) is extremely significant as it connotes emergence, the emergence and transformation of a pupa into a butterfly, a transformation which in this context happens especially through the loving nurturance and healing of Sister Agatha, whose presence in Preet's life gives him the courage to own his Sikh identity. Preet finally turns into a butterfly, ready to take his plunge into this world of violence, but a world he knows, nevertheless, is also bound with invisible kindness everywhere.

It is crucial to end this chapter while meditating on the significance of focusing on one's painful parts of existence, as incorporated in Rumi's poem, 'Wound is the place':

> Trust your wound to a teacher's (God) surgery.
> Flies collect on a wound.
> They cover it, those flies of your self-protecting feelings,
> your love for what you think is yours.
> Let a teacher wave away the flies and put a plaster on the wound.
> Don't turn your head.
> Keep looking at the bandaged place.
> That's where
> the Light enters you.

Notes

1. In my analysis, I constantly shift between calling Jagpreet Preet and Jaggi. In his childhood, Jagpreet was called Jaggi, as an adult he was known as Preet by his friends and colleagues.

2. I am in particular indebted to Prof. Honey Oberoi Vahali for her deep insights into the psychoanalytical theory related to trauma and the human psyche that I have incorporated in this chapter.

3. In film language a sonsign means a sound image.

References

Bion, W. R. 1962. *Learning from Experience*. New York: Basic Books.

Bollas, C. 1987. *The Shadow of the Object: Psychoanalysis of the Unthought Known*. New York: Columbia University Press.

Camus, Albert. 1951. *The Rebel: An Essay on Man in Revolt*. London: Routledge.

Das, Veena. 2007. 'The Force of the Local'. In *Life and Words: Violence and the Descent into the Ordinary*, by Veena Das. New Delhi: Oxford University Press.

Dickinson, Emily. 1862. 'To be Forgot by thee'. Available at https://www.eliteskills.com/c/17059 (accessed on 10 February 2017).

Eagleton, Terry. 2012. *On Evil*. Calcutta: Seagull Books.

Erikson, E. H. 1964. *Insight and Responsibility*. New York: W.W. Norton.

Felman, S., and Dori Laub. 1988. *Testimony: The Crises of Witnessing in Literature, Psychoanalysis and History*. New York: Routledge.

Garam Hawa. 1973. Director M. S. Satyu. Film Finance Corporation. Film.

Grotstein, J. S. 2007. *A Beam of Intense Darkness: Wilfred Bion's Legacy to Psychoanalysis*. London: Karnac.

Hernandez, Max. 1998. 'Winnicott's Fear of Breakdown: On and Beyond Trauma'. *Diacritics* 12 (2): 134–44.

Hollander, Nancy Carlo. 1998. 'Exile: Paradoxes of Loss and Creativity'. *British Journal of Psychotherapy* 15 (2): 201–19.

Kafka, Franz. 2016. *Metamorphosis*. London: Penguin Classics.

Kaya Taran. 2004. Director Sashi Kumar. Film.

Lacan, J. 2014. *Anxiety: The Seminar of Jacques Lacan, Book X*. Polity Press.

People's Union for Democratic Rights (PUDR) and People's Union for Civil Liberties (PUCL). 1984. *'Who Are the Guilty? Report of a Joint Inquiry into the Causes and Impact of the Riots in Delhi from 31st October to 10th November'*. Delhi. Available at https://www.pudr.org/publicatiosn-files/1984-11-Who%20are%20the%20guilty-1.pdf (accessed on 16 February 2017).

Phillips, Adam, and Barbara Taylor. 2009. *On Kindness*. England: Penguin Books.

Rao, Amiya, Aurobindo Ghose, and N. D. Pancholi, eds. 1985. *Report to the Nation: Truth about Delhi Violence*. New Delhi: Citizens for Democracy.

Rumi, Mevlana. n.d. 'Wound is the Place'. Available at https://enlightenedrumi.wordpress.com/2013/03/22/wound-is-the-place-by-rumi/ (accessed on 15 February 2017).

Vahali, Honey Oberoi. 2009. *Lives in Exile: Exploring the Inner World of Tibetan Refugees*. New Delhi: Routledge.

IV

Experience and Personal Narratives

eight

A Personal Account of 1984

Uma Chakravarti

When news about Indira Gandhi began to circulate on the morning of 31 October 1984, it was by word of mouth, so no one knew what exactly had happened to her till much later in the evening when her death was officially announced on state TV and radio. Up until then it was a day like any other. I was in Miranda House, the college for women where I was teaching, with a bunch of students rehearsing for a play that they were going to take to some inter-college event or other, and I was with them because I was the advisor to the dramatic society of our college for that year. Around 12 noon or so a colleague came and peeped in through the window of the room where we were rehearsing and asked somewhat mysteriously: 'Have you heard the news…?' I said, 'No nothing, what do you mean', but she went off, keeping the mystery to herself. This happened on and off through the next two hours; various colleagues would poke their heads in and then leave without us knowing what the mysterious event they were alluding to was. Finally, after the BBC announcement came to be circulated, the 'event' became clear. Mrs Gandhi had been assassinated by her security guards. Stunned by the news and confused by the situation, we did not know how to respond. I had a civil rights meeting in the campus that I went to attend. It was held as scheduled and then I went home. We lived as tenants in the house of a Sikh school principal and went straight to uncle, as we called him, and his wife, aunty Narinder's flat. They lived across our own door in the corridor and were like family to us and our two children for the past seven years, and we often discussed politics with them. By then they too knew about the assassination; so, as we stepped in, uncle said: '*yeh kya hua*' (what is this that has happened?). All of us were deeply concerned with the way Mrs Gandhi had played politics out in Punjab—first by setting up Bhindranwale against a perfectly justified demand by Punjab for greater autonomy, and then, when he turned on her, she ordered a military operation on the Golden Temple in Amritsar where Bhindranwale was hiding. This military assault was a deeply offensive act that would leave a permanent scar on the nation. The 'yeh kya hua' was an acknowledgement that political issues needed to be dealt with politically; assassinations simply replace one set of people in power with others who make the same mistakes, so nothing changes. Instead, things get worse.

The next morning even our middle-class colony witnessed the collection of small mobs of people who took over the streets. There were two other Sikh families on our street apart from uncle and aunty who were alone in their home as the mobs began to freely roam the streets in the neighbourhood. We tried to stave them off from attacking the Sikh houses, and as we did that I remember being outraged by a 'helpful' student who lived across from our house telling me to change from a salwar-kameez to a sari so that I would not look like a Sikh and thus be safe. Uncle and aunty, who were more visible because they lived in the front part of the house, were persuaded by us to come into our flat at the back, so that they would be less visible—it was a poignant moment because up until then we had sheltered under their protective care, nurtured by their warmth and affection. Now as uncle came into our flat he brought in with him his licensed firearm, saying with so much sadness: 'for self-protection'.

We continued to stave off the bunch of mobsters through some mobilisation of the neighbours on the streets. Even as we were successful in preventing attacks, I was shocked to hear a neighbour say: 'this street is unsafe because of uncle and aunty' who were regarded as decent. There was petty envy in the case of the other two Sikh families because they were obviously wealthy and made no effort to hide it from the rest of the neighbourhood, composed largely of modest income-holders. In the evening, a police officer who was a friend of uncle and aunty's son came and took them away to his colony where they would be safe as no one knew how the next day was going to turn out.

By nightfall there were stories of the water being poisoned. Fortunately, we did not have a phone so we were insulated from the panic phone calls people became a part of. But next morning was terrible: the papers carried news of attacks and killings on trains of Sikh passengers in the outskirts of Delhi. The emotional exhaustion of the previous day and night culminated in a collapse as I recalled stories of Partition when I was six and had heard of such killings for the first time. Partition had been traumatic for us as a family though we were never in danger ourselves. We lived across the

Bangla Sahib Gurdwara in central Delhi which we often frequented as children. At that time, it was the Muslims who were targets in Delhi and even in that middle-class government housing area where we lived we saw strange acts associated with rioting. As my father and I were going to a ration shop to buy our quota of food for the month, a group of Hindu and Sikh men came running towards us and told us to go home because there were going to be attacks in the area. My sister and brother actually witnessed the killing of a Muslim man, one among three trying to reach the shelter of a police station: two made it, but one was killed before he could get there in time before the attackers got him. My sister has never recovered from that sight. We hid at home, locking ourselves up in fear of what was to come. Soon, I had a raging fever of some kind and my mother recalls me crying out in my delirium: 'why are the Hindus and Muslims killing each other'.

Why indeed?

And so, the news of the train killings had led to a collapse. I slept for 10 hours. Our son locked himself up for a month in a room, speaking to no one, unable to deal with the violence he had witnessed in the city that he had grown up in, and loved dearly, until then. When my daughter went back to school after 10 days, she was outraged to find the school officially mourning for Mrs Gandhi but not for the Sikhs who had died—even she could see the partisan nature of official memorialising. In the meanwhile, after the curfew was lifted we went to the relief camps that were set up along with a group of people from the People's Union for Democratic Rights (PUDR). Groups of people sat dazed by the events they had witnessed; others angrily described trying to get the police to act and being turned away. This was the beginning of the process that led to the writing of the report entitled 'Who Are the Guilty?', a report that made a historic intervention in understanding the complicity of the state in the carnage in Delhi. Before the joint report of the PUDR and People's Union for Civil Liberties (PUCL) was published (within three weeks of the carnage), the report writers received threats of attacks by Congress goons, if the report was actually published. Notwithstanding these threats, the report was published and was widely circulated across India, putting the state on the back-foot. Since then the entire weight of the state's actions has been to deny its role in engineering the carnage.

Even before the curfew was lifted the first peace marches had happened as concerned citizens took out processions in colonies where hostile crowds of arsonists still had control of the streets. They went to Trilokpuri, the site of horrifying violence, and found deserted streets with only a few half-crazed souls cowering in fear. Later, Dilip Simeon, a colleague from Delhi University, recalled an event which he has never forgotten, of a child in her mother's arms crying out in fear as she saw a group of people coming towards them: '*meri ma ko mat marna*!' (Don't kill my mother!). She thought another attack was imminent—that is what groups of men did to innocent people, and I wonder if she has ever been able to get over the fear she experienced in 1984.

We all had such memories. During the course of our visits to the colonies in the periphery of Delhi (where the poor had been relocated during the clean-up of the city, master-minded by Indira Gandhi's son during the Emergency that had supposedly made them the proud possessors of 25 square yard plots, upon which they had built their homes, and which we, middle-class Delhiites, saw for the first time in our lives), we would come across people or stories that would move us in particular ways. In Garhi, in south Delhi, I saw a three-year-old girl who looked mutely at us: she had lost her speech after the attacks in her area killed her father who had been a vegetable vendor. Her face continues to haunt me to date and I do not know if she ever recovered her speech. Another young woman of about 18 or 19 lost her husband in the attacks. She had been married for less than a year and was a few months' pregnant in November 1984. The shock had resulted in a miscarriage. This young woman's story made such an impact on me that I went and pleaded with the only Sikh businessman I knew at that time to please-please give her a job so that she could be financially rehabilitated. Though he was sympathetic to her plight, he thought I was a bit touched in the head myself: he could not give her a job as he ran a truck business, an all-male enterprise if ever there was one. He gave me some money instead for the relief work we were doing.

For years afterwards, and even to this day, I come across stories of 1984. It is like an undercurrent in the life of Delhi. You get into a cab or go to a certain kind of gathering and say, 'where were you when 1984 happened' and people will tell you their stories—of landing at airports and being hidden, of hair being cut, of getting home to hear more accounts of relatives being killed, of acts of great brutality and occasionally of great generosity. Perhaps it was these stories and the need to counter the state narrative on 1984 that led to my obsession with archiving the voices of the living present. I kept talking about it to everyone until Nandita Haksar, my student from Miranda House and by 1984 a young lawyer, said:

'Okay then let's do it.' She got hold of a couple of tape recorders and a few cassettes, and we formed ourselves into a group of six people who began the process of documenting 1984. It took us three years to collect the narratives, transcribe and translate them, find a publisher, put money into the publication and then bring the work out (it was published as *The Delhi Riots: Three Days in the Life of a Nation*, 1987). This book through its narratives picks up on many threads: the terrible killings of innocent families who were mourning for Mrs Indira Gandhi because they were her supporters—she had given them plots of land that made them independent home-owners for the first time. Some were even observing a fast but were mercilessly killed nevertheless. The first narrator, Nanki Bai, described the rapes of young girls, an issue that has been unaddressed as sexual violence was buried by the complicity of every member of the community, and thereafter in every commission report. As Manoj Mitta has now written, it was inconvenient to acknowledge the rapes when the narrative of grieving mobs on a retaliatory rampage was being put in place (Mitta and Phoolka 2007: 67–73). Another account of an elderly Sikh man who had lost three sons in the killings, and was left with a daughter-in-law who went into sessions of possession after that, was almost mythic in its narration. In a slow recounting, he told us of the continuing dislocation of the Labaniya Sikhs since Partition, coming from Sindh in 1948 first to Bombay, then on to Ajmer, and then to Delhi, moving from one cluster of *jhuggi*es (huts) to another till they got the prized 25 gaz ka plot (a plot measuring 25 gaz) and thought they had finally found a home for themselves. But no: they were cruelly uprooted once more and were then in Tilak Vihar where every survivor was angry, traumatised and hurt by the massacres they had witnessed. The young were baying for revenge. But not Phanda Singh. He wanted justice, not revenge. *Kanoon dwara nyaya* (justice) he told us and so he condemned the transistor bombs that had recently exploded in DTC buses. Unfortunately, for him kanoon dwara nyaya (justice) never came. It is a burden we must all carry: the denial of justice to the victims and survivors of 1984.

The Delhi Riots was so voluminous that finally Nandita and I had to leave out some of the interviews that we had conducted, and these missing interviews are now part of my personal archive of paper. It is part of a collection of many other papers; newspaper cuttings, lists of people killed or missing which we had compiled on our visits to the colonies where the worst attacks had taken place; some photographs, and sundry other bits among which I recently found a small piece written by another student: an account of the play we had created on 1984, which had got lost among my pile of papers. Students had their own collection of stories to recount: of what it was like to be in a women's college, locked behind the iron gates of the institution, supposedly for the safety of the students, but subjected to crazy rumours inside those locked gates about students from the Khalsa College, a Sikh institution across the road from Miranda House, who were supposedly going to come and attack 'them'. Actually, no Sikh man could venture on to the streets at that time. Rumours of threatened women, whose bodies were at stake, were clearly part of the strategy for keeping the violence stoked.

Finally, when the play titled *Patan* was ready, we took it around the city. Among the many locations we performed at was the Delhi School of Economics; on the grounds of a historical monument at Nizamuddin; an elite colony that had come up post Partition; Tilak Vihar, the colony that was now home to the widows of 1984; and finally, on 8 March outside the Red Fort as part of the International Women's Day rally in 1985. After that, it was time to pack up since examinations began in the first week of April. The bonds that had been established in the group, however, stayed as did the concerns that had generated the play: when Shonali Bose made her first film, it was on 1984 and among its cast was another young actress from the group who was Sikh herself. Women students in Delhi who witnessed the days of the violence were changed forever by what they had experienced. And teachers too.

Among the activities that the Delhi University teachers were involved with in the days and months that followed was the work of collecting data on the consequences of the pogrom: the number of dead, missing and injured, the work of trying to provide immediate relief, then long-term attempts at healing the women and children, which is documented in Mita Bose's powerful account in the book Nandita and I put together. She describes poignantly the inadequacy of the attempts to support a widow who killed herself because she could never forget the little boy who was burnt in 1984. Indraprastha College stayed with the 1984 survivors, especially its children, as it ran a summer camp for two years in the college where other students, many from high schools, created activities for the children. Today, 40 years later, young researchers have picked up on a completely neglected field: the disruption of education of the children—the loss of the academic year, withdrawal from schools, especially of the girls, and the complete absence of any trauma counselling of the children who were so traumatised by the memories of what they had seen.

I also re-found one of the interviews—with Lalita Ramdas—that was left out in *The Delhi Riots*, which is now out of print, which I will include in a shorter version of the book because of its relevance to the response of women's groups to the 1984 pogrom. This interview dwells on the work of women's groups as part of the Nagrik Ekta Manch who tried to continue to work with the widows of 1984 as they sought to rebuild their lives. As the community itself closed ranks, the widows had to battle against community and kinship norms that made the women prisoners of their families or what survived of it. They were forced into marriages with brothers-in-laws and the takeover of what little compensation money they got in dribs and drabs by a state that played politics with their devastated lives, making it subject to wheeling and dealing with the Sikh political leadership. They had terrible anxieties around the marriages of daughters that led to panic marriages; the adolescent boys were in distress—many of whom slowly fell into wayward lives—as they tried to deal with their unexpressed anger at the violence they had been subjected to. The interview also describes the anger of the women when the killers of Indira Gandhi were hanged while their cases never moved, no matter which government came to power. They could see that justice for the victims of 1984 was merely a matter of rhetoric and we have seen how commission after commission and case after case has denied the substantive issue of state accountability and command responsibility and ensured that impunity for the guilty stays. Ten years later, when Urvashi Butalia and I went to Tilak Vihar to meet some of the women, one of them told us: 'We did not get justice from the courts. We got it from "rab" [God] when Rajiv Gandhi was blown to pieces by a suicide bomber.' But, for many of us, the ongoing tragedy has been that given the twists and turns of political manoeuvres when 2002 happened, 1984 simply became a way to justify impunity in Gujarat. The sexual violence too was justified as something almost inevitable in a discussion in Parliament—a statement that was so outrageous that it had to be expunged from the records. Only some of us feminists and civil rights activists have been left to point out that one does not justify the other; there are many of us who have stood against all forms of communal and state-sponsored violence and we will continue to do so, no matter what.

References

Chakravarti, Uma, and Nandita Haksar. 1987. *The Delhi Riots: Three Days in the Life of a Nation*. New Delhi: Lancer International.

Mitta, Manoj, and H. S. Phoolka. 2007. *When a Tree Shook Delhi: 1984 Carnage and Its Aftermath*. Delhi: Roli Books.

nine

The Broken Middle*

Dilip Simeon

If justice perishes, human life on earth has lost its meaning

– Immanuel Kant

Once crime was as solitary as a cry of protest; now it is as universal as science. Yesterday it was put on trial; today it determines the law

– Albert Camus

The year 1984 remains India's Orwellian year par excellence. Why? Because it is the defining moment at which the language of public life became loaded with the requirement of deceit. The gap between official and political utterances and the evidence of our eyes and ears became an unbridgeable chasm; and even the thin pretension that state institutions and the Government of India existed to uphold the law of the land and the security of citizens was dropped into a furnace and evaporated into thin air. There is nothing more terrifying than the sensation that truth itself has ceased to exist, that silence is all that is left to us because no one is listening, or none may be trusted. That was what I, and many of my friends and fellow citizens, felt in those three days in late 1984—and indeed in the months and years that followed.

The violent events that swept through New Delhi and other urban centres in 1984 were a state-enabled, politically sponsored, communally inspired carnage of Sikh citizens because they belonged to the same community as the assassins of the Prime Minister. State power rested with the Congress party. Most of the killers were ordinary people who, egged on by senior Delhi Congressmen and their local henchmen, believed in

*This chapter originally appeared as a special article in *Economic and Political Weekly* 49 (43/44), 1 November 2014, and has been carried in the present volume without any alterations.

the primitive idea of collective guilt (i.e., that all members of a community carry responsibility for the crimes committed by some amongst them). Very likely they also believed that they would neither be stopped, nor face trial for their deeds. Indeed, many rioters believed that they were engaged in patriotic activity, that mass murder was something that their political leaders and patrons actively desired. Moreover, many people with no political connections spoke in terms of Sikhs needing to be taught a lesson, etc.

In effect, we were in an atmosphere of genocidal consensus. I do not mean that everyone had become a potential murderer, but that a large section of the population that did not directly attack Sikhs nevertheless condoned such attacks or remained indifferent to the takeover of the streets by hooligans. Communal violence has been a constant feature of Indian politics since the 1920s, but a state-enabled communal massacre in independent India's capital under the aegis of the emblematic party of Indian nationalism was unprecedented.

Precisely because of this, 1984 is the year of the broken middle. Mob violence on a mass scale entered mainstream political culture. No longer could it be claimed that the politics of revenge emanated from the margins of the polity. It was the middle ground that was now shattered, giving fresh impetus to communal concepts of nationalism. The year 1984 set a new standard for the normalisation of brutality and lawlessness in the Indian polity. It undermined faith in the Constitution and gave strength to criminal elements in political parties and society at large. It strengthened communal bias within the bureaucracy and police, and generated widespread cynicism.

Having allowed the violence to rage for several days, the commanders of state institutions decided to stop the bloodletting. After that, a tidal wave of frightening words swept through society. Contemporary speech could broadly be divided into two kinds—blatant justification, as in 'they deserved it' (which had the merit of frankness); and varieties of escapism and/or self-exoneration, as in 'Sikhs distributed sweets after the assassination', 'in any family sometimes the elder brother has to slap the younger brother', 'Congress workers are responsible, not us', 'after all, they killed the prime minister, it was an outpouring of patriotic grief', 'when a great tree is uprooted, the ground is bound to shake', etc. The year 1984 prompted our opinion-makers and ideologues to indulge in a gigantic cover-up operation that was simultaneously an exercise in self-delusion. Partisan buck-passing was raised to the level of an art form. Who has not heard it said that the RSS/BJP cannot be condemned for the Gujarat carnage of 2002, because, after all, the Congress also engineered carnage in 1984? This argument acts like an opiate for some of us. Everybody is guilty, ergo nobody is. One massacre deserves another.

In 1984, one saw official bias at work precisely when the neutral authority of the state was most needed. Violent mobs were shouting communal slogans, desecrating gurdwaras and burning Sikh passers-by in the streets to assert communal superiority. And many residents of Delhi were enjoying the spectacle. Yet in the midst of all this, what we got was a passive Home Minister Narasimha Rao, delayed summoning of sufficient armed force, biased utterances and abetment of crimes by policemen on duty, non-registration of FIRs, doctoring of evidence, deceitful behaviour of public prosecutors, irresponsible behaviour by mass media sometimes amounting to instigation of violence, blatant judicial whitewash, punishment transfers of responsible functionaries, and collusion amongst bureaucrats, police and political executives to the point of granting one another impunity for criminal negligence or worse.[1] Instances of gang-rape are still being covered up. Most of these features were visible in Gujarat in 2002, including the shameless speed with which political gain (calling elections in a communally charged environment) was extracted from the revengeful climate. Advertisements issued by the Congress party during the 1984 Lok Sabha elections appealed to such sentiments by representing India's border shrinking inwards. These factors point towards criminal complicity at the highest level of state institutions. Such complicity cannot work unless large numbers of responsible officials are biased, and, moreover, unless they believe that the public at large is cynical or equally complicit.

In January 1985, newly elected Prime Minister Rajiv Gandhi entered a joint session of Parliament accompanied by President Zail Singh and H. K. L. Bhagat, a man whose constituency was the venue of some of the worst violence.[2] A resolution was adopted condoling Indira Gandhi's death. Rajiv made a mild statement of sympathy, but no one saw it fit to condole the deaths of thousands of Indians cruelly murdered for no fault of theirs. Twenty-one years later, on 11 August 2005, Prime Minister Manmohan Singh declared in the Rajya Sabha that 1984 was 'a great national shame, a great national tragedy', and that he had 'no hesitation in apologising not only to the Sikh community but the whole Indian nation'. He denied that the Congress leadership was complicit in the violence, whilst admitting that certain leaders had been implicated by the Nanawati

Commission. Jagdish Tytler was obliged to leave the ministry, and Sajjan Kumar his local government post.

The most enigmatic question that 1984 confronts us with is why and how the larger world can without warning, drag innocent people into a hell of agony and despair. At such moments, not just state institutions but the very universe reeks of injustice. In such situations, even a simple acknowledgement of our suffering can help ease the pain. But our tallest political leaders were incapable of this—in fact, their utterances and behaviour rubbed salt into the wounds of the bereaved. Whatever this says about Indian policing, it says more about the incoherence of India's conscience, even though some judges use phrases like 'collective conscience of the society'.[3] Who are we, after all? What does it mean to be a nation? The year 1984 threw these questions in our faces yet once more. Other than the assumption that might is right, no answer is as yet forthcoming.

Wool over Our Eyes

What is meant by the phrase 'requirement of deceit'? It is quite simple.

It is misleading to say that the actions of the Government of India are always grounded in law, when the police cannot be trusted to cognise terrible crimes transpiring in front of their eyes. To pretend otherwise is deceitful.

It is misleading to say that India's criminal justice system can be trusted to uphold the Constitution, if the utterances of even a single judge carry the odour of communal bias. To pretend otherwise is deceitful.

It is false to say that public prosecution is being conducted in the interest of justice and public order, when the public prosecutors seek to protect wrongdoers. To pretend otherwise is deceitful.

It is misleading to claim that political parties represent the interests of all Indians, when, in fact, we can see them working for sectional interests and/or promoting communal divisiveness. To pretend otherwise is deceitful.

It is false to claim that J. S. Bhindranwale was merely a religious preacher who was persecuted by the Indian state on account of his campaign to cleanse Sikhism and fight for justice. Such claims seek to wipe away the memory of his involvement in violent crime, contempt for moderation, instigation of hatred, desecration of the Golden Temple and pretension to speak for the entire Sikh community. To pretend otherwise is deceitful.

It is misleading to frame the question of responsibility in purely partisan language, such as 'Congress killed Sikhs'. Senior Congressmen were the prime movers of the carnage, but it is not enough to say this. Such a frame glosses over the intense and palpable communal hatred intrinsic to the violence of 1984. It disguises the fact that the killers saw themselves as patriots teaching a lesson to 'anti-national Sikhs'. It overlooks the surcharged communal atmosphere in north India in the early 1980s, an atmosphere that Prime Minister Indira Gandhi cynically manipulated from time to time. It does not explain why many people with no sympathy for the Congress applauded the violence as just retribution meted out to an entire community. It cannot explain why Sajjan Kumar, still under trial for his acts in 1984, received the maximum number of votes in India in the 2004 elections.[4] In 1984, the Congress transformed itself into a vehicle for communal ideology and violence. But ideology has origins over and beyond organisations. The ideological feature is as important to remember as the organisational one. To pretend otherwise is deceitful.

The partisan approach also diverts our attention from the acceptability of controlled mobs, private armies, vigilante groups and political assassination. Private armies have thrived in India since before 1947. In November 1947, the All India Congress Committee (AICC), which included Patel and Nehru, passed a resolution naming 'the Muslim National Guards, the Rashtriya Swayamsevak Sangh and the Akali Volunteers and such other organizations' as 'an endeavour to bring into being private armies', calling them 'a menace to the hard-won freedom of the country'.[5] However, the Indian polity has been unable to control vigilantism, which operates across a broad political spectrum.[6] Indeed, the seamless links between private armies and so-called 'mainstream' parties indicate that the ruling elites do not wish to, or cannot do away with them. Sometimes these formations acquire an autonomous or semi-autonomous existence. An examination of the political, human and financial resources of the insurgent groups of the North-East, the Khalistani armed factions of the 1980s, Islamist lashkars and mujahidin, and numerous caste-based vigilante groups can reveal these links. The Shiv Sena named itself an army and repeatedly engaged in hooliganism against ethnic minorities in Mumbai. Its leader hailed the terrorist expertise of the Tamil Tigers, aside from his numerous speech-acts of violent incitement.[7] Yet it remains a pillar of the establishment in Maharashtra.

Privatised violence is the elephant in India's drawing room. It is the clue to the phenomenon of mainstream extremism. Indian governments tend to depict 'left-wing extremism' as India's biggest security threat, whilst simultaneously sheltering armed formations such as the Salwa Judum and Ranvir Sena, and permitting RSS-affiliated paramilitaries and fronts such as the Vishwa Hindu Parishad (VHP) and Bajrang Dal, along with fanatical Islamist ulama, to freely indulge in hate speech and hooliganism. The Maoist armed groups are just one among many private armies, and they too have links with vested interests. To pretend that networks of vigilantes can operate for decades without some level of support from bourgeois civil society is to deceive ourselves.

Thus, the phrase 'requirement of deceit' implies that large sections of society, across all communities and beyond the elites, need a diet of lies to sustain themselves, to disguise their complicity in mass crime, to convince themselves of their own virtue or to enable daily life to transpire as if nothing dire had ever happened. This requirement also arises from the widespread human tendency to highlight things that buttress our arguments, and forget the things that make us uneasy. We wish good and evil to be clearly demarcated, but unfortunately, they often come in mixtures. This is another reason for the generation of necessary illusion.

Recollections

Recollections of 1984 are a means of preserving the lived experience of those events. Two important documents are the citizen's report entitled *Who Are the Guilty?* (Mukhoty and Kothari 1984), and *Delhi Riots: Three Days in the Life of a Nation* (Chakravarti and Haksar 1987), a collection of first-person accounts. Mitta and Phoolka's book on the carnage appeared in 2007. Pritam Singh's (2010) work on human rights includes a history of events prior to June 1984. All of these deserve a close reading.

I will place here some of my own memories. As a child, I had heard of communal killings from my father, an army officer posted in Fort William during the Calcutta Killing of 1946. I had never imagined I would witness anything similar. In 1984, I was a lecturer in Ramjas College in Delhi University. On 1 November, I joined a peace demonstration in Lajpat Nagar. We were confronted by *trishul*-carrying mobs on the rampage. We met Sikh taxi drivers weeping in fear and humiliation, and saw gurdwaras on fire. Columns of smoke rose from various parts of the city, which felt like a war zone. To my dismay, I heard about students participating in the violence, and some teachers speak approvingly of it. (I must add that some students sheltered Sikhs in their hostels.)

Very soon, decent-minded citizens put together a huge relief effort, named the Nagrik Ekta Manch, to deliver material/medical aid and look for trapped people. I joined a rescue operation in the Trilokpuri area, to the address of a young widow. The lane was in a lower-middle-class locality. One Sikh house was identifiable by its charred appearance. The front door was gone, and the molten blades of the ceiling fan in the main room hung downwards. My colleague Nitya and I, accompanied by a constable, climbed up the stairs to the *barsati*. It took a while for the door to be opened. Inside were a young woman, her mother and two small children. When the infant girl in her mother's arms saw the policeman's lathi she burst into tears, whimpering '*meri mummy ko mat maaro*' [Don't beat/kill my mother]. She had seen her grandfather and father being beaten and burnt to death. To this day, I remain shaken and deeply moved by the plight of these people, reduced to refugee status in their own city. Where are those children today? What sense will they ever make of what happened?

On 24 November 1984, some university teachers organised a demonstration against the carnage. It was the only one of its kind in Delhi. Needless to say, the much touted 'mainstream' was absent; nor was there any protest by the RSS family, for all their talk of Sikhs being Keshdhari Hindus and the ping-pong they play with the Congress on 1984 versus 2002. We *jholawallah*s were the only ones to protest the massacre out on the streets. About 5,000 people from all walks of life—teachers, students, auto drivers, artisans from Jama Masjid area—walked from Red Fort to Boat Club. Passers-by on the road joined in. There were no *bhai-bhai* slogans, just the demand for justice. At places, some Congress-led counter-demonstrators stood by the roadside screaming at us for being *desh-drohi* [anti-national]. I was stunned to see the hatred in their eyes. In their minds, it was patriotic to indulge in mass murder, and anti-national to ask for justice. The same perverse concept of nationalism is active today. Barring one ultra-left group, the communist parties were absent, although members of their student affiliates enthusiastically participated.

Our demonstration was blacked out by the media. Only the *Indian Express* carried three lines on an inside page (25 November 1984). Two weeks later, a commentator wrote an opinion piece in *The Statesman* on the danger of extremism. According to him 5,000 armed Sikhs had marched down Daryaganj calling for bloody revenge! Thus, many journalists spread dangerous lies. Many ordinary people appreciated our march, which remains the most significant demonstration I have ever attended.

Also, in November 1984, students of Hindu College invited comrade Sumanta Banerjee and me to address them on the events. The college seminar room was too small for the crowd, and the auditorium had to be opened. We later learned that some teachers had strongly resisted the use of the auditorium—which was packed. The mood was grim and the audience clearly opposed to communal politics, even though there was much confusion about the issue. Among other things, I said that communal violence could not be resisted by more violence, but only by a mass democratic movement for socialist goals cutting across community identities. I remember one Sikh student approaching me afterwards, with tears in his eyes, saying he wanted justice more than anything else. There was little I could say to comfort him.

Sampradayikta Virodhi Andolan

The Sampradayikta Virodhi Andolan (SVA),[8] a self-funded citizens group, was founded in November 1984 by some of the activists working in the relief camps. We wanted to engage in systematic activity to pre-empt communal violence, rather than merely react to its consequences. It fought against communal politics and demonstrated repeatedly to have the guilty of 1984 prosecuted. Over the years, we learned of shadowy 'Shakti Dals' emerging in the East Delhi colonies, which served the interests of political leaders implicated in the violence; efforts by the police to avoid the registration of FIRs, intimidation of witnesses and hypocritical behaviour by public prosecutors. All this was in the context of the Justice Ranganath Misra Commission of Inquiry (1985), whose findings we believed to be a whitewash. The SVA also hosted discussions about communalism. In January 1989, it adopted a constitution and rules of membership. Two stalwart communists, Satyapal Dang and Gursharan Singh, attended the foundation conference. That year, three members (Purushottam Agrawal, the late Jugnu Ramaswamy and I) travelled to Panjab as part of our campaign. The SVA was a direct offshoot of the violence of 1984, and lasted till 1993.[9]

On 6 February 1985, I attended the high court hearing of the People's Union for Democratic Rights' (PUDR) appeal for an order directing the police to file FIRs. Handed a copy of *Who Are the Guilty?* the judge threw it aside contemptuously and denounced teachers, journalists and civil liberties organisations. When PUDR President Gobinda Mukhoty reminded him that grave crimes had taken place, and asked for an order asking the Delhi police to register cases, the judge said, 'there was a background to it'. His words appeared to justify the murder of innocents as a form of collective retribution. There is a background to all crime, but only a fair investigation can establish whether it is relevant to the judicial process. It is not the business of a judge to make prejudicial observations, especially when the initiation of due legal process is all that is being asked for. Communal hatred was evident in his utterances. He was subsequently elevated to the Supreme Court.[10]

Until 1984, official representations of Bhagat Singh were in popular iconic form: clean shaven with moustache, hat and revolver. Then Blue Star and the massacre took place. On 23 March 1985, the usual government advertisements appeared reminding us of the great man. But this time, they depicted Bhagat Singh wearing a turban and beard, along with Sukhdev and Rajguru wearing Nehru caps. This was when Delhi police were refusing to register FIRs. In the aftermath of mass murder, our government was busy subverting the Constitution, but it also thought it fit to remind us that Bhagat Singh was a Sikh.

Early in 1986, the SVA decided to lobby members of the National Integration Council on the question of communalism and the need for justice. We drafted an appeal, which later appeared in *Mainstream* (SVA 1986). Some of us were deputed to meet political leaders. I was asked to meet a senior national leader of the BJP, to whom I was introduced by a colleague. The leader was very cordial and he and his wife had tea with me. I gave him our appeal, and sought to draw him out on the hateful nature of communal propaganda and the sheer irrationalism of campaigns around Lord Buddha's teeth, Guru Gobind Singh's horses and Lord Ram's birthplace. At one point, this leader looked at me and said, 'Indians cannot be mobilised on economic issues'. This was an astounding statement, both for its implicit avowal of utility as a factor in the choice of political rhetoric, as well as the naivety with which he said it. Perhaps he did not realise that his words conveyed a sense of the end justifying the means. The end was quite simply, power at any cost.

Among the other frank statements, he made, was the revelation that his own party colleagues in Delhi were telling him 'not to inflate' figures of Sikhs killed in the carnage. This was the most candid admission I have ever heard of communal bias against Sikhs within the BJP. (I have already argued that communal feelings cut across political affiliation. This was evident in the campus. When our staff association president proposed that we donate a day's salary for relief, the 'parivar' faction refused on the ground they had made donations in their localities.) Anyway, I appreciated this person's frankness, but was struck by the combination of cordiality and ruthlessness. For the record, RSS/BJP cadres were implicated in cases of arson, rioting, murder and dacoity by the Jain-Aggrawal Committee.[11]

Impact on Politics and Society

Communal violence in India has a long history. In his book on Pakistan, B. R. Ambedkar (1946) used the term 'civil war' to refer to communal relations in India between 1920 and 1940. Communal ideologies are based on the assumption that shared religious beliefs produce shared political interests. In essence, they embody an authoritarian impulse for the compulsory unification of ideas. Opposed to this is the view that shared religious affiliation need not produce a shared vision or sectarian inclinations. Gandhi, Abdul Ghaffar Khan, Baba Kharak Singh and Maulana Azad were all deeply religious. Their politics were based on composite nationhood, *muttahida kaumiyat*. They were also adherents of non-violence. Communalists, on the other hand would rather see a Hindu party, Muslim party, Sikh party, and so on. Religion here becomes a badge of identity, rather than a source of wisdom and moral guidance. Politicised religion tends to see people in terms of those who are 'chosen' and those who are superfluous. The politics of inclusion and exclusion leads directly to ethnic cleansing and ghetto-fication. Psychologically, it is associated with revenge and male honour. As pseudo-religion, it is obsessed with purification. Above all, fear and trauma nourish communal ideas. The Partition riots, in which up to 5 lakh people of all communities died and 14 million were forced to migrate, exemplify the genocidal implications of Indian communalism.[12]

One aspect of the Rajiv-Longowal Accord of 1985 (the references to the scope of the Ranganath Misra Commission) showed that communal assumptions had become entrenched in Indian politics. Why did either party presume that the Akali Dal was entitled to address the massacre of Sikhs in Delhi and other cities? Legally speaking, the religious affiliation of the victims was irrelevant. Indian citizens had been murdered, and the police was bound to identify and punish the guilty. As they were not doing their duty, the investigation of the allegation of conspiracy was a red herring. Meanwhile, the Misra Commission exonerated Congress leaders and passed the buck to the police. A series of inquiries were instituted from the late 1980s onwards, up until 2000.[13] When substantial recommendations were made, they led to prolonged foot-dragging by the government, or even outright defiance. It took years of pressure for the course of justice to begin and very few convictions have been secured. The process of stalling justice in cases of mass crimes received a major impetus. All this strengthened official impunity and led to a spiral of violence, which still continues.

Ordinary people are often filled with prejudices. They are quite capable of doing horrible things. In times of grave crisis, political leaders have an obligation to speak wisely, to pursue justice in a transparent manner and preserve human dignity. They ought not to reinforce popular prejudice, but should speak reasonably to calm passions. However, in the years immediately before and (long) after 1984, India's political leaders refused to practice restraint, often preferring to play with fire. In the late 1980s the 'Parivar' launched its campaign to seize and destroy Babri Masjid. This too led to thousands of deaths in 1990 and 1992. It is no secret that the 2002 violence was related to this campaign. (I find it remarkable that those who ask us to forget 2002 keep telling us never to forget 1528.[14]) In sum, the events of 1984 acted as a force-multiplier to the all-round criminalisation of Indian society.

A study of ideological factors helps avoid the errors of partisan reductionism. The back-and-forth between Congress and the BJP leads us away from a simple question: is criticism of the Congress identical with a rejection of moderation? Is it the Congress that is being targeted or the very idea of composite nationalism? There is a difference between a party that lays claim to an idea, and the idea itself. Is religion-based nationalism a recipe for a stable society? Do opponents of the Congress need to join hands with communalists (of any variety)? Should secular demands such as federalism and respect for human rights be tied up with communal antagonism? Regardless of our estimate of Mahatma Gandhi, it is undeniable that he opposed communal violence and resisted the transfer of population till his dying day. Communal politics may appear to be an opposition to the Congress, but 1984 was evidence of communal bias within the Congress. Communalism is not an opposition to a party—though many portray it as such.[15] Rather, communal politics embody the rejection of the very ideal of inclusive, composite nationhood. Those of us who refuse to see this distinction (between ideals and parties) are being taken for a ride whose destination we choose not to see. One fact told a big story—the number of BJP MPs elected to the 1985 Lok Sabha was precisely two, because Hindutva voters had switched to the Congress. This is why communalism cannot be reduced to partisan affiliations, even if some parties propagate communalism whilst others make pragmatic adjustments to it.

Rather than conflate the symptom with the root phenomenon, we must try and see what is generic. The use of 1984 as a counter to 2002 is a means of dismissing the crucial issue of accountability and the decay of criminal justice in both cases. (In Gujarat, on the few occasions when justice has been done, it entailed Supreme Court interventions and sometimes even the shifting of trials.) It also symbolises our indifference to violence. Many Indians do not believe that involvement in mass crimes should disqualify anyone from holding executive power. They distinguish 'development' from justice, forgetting that 'development' without secular norms and lawful governance will lead to tyranny. That is why our capitalists are fond of the 'Chinese model'.

Meditations

Some secularists think religion will fade away with the advance of science. This is a pipe dream, not only because science and mathematics are ethically neutral, but because it is the nature of humans to ask unanswerable questions. Religion is the sphere of absolute truth. As such it lends itself to authoritarianism. But it is also the sphere of mindfulness—an indication of the thoughtful character of the human being. We yearn for a resolution to the enigmas and contradictions of life, for simplified answers that can concentrate our experience into a single feeling. In our time, this feature of religion has been appropriated by authoritarian politics for the needs of the nation state. The subject is vast and complicated, but needs to be addressed. After 1984, I began to study communal politics seriously. In 1985, I wrote a research piece that was published in 1986. One of the issues I addressed was the decay of religious traditions:

> It is time to stop defining Indian secularism as if it meant an arithmetical total of communally defined entities. If Bhindranwale has superseded Guru Nanak, if Pakistan is the model for a truly Islamic society, and if the activities of the Vishwa Hindu Parishad, Shiv Sena and RSS amount to a Hindu renaissance … then we had better recognize that the putrefaction

> of religious traditions is just as much a part of an all-round social crisis as, say, the debt bomb or the arms race. Deprived of the refreshing oxygen of a genuine cultural and social revolution, Indian nationalism is now choking on its own poison. Since the moral fabric is so completely fragmented as to render even the quality of innocence into communally divided categories, the very first precept of any new secularism must be the inculcation of a basic respect for human life.[16]

All that I would change here is to extend the scenario to South Asia as a whole. For example, certain Buddhist monks and their organisations in Burma and Sri Lanka have been engaged in instigating violence. A notorious Burmese monk named Saydaw Wirathu has spent nine years in prison for incitement, and has (reportedly) taken the title of the Burmese bin Laden. Those interested may research the violence in Meiktila in 2013 when tens of thousands of Rohingya Muslims were driven from their homes and nearly 200 killed. Nobel Laureate Aung San Suu Kyi did not condemn the violence, but there are those like the monk Sein Ni Ta who launched cross-faith relief efforts, condemned the religious leaders who participated in the riots and denounced the 'systematic massacre' in Meiktila.[17]

In Sri Lanka, the extremist Bodu Bala Sena (BBS) or Buddhist Brigade is supported by Sri Lanka's defence secretary Gotabhaya Rajapaksa, the president's brother. (The government was also implicated in the assassination of journalist Lasantha Wickrematunge.[18]) In June 2014, Wataraka Vijitha Thero, a monk who defends religious minorities and is critical of the BBS, was beaten unconscious.[19] In January 2014, Bangladesh's political leadership was unable to prevent vicious attacks on Hindus and Buddhists by Islamist fanatics after national elections. The savagery reminded people of the massacres unleashed by the Pakistani Army in 1971. The links between the Opposition BNP and the Jamaat-e-Islami, whose cadres spearheaded the violence, are no secret.[20]

As for Pakistan, let us remember human rights activist Rashid Rehman, shot dead in May 2014 for defending blasphemy accused Junaid Hafeez, a university lecturer who continues to languish in jail. In 2011, Punjab governor Salman Taseer was murdered by his bodyguard for advocating a change in the blasphemy law and sympathising with Aasia Bibi, a Dalit Christian brick-kiln worker and mother jailed in 2010 on a charge of insulting the Prophet. Aasia was convicted by a trial court on a mere accusation and the Lahore High Court has recently upheld the sentence. She has been condemned to death before being heard. In brief, the justice system in this Islamic nuclear power is incapable of delivering due process to a destitute person.

Islamic extremism is racing towards self-destruction. The memory of Pakistan's Nobel prize winner Abdus Salam has been wiped out—even his gravestone has been desecrated because he was an Ahmediya. Bangladesh's Nobel prize winner Muhammad Yunus has been denounced by an officially sponsored campaign as being un-Islamic, for defending the rights of gay people in Uganda. In India, fanatics routinely call for Taslima Nasreen to be beheaded, Muslim youth to be mobilised for holy war, and Bangladeshi war criminals to be defended.[21]

I would like to believe that most Indian Muslims prefer to lead a peaceful life than remain in a state of outrage about Rushdie and Taslima. Yet many political leaders believe that secularism implies concessions to small-minded Muslim conservatives, in the mistaken belief that the entire community is owned by a handful of aggressive ulama. The practice of conceding an imaginary 'right not to be offended' to all self-appointed defenders of the faith, including RSS-sponsored educationists, has opened a Pandora's box of hurt sentiment. If Islam is endangered by Aasia Bibi, Mohammad Yunus and Abdus Salam, by Taslima Nasreen, Rashid Rehman and Junaid Hafeez, the very nature and purpose of religious faith need to be questioned.

Nineteen Eighty-Four

Let us now briefly recapitulate the events of 1984. Here is an extract from an article by Hartosh Singh Bal (2012):

> Many Indians outside Punjab need to be reminded that Bhindranwale was the man who necessitated Operation Bluestar in the first place. He was not alone to blame, this turn of events would not have been possible without considerable help from Indira Gandhi, who, irked by the Akali resistance to the Emergency, had propped him up to challenge the Akali hold over the Sikh orthodoxy. As she discovered, he was not a man so easily controlled and was soon enough acting on his own … Bhindranwale was no thinker. He had no coherent position on any complex issue, but was willing to mouth the rhetoric that ensured the Akalis were afraid of losing their own constituency, and he was willing to do something the Akalis had never done, use violence to achieve political ends. His hitmen, such as Surinder Singh Sodhi, assassinated a number

> of people who earned his wrath. He had also dabbled in politics, openly supporting Congress candidates against the Akalis at one point and then trying to put up his own candidates for elections to the Shiromani Gurdwara Parbandhak Committee (SGPC) … with little success … This man, a terrorist who thought nothing of using violence to terrorise and kill his opponents, whether Sikhs or Hindus, a man who never enjoyed popular support within the Sikh community … was truly converted into a sant (holy man) by the stupidity of the Indian State.

And here is Rajdeep Sardesai (2013):

> Whether you travel to the outskirts of Ahmedabad to Citizen Nagar to meet 2002 riot victims living next to a garbage dump, or to the overflowing drains of Tilak Vihar where the widows of the 1984 anti-Sikh riots live, or the makeshift homes for Kashmiri Pandit families in Jammu, the one common factor that binds these groups is the fact that their condition represents the utter failure of the Indian State to uphold the rule of law. This is not about being Muslims, Sikhs, Hindus: it is about a society that doesn't protect and provide justice to its own.[22]

The two comments summarise our predicament, and I honour these journalists for their forthright statement of unpleasant truths. What they say is relevant for all of us. Bhindranwale's early social reform activities were soon supplanted by tyrannical behaviour. Despite his affirmations of being apolitical, neither his political interventions nor his links with the senior Congress leadership were a secret. From 1978 onwards, his exhortations and the actions of his followers became extremely violent and intemperate.[23] He hailed the killer of the Nirankari leader Gurbachan Singh in 1980, and flaunted his capacity to wreak physical retribution on his detractors, many of whom were Sikhs. He remains a polarising figure and it is a serious matter that he is still lionised by sections of Sikh society and religious leaders.

One of the most moving stories from Sikh history is the legend of Malerkotla, a principality whose ruler was blessed by Guru Gobind Singh for trying to save the lives of the Guru's two sons, bricked alive by the governor of Sirhind. When told that Sher Mohammed Khan, Nawab of Malerkotla had protested vehemently, saying this was contrary to the tenets of Islam, the Guru blessed his house, declaring that its 'roots shall remain forever green'. Malerkotla was a haven of peace in the partition riots, when fleeing Muslims could find shelter there. This legend evokes the immense power of religious faith to inspire love and compassion. Why should such a tradition feel obliged to incorporate a hatemonger into its pantheon?

Delhi was where Mahatma Gandhi was murdered by a follower of V. D. Savarkar for being a lover of Muslims. Gandhi's last fast, in January 1948, was to ensure the return to Muslims of the shrine of Qutubuddin Bakhtiyar Chisti. The Delhi Declaration of 18 January 1948, inspired by him, undertook to safeguard communal harmony, return seized religious places and welcome back people who had fled their homes.[24] It was a triumph of love in the midst of an upsurge of hate. Here is an extract from Gandhi's speech on 18 January:

> Delhi is the heart—the capital of India. The leaders from the whole of India have assembled here. Men had become beasts. But if those who have assembled here, who constitute the cream among men cannot make the whole of India understand that Hindus, Muslims and followers of other religions are like brothers, it bodes ill for both the Dominions. What will be the fate of India if we continue to quarrel with one another? … Let us take no step that may become a cause for repentance later on. The situation demands courage of the highest order from us.[25] (Gandhi 1869–1948, Vol 90; 445)

How did the Congress party degenerate to the point where its senior leaders could preside over a massacre of innocents? Did their subsequent behaviour inspire confidence? Have Congress cadre even heard of the Declaration of 1948? Incidentally, some people celebrated Gandhi's assassination. Sardar Patel had rebuked RSS leader Golwalkar upon learning that 'RSS men expressed joy and distributed sweets after Gandhiji's death' (Goyal 2000: 196). A biographer of Gandhi writes:

> In the eyes of too many officials, he was an old man who had outlived his usefulness: he had become expendable. By negligence, by indifference, by deliberate desire on the part of many faceless people, the assassination had been accomplished. It was a new kind of murder—the permissive assassination, and there may be many more in the future. (Payne 2003: 647)[26]

In an echo of this complicity, on 26 February 2003, India's highest officials unveiled a portrait of V. D. Savarkar in the Lok Sabha.[27] Our representatives have chosen to honour the prime mover in the Gandhi murder case. How is this different from the glorification of Bhindranwale?

When we realise that independent India's criminal justice system was inaugurated by a denial of justice to Gandhi, we need not be surprised at its deterioration ever since. If religious faith is to be trampled upon by men such as Yogi Adityanath and Pravin Togadia, if Hinduism requires the protection of the RSS, VHP and Bajrang Dal to remain a living tradition, it is set on a path of inner strife. A great religious tradition cannot be allowed to become the property of intellectual and moral dwarves. It is one thing to be proud of one's tradition. It is quite another to confuse religious devotion with self-worship. It is vulgar to praise oneself incessantly. Praise is best when it comes from others. These groups have trained themselves in physical belligerence and the hatred of 'alien' ideas to the point of transforming nationalism into xenophobia. They relentlessly inculcate such ideas in children. They portray millions of their fellow Indians as enemies—such language always carries the potential of becoming a self-fulfilling prophesy.

A Uniform Criminal Code

India's broken middle may only be restored by moderate speech and non-violence. A great deal depends upon how Hindus conduct themselves. I suspect they know this intuitively, for despite the best efforts of such organisations most Hindus are not inclined towards religious extremism.

If various Indian governments resist violence and lawlessness only in the case of Maoists but not across the board, and not in principle, this hypocrisy will undermine state institutions. It is time for the Indian state to implement the law without discriminating between petty criminals, who sometimes get caught, and the high and mighty ones, who are never punished. Those who agitate for a uniform civil code could ask themselves whether India has a uniform criminal code.

Something more needs to be said. Permissive assassinations are coterminous with genocidal consensus. Passive acquiescence in assassination, whether of one person or thousands, is the most ominous legacy of communal ideology. It has undoubtedly been bequeathed to us by history. But have we shown the capacity to confront and overcome our history? Have our political leaders been statesman-like? A single experience of violence is enough to traumatise a person for life. We can imagine the situation if the person is a child. What happens when a society undergoes repeated cycles of violence and injustice? When thousands experience it? Violence enters the soul. Here's what a Pakistani columnist wrote last year: 'War is a tragedy but a society at war with itself and everything around, with no objective and no remorse is more than a tragedy; it is a total disaster ... Our society is at war with its own religious diversity. It is in a state of schizophrenia passing into paranoia.'[28] We may judge for ourselves if his comments are applicable to India.

Have our religious leaders reached out to the followers of all faiths? Have they spoken up against violence and inhumanity when people desperately needed moral guidance? If this has happened, I confess I have missed something. In the years following 1984 (and speaking for myself), I have gained more comfort from the words and deeds of people such as Gursharan Singh, Satyapal Dang and V. P. Singh than from any religious leaders I can think of. During the SVA days, I had the honour to meet golden-hearted individuals—ordinary citizens of all faiths, who restored my faith in humanity.[29] It is sad that despite the efforts of such humble stalwarts, the very word 'secularism' is today sneered at by the highest in the land. Messages of love and co-existence are being drowned in the noise of civil war. With honourable exceptions, religious personages have become narrow-minded and eager to acquire wealth and power. Taking such people seriously indicates delusion on the part of the believers. If they continue along this path there will be nothing left of their religions except mindless dogma and moral depravity. I do not wish to imply that we are doomed to imprisonment in a web of lies. Language itself is impossible without some ideal of truthful speech. Moreover, we humans need to make sense of our past. New generations ask questions, memories are passed on, and things bred in darkness cannot forever escape the sunlight. But, it is a long and hard passage. It is hard because mass complicity in crime—even at the level of mere feeling—perpetuates communal ideologies and generates self-deception, especially as criminal behaviour becomes normalised.

We are in the midst of such a situation now. Powerful forces in society need to cover up the truth—whether about criminal justice, the costs of 'growth', or climate change. The struggle for justice and social betterment is dependent upon an honest dialogue and recounting of the past. Without such a dialogue, we shall remain in an Orwellian labyrinth. 1984 was the point when Indian society submerged itself in propaganda, self-deception and hypocrisy. At present, we show no signs of emerging from these depths. Let us recognise that the scientists of communal identity have succeeded in inventing a machine of perpetual motion, fuelled by human ideas and emotions. The machine will continue to revolve (this is the only visible Indian 'revolution'—the cyclical return of sectarian violence) as long as we let it. Only a commitment to truth can stop it.

Conclusions

In 1949, George Orwell wrote about the totalitarian nightmare facing humanity, and named his book *1984.* Among his dystopic inventions is a fictional pamphlet about the new order. Every day begins with a Two Minute Hate prayer. The official language is Newspeak. One of its concepts is Crimestop, or protective stupidity. Then there is Doublespeak—'the ability to believe that black is white, and more, to know that black is white, and to forget that one has ever believed the contrary' (Orwell 1949[1983]: 183). This demands a continuous alteration of the past. 'This day-to-day falsification of the past, carried out by the Ministry of Truth, is as necessary to the stability of the regime as the work of repression and espionage carried out by the Ministry of Love' (Orwell 1949[1983]: 183). He goes on:

> The essential act of the Party is to use conscious deception whilst retaining the firmness of purpose that goes with complete honesty. To tell deliberate lies while genuinely believing in them, to forget any fact that has become inconvenient, and ... to draw it back from oblivion for just so long as it is needed, to deny the existence of objective reality and all the while to take account of the reality which one denies—all this is indispensably necessary. Even in using the word doublethink it is necessary to exercise doublethink. For by using the word one admits that one is tampering with reality; by a fresh act of doublethink one erases this knowledge; and so on indefinitely, with the lie always one leap ahead of the truth. (Orwell 1949[1983]: 183)

About war the pamphlet tells us:

> It does not matter whether the war is actually happening, and, since no decisive victory is possible, it does not matter whether the war is going well or badly. All that is needed is that a state of war should exist ... War, it will now be seen, is a purely internal affair. In the past, the ruling groups of all countries ... did fight against one another, and the victor always plundered the vanquished. In our own day they are not fighting against one another at all. The war is waged by each ruling group against its own subjects, and the object of the war is not to make or prevent conquests of territory, but to keep the structure of society intact. The very word 'war,' therefore, has become misleading. It would probably be accurate to say that by becoming continuous war has ceased to exist.[30]

That is the truth about modern conflict—war is not meant to be won, it is meant to be continuous. It is also the truth of what we call communalism.

Colonial India's civil war became a post-colonial international war. And, yet, civil war continues to this day in each successor state. Our condition is such that we genuinely believe our lies; it requires the lie to always be one step ahead of the truth. We, too, need to love the infallible Big Brother, 'the face on the hoardings'. Many of us are now habituated to lies and half-truths—speech has been reduced to polemic. Few wish to listen, read, think and reflect. All around us are sociopaths and criminally insane persons armed with warrior myths, whose lust for power poisons the very air we breathe. These pathological creatures do not mean to win the civil war they have generated (and in which task, alas, ordinary people assisted them). Rather, they wish it to be a permanent state of affairs. It is up to us whether we shall permit this rampaging injustice to continue unchallenged. Yes, 1984 was India's Orwellian year par excellence. After all, George was born in India.

Day after day, throughout the winter,
We hardened ourselves to live by bluest reason
In a world of wind and frost

–Wallace Stevens

Notes

1. These aspects are described in detail in three texts: Mukhoty and Kothari (1984); Chakravarti and Haksar (1987); and Mitta and Phoolka (2007).
2. *The Times of India* (1996), 'Darshan Kaur Identifies Bhagat in Courtroom as the "Neta"', 16 November, http://www.sacw.net/IMG/pdf/ToI_Nov_16_1996_Darshan_Kaur_HKL_Bhagat_sacw-net_.pdf (accessed 2014).
3. From the Supreme Court judgment awarding the death sentence to Afzal Guru, dated 4 August 2005.
4. Sajjan Kumar won with over eight and a half lakh votes (Mitta and Phoolka 2007: 73).
5. *Collected Works of Mahatma Gandhi* (henceforth *CWMG*), Volume 90, p. 541, Gandhi Heritage Portal (https://www.gandhiheritageportal.org/the-collected-works-of-mahatma-gandhi).
6. My argument about the political implications of India's private armies may be read in 'A Hard Rain Falling: On the death of TP Chandrasekharan and Related Matters' (*EPW*, June 2012) (Simeon 2012).
7. *The Times of India* (2003), 'Rope in LTTE to Stop ISI Threat: Thackeray', 27 August, http://timesofindia.indiatimes.com/india/Rope-in-LTTE-to-stop-ISI-threat-Thackeray/articleshow/150076.cms (accessed 2014).

8. SVA (1986), 'India: SVA's 1986 Appeal to the National Integration Council', Sampradayikta Virodhi Andolan, *Mainstream*, 26 April, http://www.sacw.net/article8493.html.

9. More information about the SVA may be read in this archival collection: 'Dilip Simeon's blog: Sampradayikta Virodhi Andolan', http://dilipsimeon.blogspot.in/search/label/Sampradayikta%20Virodhi%20Andolan.

10. I have found two articles that mention this hearing, neither of them bring up the communally loaded statement of the judge. But, I heard it, and I am sure others did as well.

11. Dikshit, Vineet (1994), 'BJP Move to Shield Cadres Involved in '84 Riots', *The Pioneer*, 11 April, http://www.sacw.net/IMG/pdf/Pioneer_April_11_1994_BJP_Cadres_1984.pdf; Sharma, Rajnish (2002), 'Sikh Riots: BJP Names Figure in Records', *Hindustan Times*, 2 February, http://www.sacw.net/article8089.html.

12. These figures are estimates. See Simeon, Dilip (2013), 'The Law of Killing: A Brief History of Indian Fascism', *Dilip Simeon's blog*, http://dilipsimeon.blogspot.in/2013/07/the-law-of-killing-brief-history-of.html.

13. The following is a list of the inquiries instituted: Kapur Mittal Committee, Jain Banerjee Committee, Potti Rosha Committee, Jain Aggarwal Committee, Ahuja Committee, Dhillon Committee, Narula Committee and Nanavati Commission.

14. The year 1528 was when Babar, founder of the Mughal dynasty, is alleged to have ordered the destruction of a Ram temple in Ayodhya. This event was the basis of the Ram Janmabhumi–Babri Masjid controversy launched by the RSS/BJP/VHP in the late 1980s, which led to the demolition of the Babri Mosque in December 1992.

15. A perceptive Hindutva ideologue reportedly remarked that organisationally speaking, the Congress had won the 1984 elections, but it was an ideological victory for the BJP (Singh 2010: 130).

16. Simeon, Dilip (1986), 'Communalism in Modern India: A Theoretical Examination', 13 December, http://dilipsimeon.blogspot.in/2012/08/communalism-in-modern-india-theoretical.html (accessed 5 August 2012).

17. The Nanyang Post (2013), 'Anti-Muslim Riots Haunt Shattered Myanmar City'. 8 July, http://www.nanyangpost.net/2013/07/anti-muslim-riots-haunt-shattered.html (accessed 2014).

18. 'When finally I am killed, it will be the government that kills me' – Lasantha Wickrematunge, *BBC News* (2009), 'Sri Lankan Editor Row Escalates', 13 January, http://news.bbc.co.uk/2/hi/south_asia/7827262.stm.

19. *BBC News* (2014), 'Sri Lanka Moderate Monk Critical of Anti-Muslim Violence Beaten', 19 June, http://www.bbc.com/news/world-asia-27918343.

20. Haroon, Habib (2014), 'Bangladesh Post-poll Violence Hits Minorities', *The Hindu*, 8 January.

21. Garga Chatterjee (2013), 'A Dangerous Connivance', *The Hindu*, 6 April.

Bangladesh Independent News Network (2013), 'Kolkata Muslims Protest against Anti-Islamic Activities in Bangladesh', 30 March, http://bdinn.com/news/kolkata-muslims-protest-against-anti-islamic-activities-in-bangladesh/.

22. Rajdeep Sardesai, (2013), 'Confront These Painful Truths about Communalism', *Hindustan Times*, 1 November.

23. For contemporary reference material on Bhindranwale, see Lamba (2004).

P. S. Lamba (2004), 'Jarnail Singh Bhindranwale: Five Myths', *The Sikh Times*, 6 June, http://www.sikhtimes.com/bios_060604a.html.

24. In his prayer meeting of 21 November 1947, Gandhi claimed he had received information about the near-destruction of 137 mosques in Delhi. See *CWMG*, Volume 90, p. 79.

25. *CWMG*, Volume 90, p. 445. The seven-point Declaration is on page 444.

26. Readers who wish to study Gandhi's assassination may consult the Jeevan Lal Kapur Inquiry Report of 1969. See Kapur (1970).

27. Nauriya, Anil (2003), 'Portrait as Mirror', *The Hindu*, 3 March, http://www.thehindu.com/2003/03/03/stories/2003030300371000.htm.

28. Haider, Mobarak (2013), 'A Society at War with Itself', *Dawn*, 29 January.

29. A brief account of whom may be read in my review article 'Superfluous People', Simeon, Dilip (2013), 'Book Review: Superfluous People—Rahul Pandita's "Our Moon Has Blood Clots"', *Dilip Simeon's blog*, http://dilipsimeon.blogspot.in/2013/05/book-review-superflous-people-rahul.html.

30. George Orwell, 'The Theory and Practice of Oligarchical Collectivism', Chapter 9, in *1984* (1949).

References

Ambedkar, B. R. 1946. *Pakistan or The Partition of India*. Bombay: Thacker & Co Ltd.

Bal, Hartosh Singh. 2012. 'A Community Led by Dunes'. *Open Magazine.*

Gandhi, Mahatma. 1869–1948. *The Collected Works of Mahatma Gandhi* (*CWMG*). New Delhi: Publications Division, Ministry of Information and Broadcasting, Government of India, 20002001.

Goyal, D. R. 2000. *Rashtriya Swayamsewak Sangh*. New Delhi: Radha Krishna Prakashan.

Haksar, Nandita and Uma Chakravarti. 1987. *Delhi Riot: Three Days in the Life of a Nation.* New Delhi: Lancer International.

Kapur, Jeevan Lal. 1969. *Report of Commission of Inquiry into Conspiracy to Murder Mahatma Gandhi*. Ministry of Home Affairs, Government of India, New Delhi: Jeevan Lal Kapur Inquiry Report of 1969.

Mitta, Manoj, and H. S. Phoolka. 2007. *When a Tree Shook Delhi: The 1984 Carnage and Its Aftermath*. New Delhi: Lotus.
Mukhoty, Gobinda, and Rajni Kothari. 1984. *Who Are the Guilty? Joint Inquiry into the Causes and Impact of the Riots in Delhi from 31 Oct to 10 Nov.* Joint Inquiry, Delhi: People's Union for Democratic Rights (PUDR) and People's Union for Civil Liberty (PUCL).
Orwell, George. 1949[1983]. *Nineteen Eighty-Four*. Harmondsworth: Penguin.
Payne, Robert. 2003. *The Life and Death of Mahatma Gandhi*. New Delhi: Rupa & Co.
Singh, Pritam. 2010. *Economy, Culture and Human Rights: Turbulence in Punjab, India and Beyond*. Gurgaon: Three Essays Publication.

Notes on the Contributors

Jasmine Anand is Assistant Professor, Mehr Chand Mahajan DAV College for Women, Chandigarh.

Yasmeen Arif is Professor in Sociology, School of Humanities and Social Sciences, Shiv Nadar University, Delhi NCR.

Uma Chakravarti is a feminist historian, filmmaker and a civil rights activist.

Ishmeet Kaur Chaudhry is Assistant Professor, Central University of Gujarat, India.

Nandita Haksar has worked as a human rights lawyer, campaigner and writer for more than three decades.

Anne Murphy is Associate Professor, University of British Columbia, Canada.

Anshu Saluja is Assistant Professor of History, Azim Premji University, Bhopal.

Amutha Charu Sheela is Assistant Professor of English, Department of Humanities and Social Sciences, Sri Venkateswara College of Engineering, Sriperumbudur.

Dilip Simeon is a historian and public intellectual based in Delhi.

Amritjit Singh is Langston Hughes Professor Emeritus of English and African American Studies, Ohio University.

Diamond Oberoi Vahali is Associate Professor, School of Letters, Ambedkar University, Delhi.

Index